Ken Weber   Sheila Bennett

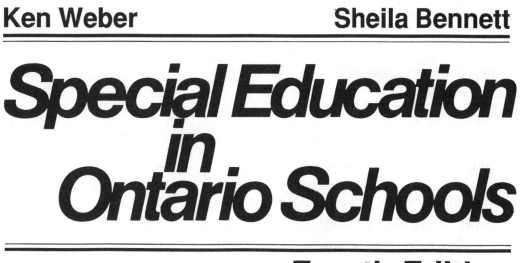

Special Education in Ontario Schools

Fourth Edition

Highland Press

Highland Press
Box 25, Palgrave, Ontario L0N 1P0
Telephone (905) 880-1277
Fax (905) 880-4134
E-mail hldpress@look.ca

Design & Cover Photo: Ron Forrester

Editors: Cecile King & Jane Rutledge

Canadian Cataloguing in Publication Data

Weber, Ken (Kenneth Jerome), 1940-
  Special education in Canadian schools

4th ed., rev.
Includes bibliographical references and index.
ISBN 0-9693061-7-2

    1. Special education – – Ontario.
I. Bennett, Sheila Marie, 1961-
II. Title.

LC3984.2.O5W42 1999   371.9' 09713   C99–900069–1

Printed and bound in Canada.

0 9 8 7
05 04 03

Table of Contents

Foreword

Classroom practices, administrative procedures, and Ontario government policies in special education are built around the ideal that it is possible to respond to the strengths and needs of every special student. Legislation in the province guarantees access to public education for all students regardless of their needs. Further, it assures that exceptional students will have access to programs and resources to meet their special needs. Individual boards and schools are set up to deliver special education service and support, ranging through simple modifications of a student's program, to allocation of complex, specialized resources, and even to changes in building design. Ministry regulations reinforce ideal professional practices such as the development and monitoring of individual education plans.

On the front lines, so to speak, classroom teachers and educational assistants draw on training in special education, and on their own resources and talents and creativity, to bring everything together for students with special strengths and needs.

Ontario teachers have long been recognized, not just in their own province but elsewhere, for their leadership and commitment in matters relating to special students. These qualities are a main reason why special education has been implemented so successfully as a fully functional and vital element in the province's broader system.

Like all systems put together by human beings, Ontario's special education reveals occasional faults. But the system is dynamic. It responds to evolving needs and philosophies; it develops; it adapts. And most of the time, it improves. In any case, special education will only be as effective as the people — at every level — who make it work. Ultimately, special education can only succeed as a concept, as a principle, and most importantly, as a practice, through the actions of professionals who are committed to the belief that every student has a right to the best that schooling can offer. Ironically, the ideal of special education is to put itself out of business. The goal for which it strives is a system of education in which adaptation and accommodation for the needs of every student is automatic, and in which the very idea of 'special' education is unnecessary.

Ken Weber   Sheila Bennett
30 June, 1999

The authors of Special Education in Ontario Schools *are grateful to the many truly professional and caring people in the field of special education who have offered much useful advice over four editions of the text. While it would be impossible to name everyone, we would like to express our appreciation to Don Dworet, Deborah Goldberg, Andrea Jack, Louise Moreau, Don Reilly, Michael Tudor, Kelly Ann Vokey, Tammy Waxman, and especially the late Helen Pogor, to whose memory this edition is dedicated.*

1

A Place For Every Student

A Brief History of Special Education in Ontario

Dateline 1957 — The Case of Ruthie

It was not until she was almost eight years old that Ruthie began attending school. To begin with, her parents knew she was, in her father's words, "something behind other young ones". Then there was the long walk down the concession and across the sideroad to the one-room school. She'd have to do it alone and well, everybody knew Ruthie had this habit of wandering off.

Even at age eight, Ruthie's future as a student was uncertain at best.

"We don't have to take this child in if you don't want," the chairman of S.S.#12 school board had said to the brand new teacher in August. "It's going to be hard enough in your first year without having a retarded child to look after. The regulations are clear. We don't have to take her. It's up to you."

But the teacher welcomed Ruthie and made her feel part of the tiny student body. Two girls in grade eight readily agreed to take her outside to the toilet every day just before recess. One of the older boys built her an extended desktop so she could more easily enjoy her favourite activity: colouring big murals on the back of discarded rolls of wallpaper. The younger children, a bit perplexed at first because Ruthie didn't speak, soon learned to ignore her strange noises. And every day after lunch, Ruthie crawled happily into the teacher's lap for the reading of the next sequence in 'the afternoon story'. By the end of the school year, Ruthie could recognize her own name in print; she understood and followed routines; could count up to ten blocks, and, most important in the teacher's view, she no longer wandered away at will.

The next year of her schooling might have shown even more development, but Ruthie got caught in a swirl of events that even her parents didn't quite follow. S.S.#12 was closed in June, along with all the other one-room schools in the township. Students were now to be bused to a brand new central school. Ruthie's teacher got married that summer and moved to the other end of the province. At 'Central', the school inspector told the staff in primary/junior that no one was obligated to take in Ruthie but if anyone volunteered, she would be admitted.

There were no takers. Ruthie never went to school again.

Bill 82: An End and a Beginning

On December 12, 1980, Ontario's new lieutenant governor, the Hon. John Black Aird, signed a bill that was to bring dramatic changes to the province's schools. The new legislation was formally known as the Education Amendment Act, but most people used its working title: *Bill 82*. Far more important than the title was the content. Prior to the passing of this new law, the province's Education Act had *allowed* boards of education to provide special education if they chose to. Now, with Bill 82 in effect, boards would be *required* to provide it. Students with special needs were now to be guaranteed a place in the regular school system. No longer would a disability be a potential barrier to their education.

It was a remarkable and courageous step for Ontario to take. Although similar mandatory legislation had been passed in the U.S.A. in 1975, its impact was still being critically examined, and the idea was not at all solidly established in most western countries. Even more remarkable once Bill 82 became law, was the relative ease — and speed — with which special education became an effective, vital, and completely accepted part of education in the province. While it would be excessive to suggest that mandatory special education was a law just waiting to be passed, it is also impossible to deny the fact that the implementation of Bill 82 in Ontario was immediately and broadly successful. And, with the slight modifications and adjustments that, quite naturally, have arisen out of experience since 1980, it continues to be successful.

Interestingly, devotees of educational history can point to a time only a decade before December 12, 1980, when the idea of sending students with special needs to a regular school was not even considered by most jurisdictions in the province. But by the same token, within only a decade *after* 1980 — even less —special education in Ontario had become a thoroughly established, integral, part of the education system. The experience makes it tempting to argue that special education therefore, should have been fulfilling its present role long before this. However, the road to the present was anything but a short and smooth one. The paragraphs that follow outline just a few of the many bumps.

The Long Road to Special Education

At First, Just Surviving

Disabled persons did not fare well in early times. This was true, even in cultures like the Greek and the Roman, which we generally view as more enlightened and sophisticated. Under Solon's law, for example, the weak and disabled children of Athens were placed in clay vessels and abandoned. In Rome, disabled children were customarily thrown into the Tiber. It was not unusual for wealthy families of the time to keep a mentally handicapped person for entertainment. No less a personage than the moralist philosopher, Seneca, reported that his wife kept a "feeble-minded dwarf", ostensibly for just that purpose. Even Aristotle, whose writings dominated western thought for more than a thousand years after his death, is known to have described deaf people as "incapable of reason", "no better than the animals of the forest" and "unteachable".

There were some exceptions to this quite universal attitude. The Talmud offered enlightened instructions regarding the blind and deaf, and Hippocrates' investigations into epilepsy and mental handicap suggested that scientific curiosity about special needs was not entirely absent. However, the impact of these exceptions was limited to small, specific groups.

In the Middle Ages too, there were a few bright spots. Saint Nicholas Thaumaturgos, fourth century bishop of Wyre, became known as a "protector of the feeble-minded", but there is little evidence of what he accomplished. (He was also the patron saint of sailors and pawnbrokers — and the prototype for Santa Claus!) Some monasteries and other clergy established hospices, but the superstitions of the day, along with a powerful belief in Satanic possession and the sheer demands of mere survival, meant that persons with disabilities were very much on their own.

A few strides were made in Europe in the post-Renaissance Era, but they were chiefly isolated, short-lived bursts of change, the accomplishments of individuals with will and drive, rather than the product of a general amelioration in attitude. And usually, when these individuals died, the fruits of their efforts died with them. Most special educators today, for example, recognize the name Ponce de Leon (1520-82), the Spanish monk who taught deaf children to speak and read (although he is often confused with the explorer who visited Florida in 1513). De Leon's techniques, although apparently very successful, are lost and unknown to us, largely, historians believe, because there was no general impetus after his death to continue their use.

Eventually, a Bit of Light

Three hundred years after de Leon, Louis Braille (1809-1852) had a far more lasting success with an alphabet for the blind that he adapted from a night-writing cipher system invented by one of Napoleon's staff officers. But then by Braille's time, attitudes toward people with disabilities were beginning to shift. British philosopher, John Locke (1632-1708) had impressed the intellectuals of the western world with his philosophy of 'sensationalism', which took issue with — among other things — the long held view that children are born with innate characteristics imprinted by God, nature, or the devil. Instead, Locke argued, they are a *tabula rasa*, a blank slate waiting to be written upon. Ever so slowly, this idea, given further impetus by other European scholars like Voltaire, Rousseau, and Goethe, began to chip away at the notion that disabled people are simply the product of some Great Plan and should therefore be left alone. At the same time, the notion that disabilities were a consequence of divine punishment, was also being called into question.

Nevertheless, the march toward enlightenment was slow, and again, very much the product of a few key motivators. Although they were actively discouraged by many of their contemporaries, Jean Marc Itard (1775-1858) who "discovered" and tried to teach Victor, the wild boy of Aveyron, and Frederick Treves (1867-1923) who "rescued" John Merrick, the Elephant Man, are among the better known personalities who tried to break new ground.

But this kind of humanism still seemed to be too advanced and radical for the times to take on practical, universal expression. Indifference, or perhaps just overwhelming inertia, is evident in the fact that carnival shows continued to offer physically unique persons like John Merrick for display, well into the mid-twentieth century.

In Canada, Some Real and Lasting Light

Curiously, although Louis Braille's successful development of an alphabet for the blind was resisted, especially in the U.S., for almost fifty years after his death, the same time period hosted a clear and lasting movement for the education of the blind. A school for the blind opened in Toronto in 1872, and one in Halifax a year later. Nor were these the only examples of major change in both philosophy and practice. In Quebec, Ronald McDonald, a reporter with the *Montreal Gazette*, had opened a school for the deaf in Champlain, in 1831. (It was, in fact, Canada's first formal special education project.) Similar schools opened in Halifax in 1856, in Toronto (1858) and Winnipeg (1884). These were followed soon after by the first Canadian residential institution for the developmentally disabled, which opened in Orillia in 1876. A few years before that, and also in Ontario, the vigorous work of John Barrett McCann had brought about the founding of two residential schools: the Ontario Institution for the Education and Instruction of the Deaf and Dumb, at Belleville, in 1870, and the Ontario Institution for the Education and Instruction of the Blind, at Brantford, in 1872. In 1893, Children's Aid societies were formed in Ontario and became the model for such practice throughout North America.

By establishing such institutions, the provincial government was reflecting the greater sense of social responsibility evident in the province's general population, as well as a developing interest in people with disabilities. Although some of the teaching methods used in the institutions seem odd today, and although the language and terminology make contemporary educators wince, the mere existence of residential schools was an especially striking development for the time, in light of the fact that education of the so-called "normal" population was still far from universal.

Still a Long Way to Go

Unfortunately, by reason of economics, not to mention Ontario's vast geography, comparatively few children were served in terms of the actual needs in the population. Resources in the schools tended to be aimed at the most overt and visibly obvious exceptionalities. And from a contemporary perspective, the curricula were very much biased toward industrial training. The idea was, in the words of one contemporary, "to make something of the students" so that graduates could seek gainful employment. On the other hand, that mission was based very much on the wishes of the students' own parents and families who, perhaps understandably, felt that "making something of the students" at least offered them some hope of employment and independence.

Not even this much was held out to the exceptional students whose needs were less obvious, and as a consequence, harder to understand or even acknowledge. Consequently, students with a learning disability (the term did not even exist until 1963) or those with what is often seen now as a behavioural difficulty, were usually early dropouts from any form of education. Right through to the final quarter of the twentieth century, these dropouts were regarded — and also saw themselves — as poor

educational material in any case, not likely to benefit a great deal from extended schooling. Pre-computer, assembly line industry absorbed them quite readily into fairly low-level employment, and reinforced this perception.

As it was, even the established schools were not always secure, especially if their faculties attempted to be innovative. The Ontario School for Crippled Children (now part of Bloorview MacMillan Centre) in Toronto had quickly established a well-deserved international reputation for its programs, and as early as 1890, faculty at the Orillia institution had developed quite advanced school programs for its clientele; yet both centres had to struggle to keep their programs going in the face of widespread criticism. Students with serious physical or intellectual needs were often described as poor candidates for education on the premise that it served little purpose, and offered only minimal return to society. In light of that hypothesis, it

Dateline 1965 — The Case of Leo

No one was more exasperated by Leo's language skills than his mother. A former teacher, she had sent his two older sisters off to grade one so well prepared they both skipped a grade. Not Leo. To be sure, he appeared to be just as bright. Certainly he was charming, and so what if he had a few odd speech patterns? That was nothing unusual in a youngster. Yet no matter what she did, Leo's mother just couldn't teach him to recognize letters.

Not that she pushed him to frustration. She was too wise and experienced a mother and teacher. But Leo — she'd never seen anything quite like it. Take the letter 'A' for example. She'd have him trace it, colour it, find 'A's hidden about the kitchen, and sing the 'A' song. Although he'd then recognize the letter without a prompt for maybe the next two or three days, after a week on 'B' and 'C', the letter 'A' would be gone. And it would be really *gone*. That was part of the exasperation. Re-introducing 'A' to Leo was not a simple matter of stimulating recall. It was as though he'd never ever seen it before!

Of course, Leo's printing was disastrous. Nor did it improve as he got older. At the end of grade one, Leo's principal boldly left the *printing* mark blank on his report card so he could pass into grade two, but the problem was still there. So was his letter recognition problem and lack of progress in learning to read. Friends of Leo's mom tried to console her with the explanation that boys are almost always slower, but Leo just didn't get any better. Nor did anybody have an explanation, although the grade four teacher had seen another boy like it once before, and he'd become a real problem because no one seemed able to do anything for him.

Still, the situation was not all bad. Leo's dad ran a successful plumbing business where Leo helped out on Saturdays, and as long as the boy was given only one instruction at a time, no one worked harder or more reliably. In fact, it may have been the plumbing business that provided an 'out' for everyone, because by grade five, Leo's behaviour was changing. He'd already repeated two grades, was facing failure again, and reading was still torture and writing an agony. By grade five, Leo was no longer getting headaches and stomach pains during language arts; he was now acting out in progressively alarming ways. That was the main reason Leo's mother reluctantly agreed to the arrangement that allowed him to leave school to work for his dad. Even so, one of her worst fears came true some years later. When Leo's dad retired, he had to sell the business, for although Leo was willing and handy, he never learned to read and write well enough to run things.

is more than a little ironic that the societal benefit factor apparently played no role at all in discussions of special education for students who were especially able. Public education for gifted students was almost unheard of until the 1970s.

The Modern Era

There is little question that special education as we have come to understand it in Ontario today, is very much a twentieth century phenomenon. And future historians will likely place its watershed point, the point at which the march to Bill 82 began, in the mid nineteen-sixties. This decade was a time when the chronology of events shifted from episodic, often unconnected attempts to somehow improve the lot of exceptional students, to a generally coherent movement that aimed to educate them according to their needs. The change occurred around this time for a number of reasons.

> "Every child has a claim on the community for the best means of moral and mental cultivation."
> —Educator, Harvey Peet, 1855.

A Shift in Thinking

The influence of two dominating ideas diminished significantly in the nineteen sixties. One was the idea that commercially produced, formally administered assessment instruments — tests, especially the IQ test — could be used as exclusive determiners of a student's potential future. Although doubts about the real value — and the abuse — of testing instruments were raised as early as the 1930s, the general public's faith in them had taken a long time to fade.

Simultaneous with the re-evaluation of the role of tests was the decline of the eugenics movement, a philosophy very much in vogue among intellectuals in the first half of the century. Eugenicists argued that 'feeble-minded' persons should be protected in institutions, in order to protect society, in turn, from genetic contamination. In 1918, a coalition of doctors, social workers and influential citizens had formed the Canadian National Committee on Mental Hygiene to pressure the government to expand custodial facilities for the 'feeble-minded', whose spread was caused, in the Committee's opinion, by "procreation by unsound stock, the numbers of which were being accelerated by the government's admittance to the Dominion, of degenerate immigrants" (sic!).

The Normalization Principle

Although both testing and eugenics still had their champions — particularly testing — their combined and somewhat mutually supportive power was minimal by the time the Ontario government passed Bill 82. In their place, the normalization principle championed in Canada by Wolf Wolfensberger through the National Institute on Mental Retardation (now the G. Allen Roeher Institute) became the widely accepted philosophy. In essence, normalization argues against institutionalization, and contends, quite credibly, that persons with special needs should be viewed more from the points on which they are similar to other persons, rather than from those on which they are different.

The philosophy of normalization holds that, if they are integrated into mainstream society, exceptional persons, such as those with mental handicaps, will take on the behaviours of the norm because they will have more normal models to follow.

It is a concept that suggests unlimited growth and improvement instead of ceilings and limitations, and it struck a powerful chord, not just in Ontario, but throughout Canada and North America. Thus in only about twenty years, government policies across the continent changed from a commitment to building and expansion of care-based facilities, to strategies that saw these centres being closed and the residents being integrated into their communities.

Empowerment of Educators

Educators in the sixties, and even more so in the seventies, began to set aside the 'medical model' approach to students with special needs. Under the influence of this model, they had been taught to concentrate on what was wrong with students. What began to replace that style was a wider, more ecological focus incorporating the whole person, essentially a perspective that takes note of what the exceptional student can do in addition to what is hard or impossible to do. At the same time, teachers also began to recognize their own

On the agenda distributed to the public at the county school board meeting, item no. 5 appeared innocuous enough. It read

Approval of funds to install elevator, renovate main entrances,
washrooms, fire exits and classroom doorways as outlined in Report 995A.

To Pete and his family, and to three other families with sons and daughters who had severe physical disabilities, no. 5 item was full of implications. Pete had muscular dystrophy. Over his years in elementary school, the condition had developed to a point where he could no longer walk for more than a few metres without risking a serious fall. The walking itself was accomplished with the help of crutches which Pete used in alternating wide swings. Increasingly, he was spending longer and longer periods in a wheelchair, and now required some assistance when using the washroom. In a few months, Pete would be eligible to attend the secondary school in his community. However, it was an old building where he would simply not be able to get around, much less get in or out, without some major structural changes to it. There would also need to be some kind of arrangement developed for Pete's personal hygiene needs. Nothing in either education or civil law obligated the board to do these things, but because it was a fairly small community where Pete and his family were well known and active, the local trustees agreed to consider the matter.

The motion was defeated, but so narrowly that Pete's family was sufficiently encouraged to press for another possibility. Since 1974, Ontario's Education Act had permitted school boards to provide special education services if they chose to, and by now, some boards in the province had undertaken to do so. A few had renovated some schools to accommodate students with physical disabilities. Thus Pete's family, supported by an advocacy group, began urging the local board to arrange — and bear the cost — for Pete to enrol at one of these. Once more the trustees listened carefully and sympathetically, but because there were a number of students in a situation similar to Pete's, they approached the proposal with great caution. So cautiously, as it turned out, that the motion kept being tabled. Pete's parents, wary of the outcome, reluctantly sold their home, moved out of the community, and relocated in another part of the province near a school that was modified for students with special needs like their son's.

strengths, and the potential power of their own contributions to an exceptional student's case. Whereas in the medical model approach, a teacher is expected to defer to some greater, outside expertise, the ecological focus grants teachers, and educational assistants, the right to exercise intuition, knowledge and experience.

An important consequence of this latter approach is that the student with special needs is seen as an educable entity, not as a custodial, medical responsibility for whom intellectual development and learning are secondary to coping with a handicap.

Perhaps more important, ultimately, is the effect of this perspective on how special education service is delivered. In a medical model, expertise is visited upon both student and teacher from above and afar. In a model that requires empiricism and hypothesis and flexibility and constant program modification, the decision-making and the delivery of service are likely to be much more current, not to mention appropriate, if they take place on site. By the time Bill 82 was only a decade old therefore, the trend in Ontario had moved clearly toward management of special needs in the local community school, and specifically in the regular classroom.

Parent Power

Social commentators frequently trace the origins of parent advocacy to the protest movements of the nineteen-sixties. Certainly, it was at this time when the parents of students with special needs found that they could achieve more for their sons and daughters by acting collectively rather than singly. The result was that political activism by parent and other advocacy groups began to have — and continues to have — a powerful effect on governments. The strength and sophistication of lobbying efforts by groups like the Learning Disabilities Association, the Association for Bright Children, the Association for Community Living, among many others, has been instrumental for decades now in motivating educational jurisdictions to improve the lot of exceptional students. In fact, there are many participants in the process that eventually gave birth to Bill 82 in Ontario, who acknowledge quite candidly that, were it not for the activity of advocates, the legislation would not likely have come about as soon as it did.

One of the important consequences of this level of advocacy is that, by the end of the twentieth century, it became accepted, indeed encouraged, practice among professional educators to involve parents or their representatives far more extensively in day by day educational decision-making of all kinds.

U.S. Public Law 94-142

A landmark piece of legislation in the U.S.A., 'The Education for All Handicapped Children Act' (which like Ontario's Education Amendment Act became better known by its legislative working title: PL (for 'Public Law') 94-142) was passed in 1975. PL 94-142 mandated appropriate education for every handicapped student, appropriate screening procedures, consultation with parents (and due process rights if they disagree with the school), a written individual education plan (IEP) for each student, placement in the least restrictive environment appropriate to the student's needs, and other features. Subsequent amendments to this law have tinkered with and upgraded it (e.g., PL 99-457, the 'Individuals with Disabilities Education Act' (IDEA) in 1990) but the legislation has, by and large, fulfilled its promise without major change.

PL 94-142 had a powerful impact on other jurisdictions in North America, giving them on the one hand, motivation to bring about legislation of their own, and on the other, determination to avoid some of its problems. One of the latter is

"The Ministry of Education and Training remains committed to the principle that the integration of exceptional pupils should be the normal practice in Ontario, when such a placement meets the pupil's needs and is in accordance with parental wishes. A range of options including placement in a special class or provincial or demonstration school will continue to be available for pupils whose needs cannot be met within the regular classroom."

— *Jill Hutcheon, Assistant Deputy Minister. Memorandum to directors, superintendents and principals, June 9, 1994.*

that although "least restrictive environment" was never intended to mean 'regular classroom for everyone', interpreting the phrase that way has engendered quite a bit of litigation. Another is the entanglements that have resulted from making an extensive written individual education plan (IEP) a legal requirement.*

Two Canadian provinces had passed mandatory legislation well ahead of the U.S.A. Saskatchewan did so in 1971, and Nova Scotia in 1973. In the Ontario legislature, a private member's bill (Bill 109) concerning special education was tabled in 1977. The bill called for mandatory legislation but did not get past first reading. These events added impetus to the movement, but it was the fanfare accompanying PL 94-142 that truly accelerated events. By 1980, the Ontario government had Bill 82 on the books.

What Bill 82 Brought to Ontario

Following are important features of Bill 82 (the Education Amendment Act) and regulations** associated with it. Although all of these features continue to apply, it is important to keep in mind that provincial legislation along with Ministry-issued regulations and policy memoranda, is regularly modified and updated.

---

*In Ontario, written individual education plans (IEPs) were not required when Bill 82 was passed in 1980, even though most of the province's educators soon began to use them as part of normal special education practice. IEPs were made a regulatory requirement in the province in 1998, but the regulations do not stipulate the kind of extensive detail originally set out in PL 94-142.

**From time to time, the Ministry of Education and Training issues 'Regulations' that give specific direction to the province's school boards on matters of policy and practice. Regulation 181, which details the composition and role of IPRCs, is an example. Although they are not legislation per se, regulations have essentially the same force. 'Program/Policy Memoranda', also issued by the Ministry, fulfill a similar function. PPM 76C, for example, covers alternative program funding for deaf, blind, and deaf-blind students.

- Every school board in the province is required to provide special education programs and services for its exceptional pupils. If a board cannot provide programs and services, it must make an agreement with another board to provide them (and compensate the other board accordingly).

- Boards are to establish Identification, Placement and Review Committees (IPRCs) whose chief function is to identify whether a pupil is exceptional, and then decide upon a placement for him or her. (This feature is a functional centrepiece of the province's special education structure. For more on the IPRC, refer to Chapter 5.)

- Parents of an exceptional pupil are to be included in the identification and placement process. A review and appeal process is available if they are dissatisfied with IPRC identification or placement decisions.

- Each school board is required to establish a Special Education Advisory Committee (SEAC) to advise on matters of special education programs and services.

- A comprehensive special education 'Plan' must be developed and maintained by each school board in which its programs and services are outlined for public and Ministry examination. The 'Plan' is updated and amended as necessary to meet the current needs of exceptional pupils.

- School boards are required to implement procedures for early (and on-going) identification of pupils' learning abilities and needs.

Meeting the Challenge of Bill 82

At the Board Office

Even critics of Ontario's legislation agree that the heady optimism engendered by the passing of the Education Amendment Act, was by and large justified over the ensuing years. When Bill 82 was passed in 1980, the province's school boards were given five years to establish their plans and systems; yet special education policies and practices were fully operational in the majority of boards well before the deadline. More subtle, but certainly crucial to the almost immediate success, was the relative ease with which special education became a natural part of every school board's function.

This phenomenon occurred in spite of some major development challenges. Prior to Bill 82, separate school boards, for example, did not have the right to provide programs and services for what were called in 1980, 'trainable retarded pupils', and most separate boards had to build these services from scratch in a very short time. Smaller boards, especially some in rural areas, likewise had to develop special education systems with little or no existing base to build on. Even boards which already had some special education services in place before 1980, usually did not offer the wide and comprehensive system that one could find almost anywhere in the province only five years later.

In the Classroom

Still another challenge was finding "front-line" staff to make the systems work on a daily basis. At the time the bill became law, there were very few teachers in the province who had undertaken special education as part of a career path. Yet a combination of teachers' inherent skills, and their ready willingness to learn on the job, supported by a mass professional development drive on the part of the Ministry and of the province's universities, soon addressed this vital component. Within only a decade of establishing mandatory special education, provincial authorities were able to point to a large cadre of professional teachers clearly committed to the field. (See Appendix for information on Additional Qualifications (AQs) in special education.)

Equally urgent was the need for resource and support personnel, most especially classroom teaching assistants, whose role soon took on more importance as schools began to deal with a variety of special needs that many had never encountered before. Fortunately, Ontario's community colleges were quick to show leadership in developing effective education programs for potential assistants, a response that paid dividends immediately, for assistants soon proved themselves invaluable in classrooms with exceptional children.

At Home and School

Although the idea of parent support for education was hardly a novel one by 1980, the manner and extent of parental involvement that grew as a consequence of special education, was something different for the province. A few senior administrators found the experience more of a challenge than they were accustomed to, but for the most part, the experience proved to be very positive.

Initially, the role of parents was very much confined to the SEAC, the Special Education Advisory Committee that school boards are required to establish, with membership taken principally from the various parent associations in the community. However, as both administrators and classroom personnel gradually came to understand through experience, parents play a role in the education of children with special needs that is qualitatively and quantitatively different from that generally required in supporting the education of other children.

Late in 1997, the Ministry of Education and Training reissued the regulation governing SEACs (Reg. 464), and in it, strengthened the role that these bodies play. SEACs are now entitled to view a board's budget, and as well, to have input in the allocation of special education finances. Some boards in the province were already doing this as a matter of course. Still, the fact that this very important right was enshrined in official provincial policy, suggests that parental involvement has proven beneficial in many ways.

Growing Pains

Despite the fact that the IPRC process guarantees the rights and involvement of parents, many were intimidated at first by its apparent complexity. The legislation very specifically requires boards to provide literature to explain the IPRC but, in the beginning especially, some of them were not quite successful at this. Over time, however, a combination of simple good will, along with cooperative effort on the part of boards, and some very effective work by parent associations and special education teachers, has done much to mitigate this concern.

Dateline 1989 — The Case of Justin

A flurry of October transfers meant that Justin's grade three class suddenly acquired a new teacher only a week before his situation was scheduled for special review by an Identification, Placement, Review Committee (IPRC). The new teacher wisely allowed the full-time assistant in grade three to work with the school's resource teacher in putting together the documentation for the IPRC. The EA was experienced and held in high regard in the school, and she had worked with Justin for the past two years. Perhaps most important, she was one of the few adults who understood and managed his behaviour effectively.

Over the past several years, Justin had been variously diagnosed as autistic, ADHD, learning disabled, cerebrally dysfunctional and mentally disabled, by a variety of clinical psychologists, either in private practice, or employed by the school board. While Justin was still in kindergarten, an IPRC took the unusual step — for a student so young — of identifying him "exceptional: behavioural". Justin's mother agreed with the identification because, as she wrote to the principal, it would allow the school to bring in extra resources for him. However, she served notice she would appeal any move to take her son out of a regular class, and maintained that position through reviews in grades one and two, in the face of growing evidence that a regular class might not be the best place for him.

The special review in grade three was arranged by the principal who, for everyone's sake, planned to make one more stab at modifying Justin's class placement. If that failed, she would initiate a process which could declare him 'hard-to-serve' and thereby excluded from the school. Fortunately, everyone, including the boy's mother, agreed to an adjustment. Justin would begin each day in the grade three class and then, with the EA, join a small resource class. He would, depending on his mood and behaviour, return to the regular class as frequently as possible, for periods as long as possible. Above all, it was agreed that flexibility would prevail and both EA and teachers would be free to make ad hoc decisions as necessary.

For Justin — and everyone — the long term outcome was most positive. Over time, he spent increasingly more time in the regular grade three class, but there was always a friendly place to go if the need arose. Perhaps most telling: the annual IPRC review in grade four lasted only ten minutes.

The appeal process too, came under criticism. Parents dissatisfied with an IPRC decision can take their case first to an Appeal Board, and then if it is unresolved at this level, to a Special Education Tribunal. The process came under fairly pointed criticism until a study of Appeal Board hearings commissioned by OCASE (Reilly, 1991) showed that the process is genuinely effective in giving parents a fair hearing. Nevertheless, a few years later, the province modified the appeal process, so that the right to choose members of an Appeal Board would be shared equally by parents and a school board.

Over several years in the mid 1990's, the appeal process — indeed the entire special education system and even the Education Act — was broached in a case that eventually was heard and ruled on by the Supreme Court of Canada (See page 19: Eaton vs. Brant County Board). However, not only did the high court's ruling uphold the board's original IPRC decision, over the course of hearings at several court levels, the province's special education legislation was also soundly affirmed.

Happily, appeal and litigation has been a factor in only a very tiny number of cases. The many thousands of IPRCs held since the final implementation of Bill 82, have generated but a few dozen Tribunals, suggesting quite strongly that the IPRC process does the job it was designed to do. Another more recent — and positive — trend, which has no basis in the legislation but is actively encouraged by the Ministry, is the use of mediation to resolve impasses. Both parents and boards are finding this technique far less costly and time-consuming than formal appeals, and usually, one that minimizes post-adversarial residue.

Constant Fine Tuning

Given the sweeping changes effected by Bill 82 and its related regulations and policy memoranda, the amount of subsequent adjustment on a province-wide basis, has been remarkably little. Indeed, much of what has been altered, has gone barely noticed except by administrators, and by parents with a specific area of interest. Typical of the latter group were parents of developmentally disabled children in 1993, when the provincial government in what was known as 'Bill 4' repealed the term 'trainable retarded' from the Education Act. The same bill

removed the 'hard-to-serve' section from the Act. This was a complicated and almost never used set of clauses that allowed a board to exclude a pupil.

The most significant modifications to official policy and practice were introduced in 1998, when the province re-issued the regulation concerning the IPRC process. The new regulation (Reg. 181) expanded the responsibilities of the committee in a variety of ways, required a written plan for the exceptional student, and generally strengthened the role and rights of parents. (See Chapter 5 for fuller details.) There have been other fine tunings as well, but the fact that so relatively few items have been altered in Ontario's official special education policy and practice, reinforces the conclusion that it works well, generally speaking. And when modifications are deemed necessary, most of these can be accomplished by individual boards and schools.

As special education practices mature, what seems more likely to occur on a more or less frequent basis are initiatives such as the special needs technologies (e.g., speech to text software and hardware) or the SNOW (Special Needs Opportunity Window) Web Site developed in 1998 as a resource centre for teachers.

Seeking Compromise on Integration*

At the time Bill 82 became law, it was customary in most jurisdictions to group exceptional students in self-contained classes according to their particular needs. This was not only considered normal, but in fact beneficial for all concerned. It was not unusual for school boards to point with pride to the number and range of special class situations it offered in its 'Plan'. However, in a very short time, the special education agenda was overtaken by pressure from some parents and professionals to integrate all exceptional students into regular classes, full time. Support for full integration was by no means unanimous, for others argued that the benefits of specialized environments are too significant to discard. The result, for a time, was quite intense conflict.

The issue, not just in Ontario, but in all of Canada, was further clouded by whether or not a board's decision to place an exceptional student

_____

*Advocates of the idea often prefer the word "inclusion".

Given that, in grade two, Onisa regularly brought clippings from the *Globe and Mail* and the *National Post* to 'show-and-tell', no one in her school was the least bit surprised when she won a UN-sponsored trip to Geneva, Switzerland, for her essay on the meaning of democracy. Still, during the promotion and placement meetings that were held at the end of the school year, both Onisa's regular grade six teacher and her 'Challenge Program' teacher were uneasy.

Onisa had been identified 'gifted' for some time, and her academic achievements were remarkable, especially during her earlier years at the school. But a standardized achievement test administered just before the end of the year in grade six suggested somewhat more modest abilities. Onisa still was clearly in the 'Superior' range, but if the language and general awareness categories were factored out, and only her results in math/science were presented, she was actually below the mean for her class. What intrigued both of Onisa's teachers was that this confirmed an unevenness that both of them had noticed: a contrast between what appeared to be her giftedness in language, and her quite ordinary ability in math and science.

It was a dilemma for the teachers because in their board, all students left for new schools after grade six. For Onisa to continue in the 'Challenge Program' and be able to develop her unique abilities, her identification as 'gifted' would need to be confirmed by the annual IPRC review. However, whereas the "Challenge Program" from grades one to six was an individualized, in-the-regular-class, enrichment offering, from grade seven on, students identified 'gifted' were generally placed in self-contained classes for an across-the-board enhanced curriculum (including advanced level math and science).

Happily, the school board's resources and the professionalism of its staff were brought to bear on Onisa's behalf. The head of the gifted program was aware of several other students with a similar math/science vs. language imbalance — and who shared Onisa's type of interests. Accordingly, they were each recommended for the same grade seven class. It would not be in a school designated for the specially enhanced curriculum, but Onisa and her peers would retain their identification so that, if in the future, it appeared any of them would be better off with the enhanced curriculum, then arrangements could be made with a minimum of fuss.

After six months in her new school, Onisa declined to make the switch when it was offered (although one of her peers accepted). After twelve months had passed, she was eligible once again to compete in the UN essay contest. This time her first step in the process was to write and request an appointment with the federal Minister for External Affairs.

in a special class, could be a violation of his or her equality rights under the *Canadian Charter of Rights and Freedoms*. The 1996 high court decision in Eaton vs. Brant County (see p. 19) did much to defuse this contention, but by this time the provincial government had already made significant strides toward a sensible and logical resolution. As early as the spring of 1991, the then Minister of Education had made a statement to the Ontario legislature that it was the position of her government that "integration of exceptional pupils into local community classrooms be the norm wherever possible". She went on to assure the assembly that inasmuch as an integrated setting is not appropriate for every child, school boards would be encouraged to offer a full range of alternative educational placements.

It was a position that seemed at once reasonable, educationally sound, and politically astute. Although no Ontario government has yet brought forward any specific legislation to reflect that position, it is in effect, the way special education works in the province today.

Policy from the Ministry supports it, and many school boards and individual schools were already operating that way in any case. Above all, it is a position that enables educators and parents to work together in an atmosphere of flexibility, something that the very notion of 'special needs' implies.

Special Education Today: A Mature Force

For Ontario students with special needs, universal access to education is guaranteed. The definite first choice of placement is the regular class. And perhaps most important, students with special needs are just that: *students*.

In short, special education has become a normal, integral and functional part of education in general. Not that continuing change and development and improvement will no longer be needed. Adjustments will always be necessary and will continue to happen. But special education in Ontario is positioned now so that changes to it occur in the larger context of all educational development. As education itself adjusts to social change, to technology and to general needs, special education will adapt with it. In that context, the future of special education in the province will most likely be expressed in positive refinements of the gains that have already been made.

READINGS & RESOURCES

For Further Investigation

Bell, C., & Harris, D. (Eds.) (1990). *World yearbook of education: Assessment and Evaluation.* Kegan Paul.

Bunch, G., & Valeo, A. (1997). *Inclusion: Recent research.* Toronto: Inclusion Press.

Council of Administrators of Special Education (1997). Position paper on delivery of services to students with disabilities. *Keeping in Touch.*

Foerter, J., et al (1991). *Special education: Bridging the centuries*, (Ontario Teachers' Federation).

Grossman, H. (1995). *Special education in a diverse society.* Toronto: Allyn & Bacon.

Hallahan, D. B., & Kauffman, J. M. (1994). *Exceptional Children: Introduction to special education.* Toronto: Prentice Hall.

Hardmen, M.L.D., et al (1993). *Human exceptionality: Society, school, and family* (4th ed.). Toronto: Allyn & Bacon.

Itard, J.M.G. (1806). *The wild boy of Aveyron* (G. Humphrey & M. Humphrey, trans.) (1962). Englewood Cliffs, NJ: Prentice-Hall.

Keeton-Wilson (1983). *A consumer's guide to Bill 82: Special education in Ontario.* Toronto. OISE Press.

Malouf, D.B., & Schiller, E.P. (1995). Practice and research in special education, *Exceptional Children, 61*, 414-424.

Oderkirk, J. (1993). Disabilities among children. *Canadian Social Trends*, pp. 22-25.

Reilly, D. Report on the OCASE Study on Special Education Appeals in Ontario (1985-1989).

Smith, D., Luckasson, R. & Crealock, C. (1995). *Introduction to Special Education in Canada.* Scarborough: Allyn & Bacon.

Winzer, M. (1993). *The history of special education: From isolation to integration.* Gaulladet University Press.

Wolfensberger, W. (1975). *The origin and nature of institutional models.* Human Policy Press.

Wood, M. (1998). Whose job is it anyway? Educational roles in inclusion. *Exceptional Children, 64* (2), 181-195.

Links

Canadian Charter of Rights and Freedoms
http://canada.justice.gc.ca/Loireg/charte/const en.html

Special Needs Education Network
http://schoolnet2.carleton.ca/sne/

Continuing Issues in Special Education

Integration*: the Great Debate

Although discussions about whether or not to place exceptional students in regular classes can still stir considerable passion, the issue is no longer the intensely polemical matter it once was. This is so because for the most part today, the majority of exceptional students are placed in regular classes, and in cases where alternatives are chosen, it is usually with the agreement of all parties involved. Nevertheless, arguments on the subject of integration continue to fill the journals, and still stir interest in administration offices, at professional conferences, and among various advocacy groups.

Essentially, what is left of the debate arises out of the premise that *all* students with special needs, no matter how unique or demanding

a particular case may be, should be placed in regular classrooms in their neighbourhood schools. Ranged somewhat apart from this view — and usually most reluctant to be put in an adversarial position — are those who do not see the matter quite so unconditionally. This group of educators and parents contends that, whereas integration should invariably be sought as a first solution, some students might be better served if they receive at least a portion of their program in a more specialized environment.

Supporters of full integration contend that the mere availability of a spectrum of settings is offensive, that the very existence of alternative settings can make integration fail for the very simple reason that it does not have to work. Supporters of a range of settings, meanwhile, argue that to be so absolute is unrealistic, that certain cases, out of sheer practical necessity, demand at least some form of special placement from time to time. What has made the integration debate so enduring is the difficulty in establishing ultimate answers. Research — a great deal of it over quite a long period of time — has been of regrettably little help, since for practically every research outcome demonstrating support for one view, an opposite research result seems to be readily available. (Note item

---

*When special education first became mandatory in Ontario, the prevailing term for placing students with special needs in the regular school system was 'mainstreaming'. Gradually, 'integration' became the preferred word, but because that term has other contexts for some people, many educators and parents prefer the term 'inclusion'. Because the Ontario Ministry of Education and Training uses the term 'integration' in its discussions and official publications, *Special Education in Ontario Schools* follows that practice.

on educational research in this chapter.) Classroom experience with integration is usually very case-specific; thus it can be misleading to generalize from the success or failure of one, or even several situations. And empirical evidence suggests that it is almost impossible to separate the success or failure of integration from the level of commitment in individual teachers.

It is ironic that a polemic should have arisen among educators and parents over integration, since in the end, both groups have always had the same objective: what is best for all students. There is even further irony in that a neutral observer, with no prior information, would have some difficulty at first, distinguishing between a school with a total integration policy and one with a range of settings policy, for both, out of sheer, practical necessity and the benefit of all, will arrange special settings for some exceptional students, some of the time.

Fortunately, a conjunction of circumstances over the 1990s, especially in Ontario, has done much to wind down the integration issue, and in the process made winners of all but a few absolutists on both sides. In the first place, early in the decade the provincial government presented policy (but not actual legislation) which declared the integration of exceptional students

to be the norm in the province's schools, a policy that continues to be affirmed in official ways by the Ministry. Secondly, the sheer fact of experience has taught both educators and parents that, on the one hand, including students with special needs in regular classes is not as difficult a task as some opponents of the idea had argued, and usually produces significant benefits for all. On the other hand, that same experience demonstrated that there really are some students who simply benefit from an alternative setting, no matter how extensive the resources in a regular classroom, nor how adapted the curriculum, nor how allegedly ideal the integrated setting. (Ultimately, experience has taught that decisions of placement lead to the best outcome when they are made on a by-case basis rather than on the basis of policy.) Thirdly, over the decade, a number of official decisions by commissions, by the civil courts, and even by the Supreme Court of Canada, have to a large extent, taken the denial-of-human-rights factor out of the debate, thereby affirming the idea that integration is essentially an educational and not a legal issue.

Taken together these factors have done much to cool the ardour of advocates on all sides of the issue.

Arguments Used to Support Full Integration
➤ Less likely to stigmatize; more natural and reflective of the real world
➤ Develops more positive attitudes and positive relationships
➤ More opportunity for inter-action
➤ Age appropriate models are more readily available
➤ Equal opportunity implies equal rights
➤ Research says full integration works better
➤ Teachers prefer full integration
➤ Parents prefer full integration
➤ Students, exceptional and otherwise, prefer full integration

Arguments Used to Question Full Integration
➤ Environment too manipulated to reflect the real world
➤ Student relationships are often unilateral, artificial, and in-class only
➤ Opportunities for intense instruction are reduced
➤ May not be able to teach and reinforce crucial special skills
➤ Equal rights do not necessarily imply equal opportunity
➤ Research says range of settings works better
➤ Teachers prefer range of settings
➤ Parents prefer range of settings
➤ Students, exceptional and otherwise, prefer a range of alternatives

In 1997, the Supreme Court of Canada handed down a decision on an Ontario case that has had a wide-ranging, and what is very likely to be a long-lasting, impact on the issue of integration, not only in the province, but throughout Canada. As well, throughout the chronology of the case in question,* a number of lower court rulings also proved to be significant for Ontario's policies and practices in special education.

Briefly, the situation revolved around the request by the parents of an Ontario child with quite extensive special needs, that she be placed full time in a regular class in her neighbourhood school. The school board granted the request and maintained the student in a regular class for approximately three school years. At the end of this period (ca. spring, 1993) an IPRC review decided that the placement in a regular class of the neighbourhood school was not in the student's best interests, and that she should be placed in a special, self-contained class. This was a class operated by the board in a different school. The parents did not agree, but instead of appealing via the procedures set out by the Ontario Ministry of Education and Training (these are detailed in Chapter 5) asked the civil court to overturn the IPRC decision. The court declined to do so and directed matters back to the Ministry's appeal process. Although the judge also ordered that the student continue in the regular class pending the appeal decision, by returning the case to the process, the court not only affirmed its validity, but also indicated its reluctance to interfere in educational matters where an official route of appeal is already in place.

The Appeal Board then upheld the IPRC decision, and in a carefully detailed written decision, so did the next — and usually final — level of appeal: the Special Education Tribunal. Through their counsel, the parents then asked the Ontario Divisional Court for a judicial review of the Tribunal's decision. This court found no error in the decision, and also dismissed the appellant's allegation that the Tribunal was not 'expert', yet another affirmation of the process.

The case was then heard by the Ontario Court of Appeal, which overturned the Tribunal, stating that regulations which allow a school board to place a child against parents' wishes are in violation of the Canadian Charter of Rights. Two years later, the Supreme Court, in what court observers described as an emphatically presented decision,** overturned the Ontario Court of Appeal and restored the Tribunal ruling, holding that the ruling was in the child's best interests and that it did not violate her equality rights under the Charter. In its written reasons, the Supreme Court offered some basic principles for school boards on the issue of placing students with special needs. Several of the more significant ones follow.

- There is no Charter presumption in favour of integration.
- The parents' view of their child's best interests does not determine the question.
- A placement decision does not impose a burden or disadvantage on a child under the Canadian Charter of Rights when the decision makers
  ✔ attempt to determine the best possible placement for the child
  ✔ act in the child's best interests
  ✔ provide for on-going reassessment so that needed changes can be made
  ✔ act from a child-centred perspective, so equality is meaningful from the child's point-of-view as opposed to that of the adults in his or her life.
- A segregated placement may be required where an integrated setting cannot reasonably be adapted to serve the child's best interests.
- 'Disability' can be widely interpreted, so that a segregated placement may be both protective and violative of equality, depending upon the individual.

---

*(Eaton vs. Brant County Board of Education, SCC #24668, 7 Feb. 1997)

**The Court gave its unanimous (9-0) decision less than 24 hours after hearing arguments.

Cultural and Socio-Economic Differences

Professional educators wince at the accusation that special education is often a depository for the children of poverty and for the culturally different. They wince because over-representation of these groups in special classes is often the case, and that flies directly in the face of everything education stands for. Yet for very real reasons, it is easy to see why the special class is often regarded as an ideal placement. Children of poverty and of some cultural minorities often have a high frequency of severe health and physical problems that affect their education. Conductive hearing loss (usually *otitis media*) among native children in Canada, for example, and eye infections affecting sight, occur at an average rate much higher than that of the general population. Children of minority groups sometimes experience linguistic difficulties that impinge on their school function in a major way. Assessment procedures that do not allow for cultural anomalies can have the effect of placing a child very restrictively in an education system.

It is not unusual for children from lower income families or from recently arrived immigrant families to have difficulties simply because they are confused by the demands of the school culture. Sometimes a family's lack of precedent for educational experience as well as lack of support for it, can have a serious effect on a student's performance. Very often, heads of the families do not manage a child's case by dealing with the school, the education system, and support agencies (or confronting them if necessary) either because they choose not to, or because they lack the sophistication.

For educators, the issue is one of delicate choice. From an educational perspective, these are indeed students with very special needs. And very frequently, the needs can be effectively met in a special education mode. However, the educational perspective must inevitably be illuminated by consideration of what is morally and socially appropriate. Identification and placement of a student in special education is a major step, one that can be taken with certainty if the basis of the decision is strictly educational. But when the basis is influenced by social, cultural and economic factors, there is, inevitably, a commensurate erosion of that certainty. It is a hard nut to crack, and no jurisdiction in Canada has yet done so to everyone's satisfaction.

The Gap Between Assessment and Program

In theory, where perfection is always more attainable, the assessment of a student is conducted not just for the purpose of identification, but also for the purpose of program planning. In fact, inasmuch as most exceptionalities are broadly identifiable without formal assessment at all, it may be more accurate to say that the principal purpose of an assessment, after it refines the broad identification, is to provide the information from which program planning can be developed.

Like so much of education, the practice often stumbles clumsily after the theory. It does so for several reasons. Chief among them is the strange combination of expertise and naivety that seems to prevail on both sides of the assessment/program planning issue. Psychologists or psychometrists or other assessors, without actual experience in teaching, often have either idealistic or simplistic notions of what actually occurs minute by minute in a classroom. Many classroom teachers, on the other hand, are not well-versed in assessment procedures, and frequently have difficulty coming to grips with the results of an assessment, most especially in translating the results into program.

> Parents of a special child . . . we don't worry quite the same way that other parents do. Sure we have all the 'what if' and 'if only' worries that all parents have. But what sets us apart is that it never stops. You see, for the parents of — can I say it? — *normal* kids, the worry pretty much stops when those kids grow up. But for us, growing up opens a whole new can of worms: *Now what's going to happen to them?* There is comfort when special kids are in school. It's a place to go, a reason to get up, a place of purpose. But once they're adults . . .
>
> Even worse, what happens when we're gone? They lose their best advocate when we die. Really, this is the disabilities issue of the next century.
>
> — *Louise Paul, parent of an adult male*

To be fair to both sides, the number of professional, concerned, caring assessors and teachers who attempt to rise above this problem is by far the majority. Yet they are frequently obstructed by matters not of their own making. The gap begins with their own training, for traditionally, neither gets opportunity to gain more than sketchy knowledge about the other. (Many universities and colleges have taken steps to remedy this.) As well, both sides argue that the gap could easily be narrowed, even closed, by direct communication: that if the teacher(s) and educational assistant(s) of the student being assessed can communicate directly with the assessor, the questions that need answers will at least be put on the table. Yet in many jurisdictions, this very simple expedient is impeded by bureaucracy and systems management. It is very common policy for assessors to obtain and report data only to a third party (coordinator, committee, principal, etc.). Then, for a variety of reasons such as privacy regulations, work loads, or in some cases, inefficiency, these data come to the classroom, if at all, in a form that is altered or diluted or summarized to the point of irrelevance.

It is the student who falls into the gap this system creates. The assessment may well be competent; the teachers may well be effective. But unless there is opportunity for some form of direct communication, the whole point of the procedure is diminished. Fortunately, a very positive outcome of the continuing experience in special education is an increased emphasis on classroom observation and assessment. It stands to reason that competent teachers and educational assistants who are "watching it live", so to speak, are in a crucial position to make perceptive, realistic evaluations of a student's strengths and needs. The fact that their observations are being given increasing credence in most jurisdictions, is a tribute to their professionalism and to common sense.

For Discussion: the Case of Parnell

On the surface, this case seems simple enough. Parnell lags behind his peers in achievement, by at least three grades. Most serious is his apparent inability to read. This might be accounted for by Parnell's own explanation that he "didn't go to school much" before coming to Canada three months ago, but the teacher of the grade 5-6 split class where he is placed, reports that the boy frequently manifests "learning disability-like characteristics"; viz; he is frequently off-task, rarely follows instructions in proper sequence, seems easily confused, and regularly loses his personal property (and the school's). A preliminary assessment by the board's special service group served only to reinforce what everybody already knows: that Parnell can't read. But the assessment was unable to identify specific reasons.

On the other hand, the (half-time) EA in the class points out that when she is able to instruct Parnell one-on-one, in skills like phonics and letter/word recognition, he grasps the material quickly. And retains it. The teacher acknowledges this. Unfortunately, neither has very much of this exclusive time available for Parnell, but time, along with the appropriate instruction, *is* available in one of the school's two special education classes. To benefit from it, Parnell would have to be identified as 'exceptional' by an IPRC, as the school board's policy is very strict on matters of this nature. (Unfortunately, a special reading program is not a viable option. The school's junior program was deleted two years ago owing to budget issues and staffing reallocation. The primary program is entirely over-extended and depends to a large extent on volunteers.)

Parnell has not expressed an opinion one way or another about a shift to special education; nor has his father. (Parnell's mother still lives in the Caribbean but plans to emigrate at some point in the future.) However, an intrusive issue of some delicacy must be dealt with in the case. Only a month ago, the senior public school that shares a campus with Parnell's school was the focus of obsessive media attention after an advocacy group accused it of "dumping" black children like Parnell into special education. An investigation revealed that the number in special education is indeed significantly disproportionate to the number in the general school population, and the school board has vowed to review all IPRC identifications carefully.

The IPRC will meet next week to discuss Parnell's case. Meanwhile, the principal has asked all members of staff to offer a comment on the best direction for all concerned.

Professional Autonomy Versus Bureaucracy and Tradition

All teachers and educational assistants regard the academic success of their students as a foremost priority. Yet very few ever stop there. Equally important for most teachers is their role in developing the full human potential of every one of their students. The freedom to pursue such a vision of combined professional purpose is essential to effective teaching and learning. Professionals with exceptional students in their classes have extra difficulty in this pursuit. Part of the difficulty is having to, wanting to, and trying to, find the time and opportunity and skill to respond to needs that appear to go beyond the normal demands one might reasonably anticipate in a classroom. Experience has taught that no matter how extensive the support available, students with special needs invariably require something extra. And while teachers and EAs are generally willing and able to do that something extra, a difficulty arises in their attempts to do so without denying the rest of the students equal treatment.

Finding a balance is extremely difficult, and the fact that so many teachers and EAs are successful much of the time is a tribute to them. However, to find the balance, they need the freedom to make decisions, and this freedom is often obstructed by traditional educational practice. Schools are run bureaucratically, with all the pluses and minuses that bureaucracy implies. Because special education seems to attract a disproportionate amount of legalism, and because it usually incorporates a wider range of professionals and a greater degree of administrative activity than regular education, the bureaucracy tends to be thicker, and often more regulatory and precise. The result is that classroom professionals are often denied the autonomy to make decisions that realistically, should be made ad hoc and on-site. The mere existence of a bureaucracy, no matter how enlightened its application, can impede the flexibility and spontaneity (and most often, simple common sense) so vital to good teaching.

The issue is often exacerbated by the not-yet-completely-dead medical model tradition, wherein classroom professionals, despite their position on the front lines, are denied expert status and must frequently yield to decisions that are made from afar. Further delicacy arises out of day-to-day parental involvement. Although the benefits are usually significant, close parental involvement holds the potential for stress, especially in the case of parents who advocate vigorously.

Taken together, or even separately, these are pressures which may deny classroom professionals the level of responsibility necessary to be effective. It is an issue that is still working its way through the special education experience, and one on which progress could well founder, for after the last bell of technical advance or service delivery or change in policy has been rung, it is only in classroom implementation where success or failure is realized. And classroom implementation is in the hands of the people who actually do the job.

The Challenge of Funding

When the cost of public education is under attack, special education is a readily available target because it is so visibly expensive and its outcomes are uncertain. The latter point becomes even more provocative when cost-benefit analysis is applied, namely: just what is the benefit to society in educating someone who may never return the costs of the investment? As reprehensible as such a question may be, and despite the fact it denies the very essence of our humanitarian spirit, it is a question that continues to arise, albeit usually in whispers, especially in times of economic downturn.

Fortunately, educators reject it for the most part. The overwhelming majority would fight to the last breath for the right of all students to be educated. Still, how to educate in the most beneficial but financially responsible way is an issue that will never go away. Only a few decades ago, funding practices followed a philosophy which held that time, effort and expense, needed to educate exceptional people offered no return, and it would take only a minor social upheaval to bring back that kind of thinking. Educators therefore, must be constantly aware of the role they play in projecting an image of responsibility.

That responsibility is reflected in yet another challenge: *how* to fund effectively and efficiently. Most jurisdictions in North America, Ontario included, offer extra monies to individual boards on a universal per pupil basis. These funds are then allocated locally according to need. Some, but not all of these jurisdictions,

Of the five students still attending the 'junior resource class' at the end of the school year, Vanessa and one other have been deemed ready by an IPRC to spend part of the school day in a regular grade five class. The other three will remain in the special resource class come September, where the resource teacher and two assistants will continue to emphasize appropriate behaviour and socialization.

Vanessa's gains, over two years in the resource class, have been considerable. She no longer screams continuously at maximum pitch when dissatisfied. She has developed appropriate toileting skills (instead of using the floor, wherever and whenever). Biting, scratching, and hairpulling seem to have been discarded as communication methods. And experimental mornings in the regular grade four class indicate that, with a little help from her favourite EA, Vanessa can sustain an age-appropriate relationship with a peer group. Interestingly, what pleases all the adults dealing with Vanessa more than anything, is that most of the time, and with supervision, she can be trusted to take a regular recess without incident.

Still, hers is a situation that will bear careful watching. A similar attempt at reintegration in grade three failed utterly, although all agree that this attempt was made too soon, and that the change was too drastic.

Assessments (two) indicate that Vanessa is of average intelligence, and there is no indication of any physical or learning disability despite the experience of her early years. From the time she was a baby until she became a ward of the Children's Aid Society at age eight, when her mother was jailed on a charge of voluntary manslaughter, Vanessa had moved seventeen times, had known six stepfathers, and had been treated for both TB and malnutrition. Her present school (from grade two) was the first one she had attended with any regularity, although her behaviour was so extreme initially, that the principal placed her in a one-on-one situation. (Three EAs, the school's full complement, spelled one another over the course of the day.)

However, a possible complication has now developed. Vanessa's birth father, whom she had never seen until a few months ago, has applied to the family court for custody. Both the court and the Children's Aid Society agree that he is a responsible, mature individual (he is married with two other children) and a good parent. However, he proposes to enrol Vanessa in the same school as his other two children. This school is in a different board in a different community and has a full integration policy. It has no designated resource or withdrawal classes. The family court judge has reserved a decision about custody until he receives an opinion from Vanessa's school as to whether or not the school change is serious enough to postpone the awarding of custody until she is able to make the change without risk.

offer additional funding over and above the universal grants, based on increments of need. Ontario moved to this style in the late 1990s, a modification which causes continuing debate. On the one hand, there is the quite laudable purpose of accountability. On the surface it seems reasonable to allocate monies on the basis of student need, with the more intense needs receiving proportionately more funding. Yet identification of special needs in a manner that satisfies fiduciary demands is extremely difficult. The fact that no jurisdiction in North America has yet found an entirely satisfactory way of making staged funding work, likely means that Ontario will not either. Just how to bring about the reasonable and responsible

funding of special education, it appears, is an issue that will never be satisfactorily resolved.

Special Education and Research

For special educators, drawing firm conclusions from research in the field can be an awkward task. For the simple, yet fundamental reason that the variables in studies involving human interaction are so extremely difficult to control, the results these efforts obtain often do not inspire confidence. Unless a study is conducted under laboratory conditions (which, paradoxically, makes it unreal at the very outset!) the researcher, not to mention the consumer, can really only speculate about the reasons for an outcome. It is a weakness that means educators can never be entirely sure they are dealing with results that would have meaning in their own situations.

Ironically, the two most important reasons for doing research in the first place, the teachers and the students, are at the same time the two most difficult variables to control. This shows up particularly in studies of integration, for example, where as a consequence, *place* is regularly confused with *what is happening in a place*. Simple logic forces recognition of the fact that the personality, the commitment, and the training of classroom professionals have a profound impact on the outcomes in their classes. Thus, if a study were to compare outcomes in two classrooms where all conditions are matched except an element of integration, that study would still not be able to duplicate the vital spirit and atmosphere that different professionals impart to the environment in which they teach. Nor could two classrooms ever be found where the collective personality generated by the students, is the same. If nothing else, this explains why there is so much contradictory research on integration.

Researchers in education face other problems, one of them being access to subjects and situations. Thus the numbers (i.e., the number of students, or teachers, or schools, etc.) are often too small or the subject groups too unique for the results to be truly meaningful — one reason why so many research reports conclude by calling for more research. (Another reason for the call is that the researchers themselves acknowledge limitations.) Even the typical claim that a "weight of evidence" generally favours one conclusion or another, is ultimately a very subjective stance.

Then there is the issue of misapplication of results and data. Usually this is not the researcher's error, but the consumer's. It has not been uncommon during the recent history of special education, for an advocate of one point of view or another to quite blithely use research results on integrating children who are

blind, for example, to support an argument about integrating children who are autistic. Nor is credibility and rational discussion enhanced by the amount of "gee whiz" literature in special education, particularly in non-refereed journals and in newspaper columns, where anecdotal reports are used to imply a general conclusion. (Although these narratives do add a powerful impetus to the reality of people with special needs and the importance of making accommodations for them.)

Taken together, all the above most emphatically does not mean that special educators, especially the professionals in the classroom, should ignore the research literature in the field. Rather, by staying in touch with the research, by following enough of it to be able to extract sensible conclusions and useful advice, teachers and EAs have a much greater chance of turning the outcomes to positive ends. Above all, by keeping informed and up to date, they will at the very least, be able to evaluate the research with far more insight and confidence. Regrettably however, 'keeping up' is a practice that many teachers acknowledge they do not follow, partly from lack of time and opportunity, but also out of inclination.

Labels, Categories and Definitions

Ultimately, the issue of labeling and categorizing students with special needs is a factor of the importance a culture attaches to language. And this importance will vary in intensity over time. There are still a few professionals in Ontario today, who can remember when the terms 'idiot', 'imbecile' and 'moron' were not only acceptable usage but were quasi-scientific categories. Today, of course, they are seen as fiercely pejorative and insulting. Yet there are jurisdictions in North America which have already abandoned contemporary ameliorative descriptors like "developmentally delayed" because of the gradual acquisition of negative connotations. Regrettably, experience tends to demonstrate that the search for ever more euphemistic vocabulary never

> "Over my many years running a school, I was always struck by the fact that the vigor of an individual's support of inclusion usually varies in direct ratio to his or her distance from the front lines. I hope it doesn't sound too cynical, but the fact is that people seem inclined to push an idea harder if someone else has to make it work. It may explain why academics tend to make more noise about inclusion than classroom teachers do."
>
> — *Jackson Tovell, Ontario principal*

ends. As new and sensitive identifiers age, they take on overtones, thereby provoking a perceived need for yet newer ones.

Still, there are indications that as the new century begins, the matter of labels and categories and definitions has declined significantly as an issue for debate. More and more generations are growing up with special people in their midst as a matter of course. More and more parents and professional educators now recognize descriptors simply as a convenience for discussion and administrative procedure. Although it is unlikely that the vocabulary of special needs will ever be entirely free of controversy for the simple reason that the meaning of words changes over time, it is equally unlikely that the issue will stir passions as it once did.

Controlling the Paper

Special education generates a lot of record keeping. The students, to begin with, have special needs that often require a wide range of personnel, who not only make their own reports, but also have to be kept advised of the work of others in the case. Funding mechanisms usually stir up a paper storm of their own, especially in situations where special students require unusual equipment or specialized instruction that take costs above the normal level of funding*. Most crucial in the education of exceptional students is the need for extensive adaptations in curriculum and teaching methods, adaptations that need to be recorded for pre-post evaluation, and for dissemination to interested parties. And looming over it all is the need for a collating plan or file to make sure the various parts work together and toward the same purpose. The consequence is a great deal of paper, and for all parties, a serious task: judging just how much is necessary?

Privacy matters aside (an issue that infuses all elements of education) it seems entirely logical, when viewed objectively, that preparing written plans for exceptional students, has

*An interesting case in point occured in Ontario in 1998, when the provincial government changed the basics of funding special education. Although the new system was presented as a simplification of the previous mix of grants and special considerations, it created whole new levels of complexity.

Against Labelling (Identification)	For Labelling (Identification)
• A single label by its very nature is inadequate, for the complexity of a human being cannot be summed up in a single concept such as *gifted*. • Labels stigmatize by emphasizing weakness and dysfunction (e.g., 'behavioural'). • Labels often mislead; someone who is described as *deaf* may only be hard of hearing. They propagate confusion, especially in the continuing search for mitigating phraseology. A classic case in point: the frenetic search to replace *mentally retarded*. • Once a person's exceptional need is classified, he or she tends to be seen in terms of the label, rather than as a human being with a special need. Thus individuals with the label 'learning disabled' for example, may innocently and unwittingly provoke lowered expectations in those who teach them. • Labels tend to stick for life.	• It is simpler to engage in academic discussion, in professional development, in in-service teacher training, in all varieties of research, when there is an accepted and understood frame of reference. • Specific identifications permit precise communication among professionals from different fields. Particularly in cases of chronic health need or physical disability, it is important that educators, caregivers, and medical personnel all work from the same text. • Identification of a group's unique needs raises its profile so that it gets the special attention it requires. • Categories facilitate differentiated responses. • Administrators need a mutually acceptable taxonomy of description if they are to account for their management of the public purse. • Experience shows that abolishing one set of labels simply produces another, often pejorative.

beneficial effects. This seems especially so if the plans detail the students' needs and then follow that detail with descriptions of how, where, and when the needs will be addressed, and further, by an account of when and how the success (or failure) of these efforts will be evaluated. Indeed, a requirement of Ontario's Regulation 181 governing IPRCs, is that such plans, called IEPs or Individual Education Plans must be completed for every student.

On the surface, the logic behind this practice is unassailable, for a specific plan brings focus and coordination to meeting a student's needs. It helps to satisfy the need for accountability: viz., if funds are being spent, personnel assigned, and effort expended, then at the very least, every one involved can follow the tracks. A plan offers a common basis for discussion should the need for modification develop, and far from least in importance, unfortunately, a documented paper trail may someday be needed should legal issues arise.

The drawbacks, however, are twofold. One is that a plan itself can easily become more important than the subject for whom it is designed. (This has been a long time complaint of special educators in the U.S. where legislation passed in 1975, has required extensive written plans.) Once a plan dominates absolutely, then flexibility diminishes, and creativity disppears, and without these components, the very essence of 'special' education is lost. Granted, the evaluation phase of a typical IEP is designed to preclude such an outcome, but once plan supremacy is established, modifications become very difficult to bring about. This is especially

> It seems that no matter how much we tried to shorten the forms our board required in special education, they always took on a life of their own. And they always *grew!* Frankly, I don't recall a single form in my twenty five years of special ed. that ever shrank. Every one just got longer and longer until we chucked it as too unwieldy. Then the process would start all over again.
>
> — *David Cone, superintendent (ret.)*

true if the exceptional student's needs are complex. The more complicated a case may be, the greater number of personnel there are to consult, and the larger the amount of resources to shift about — all with paper attached.

The second drawback is the *professional time* taken up by record keeping. As valuable as the detailing of information may be, it is rarely more important than the time a professional spends interacting with the student being recorded. (This too has been a complaint of U.S. special educators since 1975. In many states, former classroom personnel have found themselves spending their entire time maintaining files.) Ontario boards, encouraged by the Ministry of Education, have tried to benefit from the American experience by keeping prescribed forms as brief as possible, and by utilizing general administrative practices which assign one person nominal control — and thereby, some flexibility — over an IEP. Even so, experience has demonstrated that IEP forms and the many supplementary forms they seem to spawn, invariably grow in length and complexity over time.

Yet, experience has also shown that to make a significant impact on an exceptional student's situation, coordinated and recorded planning are essential. Finding the elusive balance between the logical boundaries of a specific plan, and the art of creatively and intuitively responding to a student's needs, will always be a challenge in special education. The fact that teachers and administrators continue to search for it, is to their credit.

READINGS & RESOURCES

For Further Investigation

Council for Exceptional Children (1991). "Code of ethics for the CEC". *Teaching Exceptional Children, 23,2.*

Council for exceptional Children (CEC). (1993). CEC policy on inclusive schools and community settings. *Teaching Exceptional Children, 25*(4), supplement.

Friend, M., Bursuck, W. & Hutchinson, N. (1998). *Including Exceptional Students: A Practical Guide for Classroom Teachers.* Scarborough: Prentice-Hall.

Fuchs, D. and Fuchs L.S. (1994). Inclusive schools movement and the radicalisation of special education reform. *Exceptional Children, 60*(4), 294-309.

Giangreco, M., Edelman, S., Dennis, R., & Cloninger, C. (1993). My child has a class-mate with severe disabilities: What parents of nondisabled students should think about full inclusion. *Developmental Disabilities Bulletin, 21*(1), 77-91.

Gutkin, T.B. (1996). Core elements of consultation service delivery for special services personnel: Rationale, practice, and some directions for the future. *Remedial and Special Education,17*(6), 333-340.

Harry, B. (1992a). Restructuring the participa-tion of African American parents in Special Education. *Exceptional Children, 59*, 123-131.

Harry, B. (1992b). *Cultural diversity, families, and the special education system: communica-tion and empowerment.* New York: Teachers College Press.

Inclusion Press / Centre for Integrated Educa-tion and Communication, 24 Thome Crescent, Toronto, Ontario M6H 2S5.

Kliewer, C., & Bilkin, D. (1996). Labeling: Who wants to be called retarded: In W. Stainback & S. Stainback (Eds.), *Controversial issues confronting special education: Divergent perspectives* (2nd Ed. pp. 83-95). Boston: Allyn & Bacon.

Minke, K.M., Bear, G.G., Deiner, S.A., & Griffin, S.M. (1996). Teachers' experiences with inclusive classrooms: Implications for special education reform. *Journal of Special Education, 30*, 152-186.

Palmer, D.S., Borthwick-Duffy, S.A., & Windaman, K. (1998). Parents perceptions of inclusive practices for their children with significant cognitive disabilities. *Exceptional Children, 64*, 271-282.

Perl, J. (1995). Improving relationship skills parent conferences, *Exceptional Children, 28*, 29-31.

Piorier, D., Goguen, L., & Leslie, P. (1986). The Canadian Charter of Rights and Freedoms and the right to education for exceptional children. *Canadian Journal of Education, 11*, 231-244.

Piorier, D., Goguen, L., & Leslie, P. (1988). *Education rights of exceptional children in Canada: A national study of multi-level commitments.* Toronto: Carswell.

Reynolds, M.C. (1991). Classification and label-ing. In J.W. Lloyd, N.N. Singh, & A.C. Repp (Eds.), *The regular education initiative: Alternative perspectives on concepts, issues and models* (pp. 29-42). Sycamore, IL: Sycamore.

Roberts, L.W., & Clifton, R.A. (1995). *Contemp-orary Canadian Educational Issues.* Toronto: Nelson.

Sandberg, B., & Michaelson, C. (1993, October 18). This is a sham: Parents, educators speak out. *New York Teacher*, pp.2-3.

Stainback,W. & Stainback S. (Eds.), (1996). *Controversial Issues Confronting special Education: Divergent perspectives* (2nd edition), Boston: Allyn & Bacon.

Vergason, G.A., & Anderegg, M.L. (1997). The ins and outs of special education terminology. *Teaching Exceptional Children, 29*(5), 35-39.

Vlachou, A. and Barton, L. (1994). Inclusive education: Teachers and the changing culture of schooling. *British Journal of Special Education, 21*(3), 105-107.

Wood, M. (1998). Whose job is it anyway? Educational roles in inclusion *Exceptional Children, 64* (2), 181-195.

York, G. (1990). *The Dispossessed: Life and Death in Native Canada.* Toronto: Little Brown and Company (Cananada) Ltd.

Ontario's Exceptional Students
Who and How Many?

Defining the Population: No Easy Task

Agreement on Generalities

For purposes of discussion and mutual understanding, teachers and other professionals involved with special education use variations of the following categories to describe the exceptional population in schools.

- *Intellectual differences:* includes students who are intellectually gifted and those who have some intellectual retardation.
- *Sensory disabilities:* includes the blind and deaf.
- *Communication disorders:* includes the learning disabled, and students with speech and language difficulties.
- *Physical and health difficulties:* includes students with problems that arise from birth defects, orthopedic conditions, and disabilities caused by disease. Usually, students with neurological disorders are included here.
- *Behaviour disorders:* includes students with mental illness, those who are socially maladjusted, delinquent, emotionally disturbed, and those with conduct disorders.
- *Developmental disabilities:* includes students with pervasive disorders like autism, or severe intellectual disability, and students with multiple disabilities.
- *Combinations* of the above.

Disagreement on Specifics

The previous categories appear in the literature, and they are used freely in general discussion, yet they are by no means official, or legal, or even scientific definitions of exceptionality. After more than a quarter century of in-depth experience, the field has yet to establish a set of clear, standardized definitions of exceptionality that everyone accepts and uses.

Part of the difficulty lies in the varying perspectives of different stakeholders. Administrators and jurisdictional centres (e.g., governments and school boards) use definitions for identifying candidates, and for determining levels of funding and resource allocation in a way that ensures accountability of the public purse. Parents, advocacy groups, and support associations also use definitions to identify candidates, but quite understandably, prefer definitions that trigger maximum funding and resource benefits. Some support groups are especially sensitive about the type of vocabulary used in definitions, and sometimes take the position that there should not even be definitions, because students with special needs simply do not fit into such confines. Very often, the official definitions issued by a jurisdiction (Ontario's, for example) will be different from the official definitions issued by a support association, even though the two parties may consult regularly. (Traditionally in Ontario, Ministry of

Education personnel and support groups consult and cooperate extensively.)

Still other stakeholders have very individualistic perspectives. Medical professionals have their own view, one that often has limited connection with education. Researchers often develop their own definitions in order to limit the variables in a study. Teachers want definitions to provide a practical guidance point for planning and practice. Then there is the very notion of exceptionality itself. To anyone who reflects on the fact that normalcy has never been subjected to the rigorous parameters of a definition, it is no surprise that departures from normal are hard to describe.

Definitions and the Classroom

For those who work with exceptional students on an active, daily basis — teachers, educational assistants, parents — the precision, or lack thereof, in definitions of exceptionality is a minor issue in the great scheme of things. Yet it is an issue that cannot be completely ignored. In the first place, if classroom professionals become involved with other professionals (medical, for example) over a student's case,

it is important that each understand the other's perspective. Secondly, for better or worse, special education attracts politics and advocacy, so for understanding and productive dialogue, it behooves all parties to be tuned in to all positions. Finally, and perhaps most practically, official definitions issued by a jurisdiction may well be the factor that determines which students are identified exceptional, and what resources can and will be made available for their benefit. For that reason alone, teachers, for example, must be sensitive to them.

Ontario's Official Definitions

See Appendix for definitions current at time of publication.

When Bill 82 made special education mandatory in Ontario, the Ministry of Education issued a set of quite detailed definitions of exceptionality. The idea was that boards of education would use them when identifying a student as exceptional and, initially, most boards did just that. But over time, many boards found it advantageous to modify the definitions for their own use. A few boards elected to discard definitions altogether. Others stuck to the Ministry list but made additions and deletions.

For Discussion: the Case of Hobie

According to the special education teacher, Hobie is the most loved student in the entire school. No one is absolutely certain whether Hobie knows this, but that does not matter to his classmates in grade three, who, in the words of the teacher, "have become twenty-four willing caregivers". Hobie has severe, multiple disabilities. He is blind, has no speech, and cannot move any of his limbs. His facial muscles respond to sound stimuli, a fact which convinces his parents, and the teacher and EA, that he can hear. No one has any firm idea whatsoever of his mental capacities.

Hobie has outlived every one of the medical profession's dire predictions, and despite initially grave misgivings about having him in a regular class, the school staff, and especially the students, have received him enthusiastically. He spends much of his day on a modified skateboard-looking stretcher that can be raised and lowered, and a health aide takes him out every two hours to aspirate him and see to his other, quite extensive, health and hygiene needs. No one has yet figured out how to communicate with him. The students, for their part, go out of their way for Hobie. They vie to roll him into every group situation. They take turns holding his hand during periods like "story time" and "the news". No one ever passes without patting his chest or gently putting a finger to his cheek, and instinctively, they speak to him in peer-level language (i.e., no "baby talk"). Everyone interprets Hobie's facial reactions as proof that he is thrilled by what is happening.

Despite the very positive situation, a change looms. Hobie can be in this class because the board's 'fragile health needs' unit is temporarily housed in the school. Next year, it moves to a purpose built facility in a brand new school, and all students currently in the unit move with it. When the grade three students, on their own initiative, asked their principal to keep Hobie with them next year in grade four, she, as well as the board's administration and trustees, were deeply touched. But whether Hobie's thought-to-be happy situation with the class should outweigh health, safety, and possibly legal considerations is an issue they must first resolve.

Ontario Student Population[1]

Total: 2,102,039 — Exceptional: 194,140 (**9.24%**)

	Elementary[2]		Secondary[2]	
	Total	Exceptional	Total	Exceptional
Male	716,157	65,832 (**9.19%**)	358,543	54,936 (**15.32%**)
Female	679,342	35,653 (**5.25%**)	340,037	29,759 (**8.75%**)
	1,395,499	101,485 (**7.27%**)	698,580	84,695 (**12.12%**)

[1]All publicly funded schools. [2]Not including provincial schools, C & T centres, and correctional schools (See Figure 3D).
Source: Policy Branch, MET, 31/10/97.

Figure 3A

Still others created whole new ones. Partly, this was in response to the aging of the definitions; partly it was in response to parent advocacy; and partly, the changes were made because many boards felt that as special education matures, and as philosophies, scientific knowledge, and practices change, the definitions of exceptionality should evolve as well.

The result was not the hodgepodge that one might expect from such independent forays. Granted, in some instances it became possible for a student to qualify for special education in one board in the province, but not in another. But most of the time these were unique cases that, conceivably, would have been difficult to specify, with or without a set of commonly used descriptions. In effect, the relatively independent expression by the province's school boards on the matter of defining areas of exceptionality, was simply a reflection of how difficult it is to describe accurately, students with special needs. Many fit several definitions; others fall into cracks between definitions; still others resist the confines of qualifiers like 'mild', 'moderate', and 'severe'. And, there is the reality of change. Exceptional students, like all students, grow and develop. Their special needs are not immutable.

When Ontario's Bill 104 reduced the number of school boards in the province from 129 to 72 in 1998, the number of local descriptive variations, quite naturally, was reduced as well. Also, new funding mechanisms increased the importance of using and co-ordinating definitions more precisely. Most important, in 1998, the regulation governing IPRCs was modified and re-issued with more specific direction to school boards that the province's definitions be used. Taken together, these conditions brought about more careful attention to centrally established descriptions of exceptionality, with all of the pros and cons such practice involves.

Exceptional Students: Just How Many?

In 1983, the Canadian Council of Ministers of Education issued data indicating that 15.5 per cent of the school age population in the country is exceptional. That figure, which was arrived at by less than rigorous science, became fixed in the consciousness of the general public, not to mention many educators who usually have access to more accurate information. Despite the fact that both incidence data (number of new cases over a time period) and prevalence data (total number of existing cases) are notoriously difficult to collect and collate, there is sufficient experience in special education practice now, along with some useful studies, to suggest that the real figure is much lower.

Figure 3A shows that, in Ontario, the percentage of students actually identified exceptional as of October, 1997, was 9.24. MET's data issued in 1995 showed the percentage at 8.9. In 1990, the figure was 7.9. Although the number of students identified exceptional in the province appears to have been steadily increasing, the rise in numbers is at least partly a consequence of improved procedures of identification, along with the expansion of special education in areas where it had not previously been offered. In 1986, for example, at the end of the first year of mandatory special education in the province, Ontario's boards, many of whom were still feeling their way through the process, had identified 6.5 per cent of the school population as exceptional.

Although current Ontario data appear to show significantly fewer exceptional students than the widely accepted 15.5 figure implies, they are substantiated by data from the U.S.A, where collection of special education information is rigidly controlled by legislation, and where it is also *centralized*. (Canadian data are collated from the various provinces, almost none of which use the same collection methods or even terminology!) After the first year of mandatory legislation in the U.S.A., (1976) approximately 7 per cent of American students were identified as receiving special education. By the mid-nineties, this figure grew to and generally hovered at just under 10 per cent. U.S. figures for the number of identified exceptional students thus show a similar path to that of Ontario, where the figure seems to have stabilized at between 9 and 10 per cent.

Numbers from Statistics Canada

Although *StatsCan* has no vested interest in driving a popular perception of any kind, it is entirely possible that some of the data it publishes contribute to a perception of ever-higher incidence of special needs. In the 1991 census for example, about 4.2 million Canadians, or about 16 per cent of the population, reported some level of disability. However, the widely recognized publication, *Disability Today* (1995, *winter*, p.7) using the same StatsCan data, stated that 390,000 Canadian children (i.e., those most likely to be counted in student populations), or about five percent, had some form of disability. Taking into account the fact that some high prevalence disabilities usually go unreported in StatsCan-type data collection —

For Discussion: the Case of Teresa

An IPRC will meet next week to discuss identification and placement of Teresa, aged 13.4. Teresa has been 'home-schooled' for the past six months, although her mother, the school counselor, the social worker from family services, the probation officer, and Teresa herself, all agree the situation has been less than satisfactory, and for the most part, unproductive.

Seven months ago, Teresa was arrested along with two other girls. Although the Young Offenders Act is protective of the details, the IPRC is aware that the three assaulted a fourth girl who is still in hospital. She sustained a brain injury in the beating that, according to the most recent assessment, will likely be permanent. Teresa spent a month in custody and was released on probation. One condition of the release was the home schooling. (The two other girls remain in custody; neither, upon release, will be returning to this school board.)

Teresa has a history of violent behaviour (first official encounter with police at age 8) and an extensive list of suspensions and disciplinary actions from her school. Children's Aid has been involved in her situation for years, and has twice removed her from her mother's care. Each of the adults concerned with Teresa's out-of-school care has given a written statement to the IPRC indicating their unanimous opinion that it is best for Teresa that she return to school, and that in their collective opinion, she has "learned a valuable lesson", is "remorseful", and "will benefit from the opportunity for a fresh start".

During an informal, preliminary discussion, the members of the IPRC agreed that Teresa could be identified 'Exceptional-Behavioural' and be placed in a resource class with a teacher and educational assistant who together have a history of success with both boys and girls like her. Teresa's mother objected to the 'Behavioural' designation on the basis that it stigmatizes her daughter and runs counter to the idea of a fresh start. She went on to state she would not agree to the designation, but would accept the designation 'Learning Disabled', inasmuch as Teresa cannot read in any case. However a community advocacy group is now privy to the mother's wishes and plans to object strenuously — through legal avenues if necessary – to the LD designation. Their argument is that such an identification stigmatizes students who are genuinely learning disabled, and further reinforces, negatively, a widening public perception that all learning disabled students have behaviour problems.

The IPRC is now looking for a solution.

most especially learning disabilities which, if fully reported, would double the number of children with a disability — Ontario's 9 to 10 per cent figure seems even more convincing.

Pros and Cons in the Numbers

Because definitions of exceptionality vary, it follows that figures showing the number of students in a particular category may not always be reliable, especially if the data are used to make comparisons across very wide jurisdictions (like whole provinces). Quebec, for example, reported a learning disability prevalence in 1989, that was three times that of Ontario and eight times that of B.C.! In two equally difficult-to-define categories, Behaviour Disorders and Multiple Disabilties, Quebec numbers were greater than Ontario's by factors of 4.5 and 2.6 respectively.*

There are other data problems too. Some jurisdictions report faithfully; others fail to do so. (For the data in Figures 3B and 3C, for example, of the 4762 schools concerned, 247 failed to report to the Ministry of Education by the due date.) Privacy regulations intervene, and geography in a province the size of Ontario can be a barrier. Then there's the issue of relevance when data apply to a large and varied population. The now defunct Metropolitan Toronto School Board, for example, in its final year (1997) pointed out among other things, that 42 per cent of its school population spoke a language other than English, double the provincial average, a fact which, the board argued, would skew requirements not just for special education but regular education as well.

*Council for Exceptional Children, 1989

On the positive side, in Ontario, the Ministry of Education and the province's school boards have some considerable experience now in collecting, collating, and sharing data about special education. While recognizing that difficulties will never be surmounted completely, it is nevertheless reasonable to regard the data in such tables as Figures 3B and 3C as a reliable overview, and therefore valuable as a tool in policy planning.

Looking At Ontario's Numbers

Few educators are surprised by data that show males outnumbering females in the exceptional student population. What often does surprise is the extent of the difference (see Figure 3A). In both elementary and secondary panels in Ontario, the number of males is almost double that of females. To a degree, the apparent inevitability of the difference is supported by

Ontario Exceptional Student Population[1] (Elementary)

Exceptionality	Male	Female	Total	Per cent
Socially maladjusted/ Emotionally disturbed	6141	1123	7264	7.2
Autistic	1473	445	1918	1.9
Hearing Impaired/ Deaf	900	1114	2014	2.0
Learning Disabled	32,403	16,024	48,427	47.7
Speech & Lang. Impaired	4300	2000	6300	6.2
Gifted	8488	6543	15,031	14.8
Developmentally Disabled (Mild)	5227	4048	9275	9.1
Developmentally Disabled	2917	1992	4909	4.8
Visually Impaired/ Blind	332	228	560	.5
Deaf/Blind	44	35	79	-
Other Physical Disabilities	784	569	1353	1.3
Multi-Handicapped	2823	1532	4355	4.3

[1] All publicly funded schools except provincial schools, C & T centres, and correctional schools.
Source (and terminology): Policy Branch, MET, 31/10/97.

Figure 3B

evidence of pre-existing conditions. Note, in Figures 3B and 3C, for example, those populations where a physical condition exists. In every one of the categories except Hearing Impaired/Deaf, males outnumber females by a significant measure, suggesting that the disproportion in gender distribution is simply a reflection of the real world. Schools, after all, can hardly be blamed if more boys are physically disabled than girls.

But also worth noting is that in some of the categories of exceptionality where the schools make the basic determination (e.g., learning disability, socially maladjusted/emotionally disturbed) males outnumber females by even greater percentages. Discrepancies of this magnitude give pause to educators, for they make it difficult to refute the long-standing criticism that schools are less friendly to boys than to girls. Of even further interest, the latter accusation has traditionally been directed at elementary schools,

but the data here show that learning disability percentages *increase* in the secondary schools of Ontario, not the other way around! Even more perplexing is the sheer number of students identified learning disabled.

The gifted category merits some reflection too, not just for the high numbers but for the increase in secondary numbers over elementary, even though accepted wisdom has it that high school is a weightier challenge. As well, the relatively higher proportion of secondary students identified exceptional provokes a series of questions that, albeit uncomfortable, are nevertheless useful. E.g., is special education too convenient an alternative in secondary school for students who don't fit the mold? Or, does elementary school send on too many students who are inadequately prepared? Do the significantly lower numbers in deaf/blind at the secondary level mean that this panel is less hospitable to that special need? Or, is special schooling more productive, and thereby a better setting for older students with that special need? Would this be the case then, for the majority of older students with special needs?

The discussions that such questions stir is one of the benefits of making data available. If numbers like those in Figures 3A, 3B and 3C enable educators to reflect with more insight on their objectives and their methods, indeed even on their mission, then the numbers have value. Not that the outcome is always a polemical matter, for the revelations can be encouraging too. A comparison of numbers from elementary to secondary panels in categories like Autistic and Speech and Language Impaired, for example, supports the conclusion that the special needs of some exceptional students do in fact decrease, that students do "get better".

Ontario Exceptional Student Population[1] (Secondary)				
Exceptionality	Male	Female	Total	Per cent
Socially maladjusted/ Emotionally disturbed	3412	915	4327	5.1
Autistic	549	152	701	.8
Hearing Impaired/ Deaf	408	501	909	1.1
Learning Disabled	31,578	14,350	45,928	54.2
Speech & Lang. Impaired	1799	925	2724	3.2
Gifted	9303	7443	16,746	19.7
Developmentally Disabled (Mild)	4314	3195	7509	8.9
Developmentally Disabled	1320	984	2304	2.7
Visually Impaired/ Blind	249	164	413	.5
Deaf/Blind	2	5	7	-
Other Physical Disabilities	367	315	682	.8
Multi-Handicapped	1635	812	2447	2.9

[1]All publicly funded schools except provincial schools, C & T centres, and correctional schools.
Source (and terminology): Policy Branch, MET, 31/10/97.

Figure 3C

A Very Special Population

The Ministry of Education and Training has direct responsibility for a number of very special schools in the province. The examples of longest standing, and certainly the best known, are the *provincial schools*. These are residential schools (with a few day students where feasible) geared to specific exceptionalities.

In Brantford, the W. Ross Macdonald School, named after a former lieutenant-governor, has programs for blind and deaf/blind students. In London, Belleville and Milton, schools named after former Ontario premiers — the Robarts School, Sir James Whitney School, and Ernest C. Drury School respectively — offer programs for deaf students. The Ministry also maintains what are called *demonstration* schools at the latter three locations, for students with ADHD and severe learning disabilities. Each with a fairly small population, these are residential schools known, respectively, as Amethyst, Sagonaska, and Trillium. In Ottawa, the Centre Jules-Léger offers programs for the deaf and severely learning disabled in French.

Ontario Special School Enrolment[1]

	Hospital Schools	Provincial Schools, Care/Treatment Ctrs., Correctional Facilities
Male	576	5070
Female	440	1874
Total	1016	6944

[1]*Source: Policy Branch, MET, 31/10/97. Data amalgamates elementary and secondary.*

Figure 3D

Also, the Ministry maintains a number of *hospital schools*, as well as *care and treatment centres* at various key locations in the province, and schools in a number of correctional facilities. Unlike the provincial schools, where education is the primary mission, in these latter locations the 'school' aspect functions in tandem with other purposes.

In 1997, there were 412 of these very special schools.

READINGS & RESOURCES

For Further Investigation

Adelman H.S. (1992). LD: The next 25 years. *Journal of learning Disabilities, 25,* 17-21.

Canadian Council for Exceptional Children (1989). Status of education service delivery to exceptional students: A provincial survey. *Keeping In Touch.*

Deno, E. (1994). Special education as development capital revisited: A quarter century appraisal of means versus ends. *The Journal of Special Education. 27,* 375-392.

Huntington, D. D., & Bender, W. N. (1993). Adolescents with learning disabilities at risk? Emotional well being, depression, suicide. *Journal of Learning Disabilitities, 26,* 159-166.

Maag, J.W., & Reid, R., (1994). Attention deficit hyperactivity disorder: A functional approach to assessment and treatment. *Behavioral Disorders,* 20(1), 5-23.

Mazurak, K. and Winzer, M. (1994). *Comparative Studies in Special Education,* Washington, DC: Gaulladet.

McKenzie, R. G. (1991). Content area instruction delivered by secondary learning disabilities teachers: A national survey. *Learning Disabilities Quarterly, 14,* 115-122.

Nessner, K. (1990, winter). Children with disabilities. *Canadian Social Trends,* pp. 18-20.

Raskind, M. H., Herman, K. L. & Torgeson, J. K. (1995). Technology for persons with learning disabilities: Report on an international symposium. *Learning Disability Quarterly, 18,* 175-184.

Richardson, S. (1992). Historical perspectives of dyslexia. *Journal of Learning Disabilitities, 25* (1), 40-47.

Seigel, L. S. (1992). An evaluation of the discrepancy definition of dyslexia. *Journal of Learning Disabilitities, 25,* (10).

How Ontario's Special Education Works:
An Overview of Service Delivery

> **In Simple Terms . . .**
>
> When matters like legislation, official policy, authorized practice — and politics — are set aside, special education is essentially a three part process:
>
> **I:** Identifying a student's special needs.
>
> **II:** Choosing the most appropriate setting to meet the needs.
>
> **III:** Planning, implementing, and regularly evaluating an individualized program to meet the needs.
>
> Needless to say, because our education system is publicly supported and bureaucratically organized, and because special education is a field where diverse opinions prevail and advocacy plays a large role, it is not surprising that these three components seem remarkably uncomplicated, compared to what actually goes on day by day. Nevertheless, these elements summarize precisely what is required in the delivery of special education service: determine the needs and the appropriate setting, then plan and deliver the appropriate response.

I: Identifying a Student's Needs

In many classroom situations, there are students who come with their special needs already determined. Because they are students in the school or school board, they will already have been assessed, and quite possibly, will already be officially identified as exceptional and have a program plan in place. Others, especially in the case of students with physical or medical exceptionalities, will often come with these needs clearly established and detailed. A few students may have come from another school or from another class in the same school, tagged so to speak, for "careful watching", to see whether suspected needs are genuine enough to be addressed. Still others, most especially the very young, will arrive with (usually informal) information about their needs supplied by parents or nursery school personnel. Then there are the students whose special needs become apparent for the first time during the course of a school year.

Some or all of the above students will be continuing candidates or new candidates for special education. If their specific needs have not

Both Sheldon and Jean-Marc were accepted in a pre-school, regional centre day program when they were 4.4 years and 4.2 years old respectively. Although both boys presented almost exactly the same behaviours, Sheldon had been diagnosed as 'autistic' while Jean-Marc was diagnosed as having 'pervasive development disorder'. Both boys were totally introverted; they engaged in harmful self-stimulation; neither used intelligible speech, and both were instant runaways if left unsupervised. Happily, the program at the centre was successful in quickly effecting some changes. After about three months, both began to use some meaningful speech, and as well, appeared to understand much of what was being said to them. By the end of one full year, their echolalic habits diminished significantly, and Jean-Marc (but not Sheldon) began to refer to himself in the first person (rather than calling himself "he" or "Jean-Marc") and would directly address his favourite educational assistant by name rather than as "she".

In their second year at the centre, Sheldon and Jean-Marc are now enrolled in what the staff at the centre casually calls the 'top' group. It took a psychometrist three tries, but she succeeded in completing a pre-school assessment of Jean-Marc and found him to be of average to just below average intelligence, with speech, although delayed (at 6.4, he is at the norm for 4-year olds) improving at an accelerated pace. Jean-Marc makes eye contact spontaneously about half the time, and when directed to "Look at me" will respond appropriately every time. He still exhibits some unusual behaviours (e.g., he will compulsively stroke any clothing that is red in colour, no matter who wears it; music of any kind will take up his total attention, not only during its playing but after. On occasion he will hum a melody over and over for the remainder of the day.) Staff at the centre point proudly to his ability to relate to others. On the thrice-weekly field trips (to shopping malls, parks, etc., anywhere that people gather) Jean-Marc follows directions, takes responsibility, and spontaneously assists with the group.

In Sheldon's case, the field trips are a weak point. Wide open spaces threaten him, as do large numbers of strange adults. While he copes with these situations as long as there is familiar adult support, he still turns to the comfort of repetitive, stereotyped behaviour at these times (alternately patting his cheeks and then his ears; another is spinning round and round, with eyes closed and arms extended; staff has noted several times that he can persist at this indefinitely without getting dizzy.) On the other hand, Sheldon's use of appropriate language has increased dramatically. Although he refused absolutely to cooperate with the psychometrist who successfully assessed Jean-Marc, she reinforced — off the record — the opinion of staff that his language usage was at, or just below, age-appropriate level.

Now, notwithstanding a setback incident (after a fire drill, Sheldon was found inside a heating duct in a no-go area of the building; Jean-Marc imitated the alarm bell continuously for several days) both boys are going to be transferred to grade one classes in their neighbourhood schools. The receiving principals have asked for advice on how to best make the transition smooth.

yet been identified, then that is the first step. Usually, this happens by means of an assessment that will vary in its degree of formality, depending on the policy and practice of the school board, and on the particular student being assessed.

What Happens In An Assessment?*

An assessment is a gathering, and then interpretation of relevant information about

*Note that this section offers only a brief, initial overview. For detailed information about assessments, see Chapter 14.

a student. Generally, what is revealed in an assessment, at least theoretically, is some insight into an individual's intelligence, abilities, strengths, needs, behaviours, and so on. In the case of students with special needs, the procedure is aimed primarily at uncovering or confirming information that will help meet those needs in the most effective way. Hence, an investigation of an exceptional person may go beyond basic educational parameters into areas like health matters, or psychological and behavioural profiles.

Who Conducts Assessments?

The classroom teacher, and very often the educational assistant, play crucial roles here. They are, after all, in the best position to observe a student's needs — and strengths — *in the classroom.* In many boards, the core of an assessment is in the observations, commentaries, and anecdotal summaries written by classroom teachers, along with standardized tests they may (sometimes) administer, and possibly, formal checklists or rating scales they may complete. In the case of some students, this may be all that is necessary. In other cases, additional, more formal, information will be gathered, perhaps by one of the school's special education teachers, or by personnel from the board's special services department. Where medical or other specialized information is deemed helpful, this is usually supplied by the appropriate professionals (provided the information is available, the professionals in question are forthcoming, and privacy regulations are satisfied). By and large, the nature and extent of an assessment is directly reflective of the complexity and demands of the case.

What Happens With the Assessment Results?

Unless some prohibitive factors have arisen during the gathering of information, assessment results will be used to assist in deciding an appropriate placement for the student (although this decision may already have been made). Most importantly, they are used to guide the development of an individual education plan (IEP). Generally, the assessment then becomes part of a student's 'file', from where it can provide a useful baseline when the student's IEP, and possibly the placement and

even the needs, are re-examined at intervals in the future. Because of the time and costs involved, especially in the more formal and complex procedures, it is not customary to repeat full-scale assessments on a regular basis. This is likely to occur only when a particular situation demands it.

II: Choosing a Class Placement

An important and oft debated matter to resolve in special education service delivery, is just where to do the work. As the data in Figure 4A suggest, the majority of students with special needs are based in a regular classroom with all other students, and receive their special education via administrative arrangements made in that setting. Figures 4B and 4C confirm this as a general truth. However, for a minority of exceptional students, a more specialized setting is chosen. (Usually, these more specialized classes are called 'self-contained'.) Very often, but not always, the choice of one of these latter settings is based on the intensity of a student's particular needs. Again, in Figures 4B and 4C, the distribution of percentage enrolments by area of exceptionality suggests that this is certainly the case in those areas where more intensive or more remedial instruction is usually necessary. Between the two ends of the placement spectrum, most boards of education offer a range of modifications that incorporate features of both. Whatever the choice of setting for the student, it is always, within reason, subject to review and modification.

A description of the typical settings available in most boards (with local variations and terminology) follows here.

	Reg. Class & Dir./Indir. Support	Reg.Class & Withdrawal Assistance	Part Time Self-Con. & Reg.Class	Full Time Self-Con.
Elementary	29.9	33.3	18.2	18.6
Secondary	51.5	28.1	11.8	8.6
Elem. + Sec.	40.7	30.7	15.0	13.6

Placement of Exceptional Students (Ont.) by Percentage of Exceptional Population[1]

Reg. Class = regular classroom.
Dir./Indir. Support = student and/or instructors receive resource support in regular class.
Withdrawal = student receives support/instruction outside of regular classroom for part of day (or week).
Self-Con. = self-contained class devoted to special education.
[1]All public and separate schools. *Source: Policy Branch, MET, 31/10/97.*

Figure 4A

Regular Class with Direct/Indirect Support

Very often, what is special about a student's education is a simple and straightforward adjustment in his or her program *within the regular class*. An example would be a student who has a condition like spina bifida and does not walk. If this student has learned to manage her own condition, as most do, she will participate in every aspect of the regular classroom in an entirely normal way, but for certain parts of the curriculum, perhaps for some parts of the physical education program, there would be some accommodations made. Or should she need extra time for, say, personal hygiene, the teacher would again make sensible arrangements, like planning to present new or difficult material at times when she is normally expected to be present.

Although the above is sometimes known as indirect support, that feature, along with direct support, is delivered in a variety of ways, to either or both the teacher and the student. In the case of a regular class where a deaf student, for example, is placed, there may be direct support to the student, ranging from special technical equipment to the presence of a signing interpreter. At the same time, a teacher or consultant with specialized knowledge about deafness may provide indirect support to the classroom teacher in everything from program preparation to in-service training. One of the most effective and certainly very popular forms of classroom assistance is the educational or teaching assistant. Graduates of Ontario's community colleges have proven singularly valuable in this role.

Regular Classroom & Withdrawal Assistance

For part of their program, some exceptional students benefit from a more intense, individualized learning experience, one that can best be delivered in a setting that is less distracting or competitive, or in some cases, more specially equipped than the regular classroom. Thus a student may be 'withdrawn' to a 'resource room', for example, where a different instructor, who works in close concert with the regular teacher, will deliver the modified learning experience called for in the student's IEP. Significant in this arrangement is that the student remains a regular member of the regular class. He simply does part of his program elsewhere on a formally scheduled basis. A fairly typical example of a student who uses this type of placement is one with a learning disability for whom reading and writing pose extra difficulty.

Percentage Placements by Area of Exceptionality[1] (Elementary)

Area of Exceptionality	Reg. Class & Dir./Indirect Support	Reg. Class & Withdrawal Assistance	Part Time Self-Con.& Reg. Class	Full Time Self-Con.
Socially maladjusted/ emotionally disturbed	42.5	17.9	17.7	21.9
Autistic	41.4	22.0	16.2	20.2
Hearing Impaired/ Deaf	35.8	20.0	22.9	21.3
Learning Disabled	32.1	40.3	18.5	9.1
Speech & Language Impaired	29.1	37.9	20.4	12.6
Gifted	25.5	33.4	8.7	32.4
Developmentally Disabled (Mild)	17.5	30.8	31.7	19.9
Developmentally Disabled	12.4	9.7	20.1	57.8
Visually Impaired/ Blind	60.4	25.7	7.1	6.8
Deaf/Blind	67.4	12.8	12.6	7.1
Other Physical Disabilities	66.3	21.9	5.7	6.1
Multi-Handicapped	24.1	19.8	19.7	36.4

[1] All public & separate schools. *Source: Policy Branch, MET, 31/10/97*

Figure 4B

Often, the structure and opportunity for practice and repetition and one-on-one coaching, strategies that usually benefit the learning disabled as well as others with special needs, can be very effectively delivered in this type of resource arrangement.

Incidentally, taking a student out of a class for one-on-one instruction is by no means a novel idea. It's a time-honoured practice, especially in the elementary grades. What distinguishes the practice in the special education case, is the specificity of the arrangement, and the relative guarantee of its regular delivery in the student's plan.

Part Time Regular & Self-Contained Class

As the designation would suggest, this is simply an arrangement whereby a student spends her day — or possibly her week — in two settings. It is a frequent arrangement for students who are making a transition from the full time self-contained class to the regular class. (Students gaining control of behaviour issues are a good example.) As well, this is a setting that offers an effective combination of intensive instruction opportunity, together with a normalized experience. Note, for example, in Figures 4B and 4C, the relatively larger percentage of part time enrolments in areas like autism, speech and language, and developmental disability, where such a combination can be very beneficial. Students identified as gifted are often seen in the part time setting, as Figures 4B and 4C suggest.

Full Time Self-Contained Class

In order to generate a very specific kind of learning experience, it may be deemed appropriate to place an exceptional student in a special setting full time. These placements are found in many, but not all, regular community schools. Ideally, exceptional students who take their entire program in such classes, participate in general school activities in the same way as other students.

Students identified as gifted are often found in these settings because it is simpler to arrange the kinds of experiences that will challenge them in the most productive way. (The percentages for gifted in Figure 4C may suggest otherwise, but these data are slightly skewed because Roman Catholic secondary schools in Ontario, thus far, do not report having self-contained classes for the gifted.)

Percentage Placements By Area of Exceptionality[1] (Secondary)				
Area of Exceptionality	Reg. Class & Dir./Indirect Support	Reg. Class & Withdrawal Assistance	Part Time Self-Con. & Reg. Class	Full Time Self-Con.
Socially maladjusted/ emotionally disturbed	42.3	35.8	11.4	10.4
Autistic	16.8	17.0	11.2	54.9
Hearing Impaired/ Deaf	48.9	31.8	12.4	6.8
Learning Disabled	54.8	34.8	6.3	4.1
Speech & Language Impaired	64.8	19.3	7.2	8.7
Gifted	56.2	15.7	22.4	5.6
Developmentally Disabled (Mild)	42.4	20.4	17.5	19.7
Developmentally Disabled	10.8	15.6	28.1	45.5
Visually Impaired/ Blind	62.5	27.6	3.1	6.8
Other Physical Disabilities*	60.0	26.8	2.2	11.0
Multi-Handicapped	32.8	18.2	18.5	30.5

*Includes seven Deaf/Blind students
[1]All public & separate schools. *Source: Policy Branch, MET, 31/10/97*

Figure 4C

Special Day or Residential School

These are purpose-run schools. Some are specifically targeted to the education and life-style development of students with a special need such as deafness. Other schools are established in correctional facilities or are set up as care and treatment centres, where health and education are a combined focus. For the most part, these schools are administered by the Ministry of Education and Training and, obviously, are very much self-contained settings. (See also Chapter 3.)

Which is Better: Range of Settings, or Total Integration?

All boards of education in Ontario regard the integration of exceptional students into regular classes as normal practice. This is consistent with Ministry of Education and Training policy. At the same time, Ministry policy states that a range of settings (such as those described above) should be available for students whose needs are best addressed in alternative settings. The policy reflects what has been pretty much standard practice for most — but not all—school boards in the province, since special education was first established. (Some boards have maintained a policy of total integration. More on this below.)

This standard practice has long been based on variations of a placement model often called the Cascade (Figure 4D).

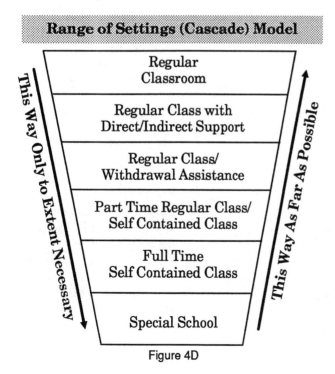

Range of Settings (Cascade) Model

This Way Only to Extent Necessary

This Way As Far As Possible

Regular Classroom

Regular Class with Direct/Indirect Support

Regular Class/ Withdrawal Assistance

Part Time Regular Class/ Self Contained Class

Full Time Self Contained Class

Special School

Figure 4D

The distinguishing feature of this model is that a range of different settings for exceptional students is available on a formal, more or less permanent basis. The settings, or learning environments, are progressively more specialized, and students therefore, if it is deemed necessary and beneficial, may be administratively placed in these alternative settings on a short or longer term basis. Important philosophical principles of the model are that students always be placed in the most enabling environment, and that no restricted placement ever be regarded as permanent.

In a province the size of Ontario, geography has an influence on setting models. Geography, and inevitably, costs. For example, in the case of a setting that is organized to deal with, say, extremely difficult behaviour, a board might arrange that only one school in an area containing several schools, would offer this special environment on behalf of all. Another school then, might be the only one with a special setting, along with appropriate technology and personnel, for blind students. Every school, however, would likely have its own 'resource room' or similar, moderately specialized setting for part or full time placements. (As the data in Figures 4B and 4C imply, it is a very rare school that does not have arrangements for students identified learning disabled.) In the range of settings model, all students in the board have access, if necessary, to the appropriate setting.

Placement arrangements built on the principle of total integration, tend to be quite flexible and, sometimes, quite ad hoc (see the looping arrows in Figure 4E). Very often, arrangements are created — and collapsed — entirely according to needs of the moment. In fact, there is probably good reason to conclude that placement arrangements are generally so individual, and so tailored on a by-case basis, that there really is no such thing as an integration model at all. It is important to recognize that most systems that have total integration as their underpinning philosophy, nevertheless do make at least minimal use of alternative settings, if only informally. A board that has every single one of its exceptional students in regular settings, full time, is very rare. However, the fundamental principle of integration is not diluted: an exceptional student, no matter where her special

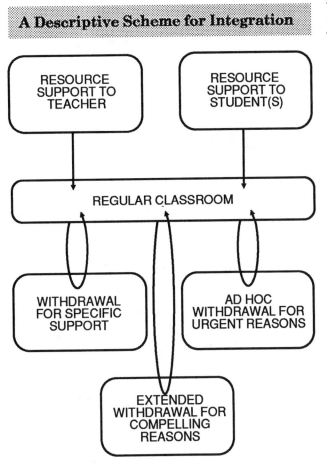

Figure 4E

III: Planning the Program

Along with identifying the needs of an exceptional student and choosing his or her most appropriate placement, there is one more crucial element in the process. Many educators see it as the most crucial. This is the student's individual education plan, or IEP, a written plan of action developed by the school staff that becomes everyone's road map. The IEP summarizes a student's strengths, interests, and needs, and presents particular expectations for him, expectations that are usually somewhat different from the demands of regular curriculum, in recognition of his special needs . (In Ontario, for students fourteen years and older, in addition to an IEP, a plan is also developed for transition to work, community living, and further education.)

The IEP is intended to help teachers monitor a student's development, to make it easier for them to communicate with parents and with others involved in the student's life, and to provide a benchmark for continuing evaluation and modification. As a practical tool, this document is vital to an exceptional student's program. *(Chapter 15 is devoted to detailed explanation of the individual education plan.)*

Getting Special Education Under Way

In the earlier days of Ontario's special education history, boards of education tended, quite understandably, to rely quite exclusively on formal procedures to get the process going. Hence, most decisions were made by officially constituted Identification, Placement and Review Committees (IPRCs)*. A committee would make a determination of exceptionality (if appropriate), decide on a placement, and in some cases make recommendations regarding support. Then if the parents agreed, the student's special education program would begin. As special education practice matured, many schools began to adopt simpler, alternative procedures for some exceptional students, and reserved the more time-consuming and demanding formality of the IPRC for the more complicated cases.

---

*In jargon exclusive to Ontario, IPRC is frequently used as a verb (e.g., "Jim was *IPRC'd* on November 10.")

education service is delivered, is considered a full time student in her regular classroom. She is never administratively 'placed' elsewhere.

Debate over the relative moral and practical superiority of total integration versus range of settings (see Chapter 2) raged hotly for several years, but has very much diminished in the light of experience. Most educators in Ontario, even before provincial policy was clarified, were operating from the position that integration, i.e., regular class placement, should be a first choice as a matter of course. And supporters of total integration gradually acknowledged the accumulating evidence that some students with special needs do indeed benefit from specialized settings. Ironically, by the mid-1990s, it would have been difficult for an untrained observer to distinguish between the two positions, so similar had they become in day to day practice. What seems to have taken place then, in the debate over total integration and range of settings, is an amalgamation of the best of both.

Throughout the province, individual boards have tended to design their own models for these procedures, or for what is called 'service delivery'. Although these models (they are also called 'flow charts') vary from board to board, sometimes significantly, they all pay heed to Ministry regulations, and all are designed to benefit the student. While the three examples that follow here do not reflect *specifically* what happens in every board (board service models are generally more complex because they reflect local practices and policies) they nevertheless outline the basics of how special education gets under way.

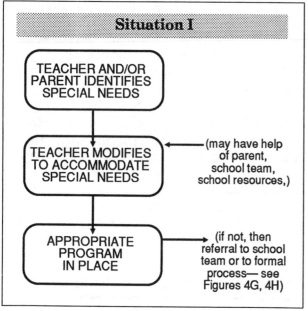

Figure 4F

Figure 4F presents a situation that occurs frequently both inside and outside formal special education practice. It begins when the teacher and/or educational assistant become aware of a student's special need(s). When it is possible to bring about appropriate modifications to meet the needs in the classroom without bringing formal processes to bear, a matter can be resolved quickly, simply, and with reasonable hope of immediate benefit. In Situation I, it is very likely that assessments would be informal and carried out by the teacher, perhaps with assistance from in-school personnel. Also, the individual education plan (IEP) in this case, as well as the continuing evaluation, may be more informal.

Whether or not practices like the one described in Situation I are used by a school, depends very much on the philosophy of its administration and staff. Both technically and legally, the student here is not identified exceptional, although for school purposes only, he or she may have an IEP.

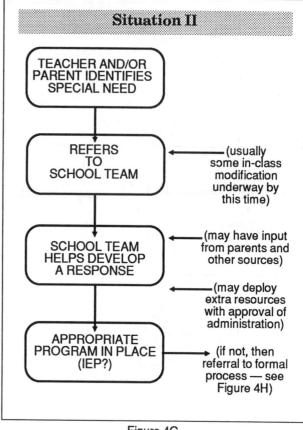

Figure 4G

Situation II (Figure 4G) is somewhat more complex in that it will likely involve more personnel. Following this procedure does not result in formally identifying the student as exceptional, but this style will likely call for somewhat more standardized procedures than in Situation I. The assessment of needs will usually be more detailed, and may even be supported with school-administered standardized test results. Likewise, the IEP is likely to be more fully developed and maintained, with more specifics in matters like amount and nature of resource support, the date for a review of progress, etc. As with Situation I, the student may be considered by the school as nominally part of its special education population. Also as with Situation I, the use of this particular model or any similar model that incorporates resources like a 'school team' is very much a reflection of how the school approaches special education philosophically.

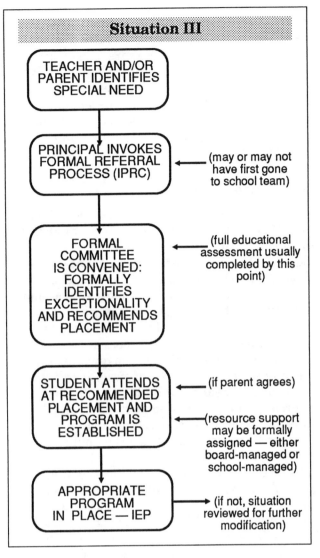

Situation III

TEACHER AND/OR PARENT IDENTIFIES SPECIAL NEED

PRINCIPAL INVOKES FORMAL REFERRAL PROCESS (IPRC) ← (may or may not have first gone to school team)

FORMAL COMMITTEE IS CONVENED: FORMALLY IDENTIFIES EXCEPTIONALITY AND RECOMMENDS PLACEMENT ← (full educational assessment usually completed by this point)

STUDENT ATTENDS AT RECOMMENDED PLACEMENT AND PROGRAM IS ESTABLISHED ← (if parent agrees)
← (resource support may be formally assigned — either board-managed or school-managed)

APPROPRIATE PROGRAM IN PLACE — IEP → (if not, situation reviewed for further modification)

Figure 4H

As the Situation III model implies, this procedure is more complex. Also, it reflects the official, regulatory practice for the province, and is the approach necessary to have a student formally identified exceptional (i.e., the IPRC). Naturally, it is far more time-consuming than the Situations I and II, and subject to specific standardized procedures, not only those required by provincial regulations, but also to processes required by the board. (Chapter 5 offers a detailed explanation of the IPRC.)

Who Delivers the Service?

The number and type of personnel involved in the delivery of service to an exceptional student is usually a factor of just how extensive that student's needs happen to be. Naturally, the service can only be delivered if the necessary personnel are available, and it can only be delivered effectively if the system is organized to flow the service to the need, and if the ever-so-crucial element of *cooperation* prevails. Fortunately, the combination of professionalism among educators and members of related fields, and the natural disposition to ameliorate the situation of students with special needs, means that most of the time, the right things happen.

The list of personnel — of *service providers* — who work with exceptional students in an exceptional setting can be as varied as there are variations among students. By far the most heavily involved personnel in literally every educational situation are combinations of the following:

* classroom teacher
* educational assistant
* resource teacher, a.k.a. special education teacher. (There are many local terms for this role.)
* special consultant

with input from:

* parents
* school teams
* advisory groups
* advocacy groups
* social agencies
* specialists

Other personnel, usually employed by a community services agency, or who have independent practices, typically become involved with exceptional students in cases where special needs require a particular expertise. These include members of such fields as psychiatry, psychology, psychometry, social work, health, speech, physical and occupational therapy.

Some boards of education, particularly larger ones, employ members of these professions directly. This is most frequently the case with professionals in the speech area, and with what is often called 'psycho-educational services' (or a variation thereof) generally consisting of professionals who specialize in assessment and counseling. The latter are usually quite heavily involved at the assessment and program planning stages, although to an extent, they will also become involved in ongoing delivery of service in situations where exceptional behaviour, for example, is a factor.

Deploying The Personnel

Within a single school, or within a single jurisdiction, an abiding concern of administrators is to get the appropriate resources into the appropriate settings as efficiently and effectively as possible, all with a view to cost, cooperation, and availability. To accomplish this, schools and boards generally organize deployment models, or service models, schemas for managing the various elements in delivering service. For once it has been decided that a student is exceptional and is to receive support, there are certain management factors that cannot be ignored, such as:

• What personnel are involved?
• How much support will be available?
• Who determines the amount of support?
• How long will the support continue?
• Where does the support take place?
• Who has primary responsibility for the student?
• When and how frequently will the case be reviewed?

School-Based vs Board-Based Deployment?

Many boards turn over management of resources to individual schools. Whereas in board-wide management of service delivery, resources are allocated across an entire jurisdiction (theoretically according to need and availability, but in practice, usually according to a formula), a school-based delivery system is one which uses available resources according to its own, site-determined priorities. Both styles have merit. The board-wide system, because of its wider purview and financial capability, can usually tap into a deeper pool of expertise, and allocate it fairly. School-based management however, because it circumvents time-consuming bureaucracy, can bring service to bear quickly and flexibly, along with a greater likelihood of informal but immediate cooperation and approval from parents. Many boards find a compromise in a marriage of the two approaches. The majority of exceptional students' needs require immediate, flexible, varied responses that can best be arranged when there is local control. As well, under these conditions of service delivery, it is much easier for a school to reflect whatever the community attitude may be to integration. At the same time, special needs that require expert response — blind-ness for example, or cases of unique physical need — which tend to be more costly to meet, but are also relatively more rare, can continue to be managed in a board-centred delivery system if necessary. Integrating board and school service delivery seems not only fiscally reasonable and responsible, but also addresses the issues of immediacy, flexibility, and optimum use of resources.

The School Team

One of the most significant developments of the late 1980's and early 90's was the gradual realization that the mystery of educating most students with special needs is not all that different from the mystery of educating any student. Experience has also taught that most educational matters which at first glance imply an elaborate response, can actually be addressed *in-house*. No one denies that expertise continues to be important, and there is no question that dealing with certain types of exceptionality such as, say, hearing or blindness, often requires specialization of some kind. Nevertheless, the needs of most exceptional students can usually be met through a healthy application of common sense, the kind of approach that all effective teachers use in all of educational practice. At the same time, teachers have found that cases of special need are almost always more effectively addressed when they are the focus of broad concern, of general cooperation and support, rather than the sole responsibility of a single individual. In many schools, this combination of insights has borne fruit in a more or less formal arrangement known as the In-School Team, School Assistance Team, or the Teacher Support Team or School-Based Support Team or similar title.

The School Team Concept

Described in its simplest terms, a support or assistance team is a committee of staff members whose purpose is to consult with individual teachers who request assistance regarding students perceived as having special needs. The team neither precludes nor replaces formal special education nor diminishes it in any way. Rather, it supports special education, and helps it function more effectively in a school, and more efficiently. In many schools, the team is a forum of first resort, to which teachers and parents may bring concerns about the special needs of particular students, without formally invoking special education procedures. This practice not only tends to keep students in the mainstream, but also, by offering this pre-referral opportunity, a team helps to free its school's special education personnel to bring resources to bear where needs are greatest. A team can also enhance service delivery simply by offering broader involvement. Perhaps most important — to teachers and students equally — a team can be a vital instigator of professionalism: the kind of drive that leads a staff to seek solutions. (*More developed information about the school team appears in Chapter 15.*)

The Multidisciplinary Team

For particularly demanding exceptional cases, some school boards may choose to deal with service delivery by first convening a *multidisciplinary team*. Usually, such a team will be made up of educators along with a number of professionals from areas outside education itself. The situation, for example, of an exceptional student with multiple needs such as a severe developmental disablity and physical disabilities, along with serious emotional adjustment difficulties, may well require the services of a variety of personnel. For this student, a multi- disciplinary team may come together only once or twice on a more or less ad hoc basis, usually at the initial stages when the student's placement and programming are being established. Ongoing delivery of service then becomes the responsibility of only certain members of the team.

An area of difficulty with the multidisciplinary team approach in educational settings is management and organization. Since the approach is used almost exclusively in cases of extensive need, there is sometimes disagreement over priority in meeting the needs (education? social? physical well-being?). Also, the mere task of bringing together a team of otherwise occupied, diverse professionals is awkward and time-consuming, and usually requires the authority (i.e., for budget, for freeing personnel from other obligations, etc.) of someone in an upper-level administrative role. As well, because there is such wide involvement, ultimate responsibility for the student — even legal responsibility — may become an issue. Difficulties like these often force serious consideration of a quite restricted placement like special day school or residential facility simply because the situation is easier to manage in such a setting.

READINGS & RESOURCES

For Further Investigation

Baker, J. & Zigmond, N. (1990). Are regular education classes equipped to accommodate students with learning disabilities? *Exceptional Children, 56*, 515-526.

Canadian Council for Exceptional Children (1989). Status of education service delivery to exceptional students: A provincial Survey. *Keeping in Touch.*

Hunt, P. & Gotez, L. (1997).Research on inclusive educational programs, practices and outcomes for students with severe disabilities. *Journal of Special Education , 31*, 3-29.

Jones, K. H. & Bender W.N. (1993). Utilization of paraprofessionals in special education: A review of the literature. *Remedial and Special Education 14*(1), 7-14.

Lusthaus, E. & Lusthaus, C. (1992). From segregation to full inclusion: an evaluation. *Exceptionality Education Canada, 2*, 95-115.

Minke, K.M., Bear, G.C., Deemer, S.A. & Griffin S.M. (1996). Teachers' experiences with inclusive classrooms: implications for special education reform. *Journal of Special Education, 30*, 152-186.

Morsink C.V., & Lenk L.L. (1992). The delivery of special education programs and services. *Remedial and Special Education, 13*, 33-43.

Simon, L. (1992). Mainstreaming: Is it in the best interests of all children? *B.C. Journal of Special Education, 16*(2), 131-137.

Wang, M.C. Walberg, H. J. & Reynolds, M.C. (1992). A scenario for better – not separate- special education. *Educational Leadership, 50*, 35-41.

Identification and Placement of Exceptional Students

How the IPRC Works

This schema outlines main features of **Ontario Regulation 181/98, Identification and Placement of Exceptional Pupils,** which came into force on September 1, 1998. (Copies of the complete regulation are available at the Ontario government bookstore (1-800-668-9938 — www.gov.on.ca), at school board offices, and at public libraries.)

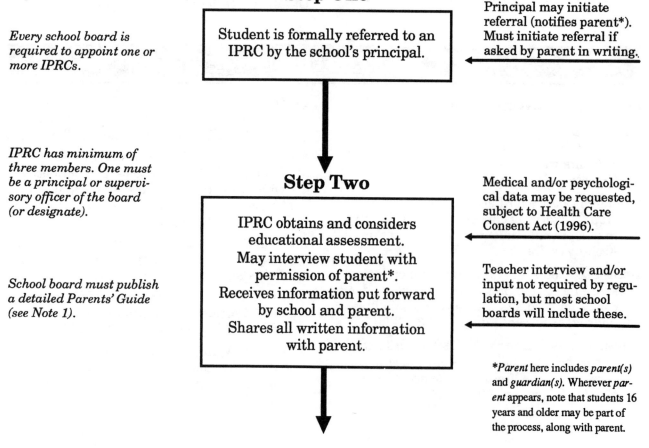

Step One

Every school board is required to appoint one or more IPRCs.

Student is formally referred to an IPRC by the school's principal.

Principal may initiate referral (notifies parent*). Must initiate referral if asked by parent in writing.

IPRC has minimum of three members. One must be a principal or supervisory officer of the board (or designate).

Step Two

IPRC obtains and considers educational assessment. May interview student with permission of parent*. Receives information put forward by school and parent. Shares all written information with parent.

Medical and/or psychological data may be requested, subject to Health Care Consent Act (1996).

Teacher interview and/or input not required by regulation, but most school boards will include these.

School board must publish a detailed Parents' Guide (see Note 1).

*Parent here includes *parent(s)* and *guardian(s)*. Wherever *parent* appears, note that students 16 years and older may be part of the process, along with parent.

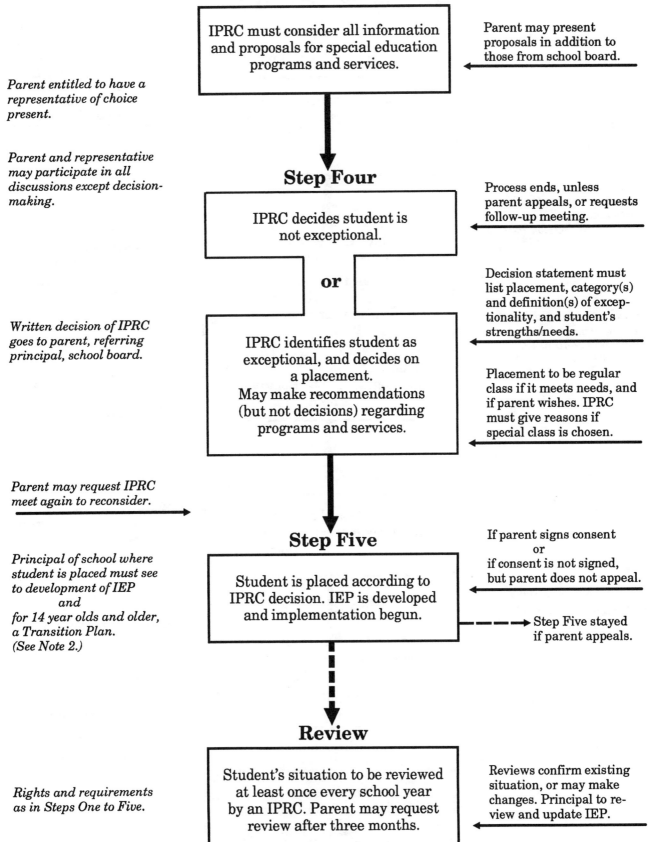

Step Three

IPRC must consider all information and proposals for special education programs and services.

Parent may present proposals in addition to those from school board.

Parent entitled to have a representative of choice present.

Parent and representative may participate in all discussions except decision-making.

Step Four

IPRC decides student is not exceptional.

Process ends, unless parent appeals, or requests follow-up meeting.

or

Written decision of IPRC goes to parent, referring principal, school board.

Decision statement must list placement, category(s) and definition(s) of exceptionality, and student's strengths/needs.

IPRC identifies student as exceptional, and decides on a placement.
May make recommendations (but not decisions) regarding programs and services.

Placement to be regular class if it meets needs, and if parent wishes. IPRC must give reasons if special class is chosen.

Parent may request IPRC meet again to reconsider.

Principal of school where student is placed must see to development of IEP and for 14 year olds and older, a Transition Plan. (See Note 2.)

Step Five

If parent signs consent
or
if consent is not signed, but parent does not appeal.

Student is placed according to IPRC decision. IEP is developed and implementation begun.

Step Five stayed if parent appeals.

Review

Student's situation to be reviewed at least once every school year by an IPRC. Parent may request review after three months.

Reviews confirm existing situation, or may make changes. Principal to review and update IEP.

Rights and requirements as in Steps One to Five.

In Cases of Appeal

Step One(A)

Parent may appeal identification as exceptional, or placement or both.

School board convenes a three member Appeal Board to review the IPRC material and decisions.

One member chosen by board; one by parent; the two select a third as chair (in case of disagreement, chair is chosen by MET).

Parent and / or representative entitled to participate in all discussions except decision-making.

Step Two(A)

Appeal Board agrees with IPRC and recommends its decisions be implemented,
or
disagrees with IPRC and makes recommendation to school board about identification or placement or both.

May interview anyone whom Appeal Board chair feels has information to contribute.

Written recommendation to parent, principal, school board and chair of IPRC.

Written reasons must accompany written statement of recommendation.

Step Three(A)

School board considers recommendation and decides what action to take.

School board is not limited to recommendation of Appeal Board.

Written decision of school board goes to all parties.

Step Four(A)

School board decision is implemented.

If parent signs consent
or
if consent not signed but parent does not appeal.

Step Four(A) stayed if parent appeals.

Final appeal stage is to Special Education Tribunal (see Note 3).

- Regulation 181 sets time limits for parts of the IPRC procedure (e.g., response periods, appeals, etc.). See Regulation for details.
- With a parent's acknowledgement, minor adjustments are sometimes made to a situation without holding a formal IPRC meeting.
- Only a small percentage of IPRC decisions go forward to Appeal Board hearings. Tribunal hearings are rare. The vast majority of IPRC procedures end satisfactorily at Step Five.

<u>Note 1</u>: Each school board must prepare a guide that explains all elements of the IPRC process, including rights of consent, rights of appeal, how to appeal, etc. The guide must list parent organizations that are local associations which may be of assistance, and outline the board's own special education services and those it purchases from other boards. This guide is to be available at every school in the jurisdiction. If requested, the board must make the guide available in braille, large print, or audio-cassette.

<u>Note 2</u>: The IEP is summarized in Chapter 4 and detailed in Chapter 15.

For students 14 years and older, a principal is responsible for developing a Transition Plan to further education, employment and community living. The requirement to have a transition plan does not apply to students whose sole identification is 'gifted'.

<u>Note 3</u>: The Special Education Tribunal is a body appointed by the province to hear appeals from decisions of IPRCs that are upheld by Appeal Boards and in turn by the school board. The Tribunal hears the cases under the Statutory Powers Procedure Act of Ontario. The hearing is adversarial in structure and both appellant (parent) and respondent (board) frequently retain legal counsel. The Tribunal's decision is final and binding. (Parties may refer to the civil courts, although experience suggests that if proper IPRC procedure is followed, they are reluctant to become involved.) See also Section 57 of the Education Act.

<u>Note 4</u>: The original IPRC regulation was No. 554, first issued in 1981. It was slightly modified and reissued as No. 305 in 1990, then reissued with some significant modifications as No. 181 in 1998.

For Discussion: the Case of Luis and Estella

Although Luis and Estella are almost nine years old, their mother continues to dress them in clothes with matching material and designs. It is her contention, as she explained to an IPRC, that the more Luis and Estella are perceived as "cute", the more readily they will be "welcomed by normal society." The two children are fraternal twins and are developmentally disabled. Luis has Down syndrome, while Estella sustained serious brain injury at birth. Although both speak in a baby talk style, they are otherwise quite socially adept. Their mother has devoted her life to their care and to integrating them into "normal society". The twins attended nursery school. They were enrolled in clubs and sports; and from kindergarten to grade three were placed full time in the same regular class in their neighbourhood school.

No one has questioned their placement until now. With two months to go in grade three, the school has requested an IPRC review. Although the majority of their class reads and writes at an age-appropriate level, neither twin writes his or her name as yet. (Luis can recognize his, but Estella does not.) Luis can identify about half the letters of the alphabet; he counts to one hundred by rote but does not appear to associate numbers with amounts or quantities. Estella, when asked, will count to five or six and then, as she always does when challenged, will produce a totally engaging smile. The school board psychologist feels that Luis especially, but Estella too, has far greater ability. Experience shows that both learn from very structured teaching and frequent repetition. However, the regular grade three class does not provide much opportunity. It is a large, busy class, with one EA who also has responsibility for the health needs of a girl with cerebral palsy.

Next year presents even more concerns. The school's junior division places several classes into one large pod-style room, where individual study is emphasized and small group projects prevail. Some, but not all, of the school team believe it would be a disservice to place Estella here, and possibly Luis too. The alternative, at least part time, would be placement either in the school's primary resource room, or the junior one. Current enrollment in the primary room is six. There are three children with severe developmental disabilities, two with physical disabilities, and one child identified autistic. Only one of the six has normal speech. The resource teacher and full time EA emphasize language development. The junior room is almost a mirror image of the primary. The twins' mother objects to placement in either setting.

6

Students With Learning Disabilities

"Why I Hit Amy
I got to cocentrate. I got to shut stuf out. Like when you talk to me other stuff gets in
the way if I don't cocentrate. Lke sometimes its like your voice is far away somwplace
or like yesterday whenyou did the maps you had a diffrent voce for part like you
where aa different person So Im sorry I hit Amy she talkd the same time you did"
— Jordan (age 11)

Misconceptions About Learning Disabilities

1. Most children grow out of a learning disability.

With effective instruction, most learning disabled children learn to manage their needs, but the disabilities usually endure into adulthood.

2. It is possible to detect the presence of a learning disability by testing.

No test yet available can detect a learning disability in the same way that a hearing test, for example, can specify the nature and seriousness of a hearing loss. A learning disability is identified through teamwork by educators, parents, and sometimes other professionals, using observation, curriculum-based assessment, informal tests, and to some extent, standardized, formal tests.

3. There is no connection between learning disabilities and the brain.

Neuro-anatomical research points to a fairly certain connection between learning disability and anomalous structures in the brain. Magnetic resonance imaging (MRI) particularly, has revealed subtle abnormalities in the parts of the brain that process language.

4. Dyslexia and learning disability are the same thing.

'Dyslexia' and 'learning disability' tend to be used interchangeably, a practice which muddies the waters in this area of special need. People who have dyslexia appear to have fundamental difficulties with integrating the sight, sound, and meaning of print, despite apparently normal intellectual ability and sensory capacity. Not all people who are learning disabled have this problem.

5. Poor eye-hand coordination is a sign of learning disability.

A now discarded theory once held that some students failed to achieve because of poor perceptual integration: viz., poor eye-hand coordination and body awareness, confusion of left-right, confusion of the self in space, etc. However, many people who are physically inept have no difficulty learning, and many students who find academic learning difficult, are well coordinated.

6. Learning disabled students have highly developed/poorly developed memory capacity.

They seem to have significant difficulty transferring information from short-term to long-term memory, but there is no clear evidence that the long-term memory capacity of learning disabled people is any different from that of the rest of the population.

7. Learning disabled students are highly intelligent.

There is little evidence to substantiate this claim. In fact, the weight of evidence suggests that on IQ tests, the learning disabled score across the same range as the rest of the population, but with what seems to be a tendency to fall in the average to below-average categories.

8. Left-handed students are more likely to be learning disabled.

"Lefties" are sometimes over-represented in classes for the learning disabled, but no hard data exist to connect left-handedness and learning disability.

9. Hyperactive (AD/HD) students are learning disabled (and vice versa).

Hyperactivity and learning disability have become very much interwoven over the past several decades. (See page 65.) The connection, however, is not absolute. A person with AD/HD is not always learning disabled, or vice versa.

10. Learning disabled students are more likely to become delinquent or criminal.

This claim originated in the 1960s and, if nothing else, contributed to the high profile that learning disabilities acquired after that time. Some research shows a slightly higher incidence of learning disabilities in prison populations, but definition problems weaken those findings.

11. Hereditary factors have no bearing on learning disabilities.

Both research and an accumulation of empirical evidence point to a pattern of learning disabilities in families.

What Is a Learning Disability?

This is the most elusive of all areas in special education. The only criterion that all learning disabled students seem to share, is loosely described as a difficulty in dealing with information, particularly language-based information, despite apparent freedom from any intellectual or sensory handicap. The difficulty may be in taking in the information, or, in integrating it with what they already know and understand, or, in expressing what they now know as a result of taking in and integrating the information. Or — and this is where the elusiveness begins — it may be a combination of the previous three elements (or just two of the three!). Learning disabled students may be disorganized, unable to focus attention, forgetful, and disoriented. They may be hyperactive — or *hypo*active. They may be highly resistant to changing counter-productive behaviours, or, so compliant that they are easily led astray. One student may manifest all of these characteristics; another student, while functioning at the same low academic level, may manifest only one of them. And either student may demonstrate some of these characteristics on one day, and on another day, show absolutely none of them. Or all of them!

Defining the Undefinable?

When the late Samuel Kirk proposed the term 'learning disability' to a conference of parents seeking information about their "mystery kids" in the early 1960s the response was immediate and positive. The fact that the term became widespread very quickly, indicated the extent to which large numbers of concerned parents were seeking an explanation as to why their children did not succeed in school, despite what they, the parents, knew was not lack of intellect. (And it was parents, far more than academics, who were responsible for placing learning disability front and centre, in education.) The

After his parents' separation, Cory lived with his mother in an inner city area. For a period of about four years, she regularly obstructed the father's visiting rights, contravening a string of court orders. On the day Cory entered grade one, his father picked him up from school at lunch hour and the two disappeared. Eighteen months later his maternal grandparents appeared at Pearson Airport with the boy in tow, claiming they had rescued him from an abusive situation abroad. Children's Aid intervened and placed him with foster parents for six months, after which his mother was again awarded custody. One year later, Children's Aid again intervened and Cory was returned to the foster parents who had maintained him previously. Meanwhile, Cory's father returned to Canada and applied for, and was denied, permanent custody. But contrary to the recommendations of the CAS, the court granted him weekly visitation rights. At about this time, Cory's mother suddenly remarried, abandoned her suit for restoration of custody, and moved to South America. Her parents (the maternal grandparents above) have now applied for custody, and CAS has entered an application to make Cory a permanent ward.

Cory is now almost ten. He is in a split grade three/four in his eleventh school, and has missed about a full year of schooling. He takes medication for TB, and he has a slight hearing loss. Cory reads very poorly. Both his printing and the language and content of his stories can be easily mistaken for that of a much younger child. His math skills are inconsistent. Although his teacher suspects he may have an articulation problem, a speech consultant feels his odd way of talking is a product of mixing English and Spanish early in life. Everyone agrees that at least part of his learning problem is the result of timidity. A psychologist described Cory's manner as "juvenile shellshock".

The social worker responsible for Cory (a former teacher) believes the evidence clearly indicates a learning disability and that if he is so identified, he'll get some of the help he so obviously needs. The School Team believes Cory's status is a result of his personal history and that what he needs is security and above all stability. To identify him as learning disabled, they argue, will add yet one more change. The principal is strongly opposed to what she calls "using the learning disability category as a dumping ground for problems that have alternate solutions." The IPRC considering the case says it will listen to any argument that clarifies whether or not Cory has a learning disability, and will consider any and all recommendations.

new term was non-pejorative and all-encompassing. It avoided altogether, implications of low intellect and ineptitude, and successfully subsumed a variety of unsatisfactory general descriptors like *dyslexia*, *perceptual handicap*, *minimally brain-injured*, *maturational lag*, even *slow learner*. The dark side, however, is that 'learning disability' is loose enough to permit a variety of interpretations, and although it offered a sense of focus and direction, and put a consensual face on an issue that had been running in all directions, making the next step to a clear and widely accepted definition, proved then — and still is today — a challenging task.

In the dozen or so definitions* that enjoyed currency since the 1960s, four elements prevail.

---

*For Ontario's official definition, see Appendix.

IQ Score – Achievement Discrepancy

A difference of two years or more between the mental age obtained from an intelligence test, and the grade-age equivalent obtained on a standardized achievement test indicates a learning disability. The flaw in this still popular element is that it reduces the complexity of an individual to numbers. Also, a two-year discrepancy has different meanings at various age and grade levels.

Presumption of CNS Disorder

Much of the early work in learning disabilities grew out of central nervous system and brain injury research of the 1930s and 40s. Researchers, because they noted similar behaviours between children known to have brain injury, and those in the new subject pool, tended to make a leap of attribution so that learning disabled students were seen to have CNS disorder. Although the field has moved away from brain *injury* toward brain *dysfunction*, or *difference*, a means of clearly establishing neurological cause in a way that implies educational response, is still not available.

Processing Disorder

Psychologists especially, were responsible for promoting a notion of diminished 'psychological processing', a theory that a learning disabled person is one who does not properly perceive and integrate stimuli such as visual information. Of all learning disability theories, this one has turned out to be, not just unsupportable, but also one of the most disappointing. (In its defence, the disappointment may be owing to the fact that it is a theory that implies specific instructional responses. Thus teachers were given something to do about a learning disability. Unfortunately, it did not seem to have value.)

Exclusion of Environment, Culture, Mental Retardation, Emotional Health

If a learning problem is caused by one of the above, the problem is not a learning disability. Unfortunately, the connection between these factors and low, generalized academic achievement is well established, so separating them from the fact of a learning disability is difficult.

Characteristics of Learning Disabilities

Processing Language

Many learning disabled students are very challenged by the task of processing language. At the *receiving* stage (when the student is hearing language or attempting to read it) or at the *sending* stage (speaking or writing), or at the *elaboration* stage (when the student attempts to integrate some language with what he already holds), a learning disabled student often has real problems. For some students, it's only at one of the stages; for others, difficulty arises at two or all three stages. For example, a younger student may not be able to process an incoming set of instructions like: "Use your red crayon to colour the robins, and then your yellow one to draw a line under the 'r-r-r-r' sound." He will *hear* the instruction all right, but all the linguistic information: robins, crayons, red,

yellow, 'r-r-r-r' sound, not to mention the activity, may be too much to process. He may miss the instruction altogether, or miss a piece of it, or confuse red and yellow, or interchange pieces of information. The result will likely be a poor performance or a non-performance.

An older student may have an equally difficult time with something like this from, say, a geography teacher: "If you refer to your maps of West Africa, you'll notice a good example of how Africa was fragmented by decolonialization. Notice how Gambia is literally inserted into Senegal, and then further down the coast you'll see even more examples with Guinea-Bissau, Guinea, Togo, and Benin all sitting side by side." The older student may have more sophisticated language ability than the one colouring robins, but then he is expected to deal with more sophisticated language, and relatively, is going to have just as much or even more trouble.

It is not unusual for an adult working with a learning disabled student to confuse the student's weakness in processing of language with weakness in visual or auditory discrimination. For example, unless she has a vision or hearing loss, this student will have no difficulty visually discriminating the letter A from a picture of a teepee, or the sound of "book" from the sound of "hook". Where she will manifest difficulty, however, is recognizing the letter A as such, and giving its name (or recalling the word teepee and saying it). It is not distinguishing between the sounds of "book" and "hook" that is hard; it is recognizing the words and the meanings; or, giving the right answers even if she knows them. A learning disabled student may also have difficulty in *producing* the letter A on paper (or the words "book" or "hook"). He may draw a teepee, but it may be disproportionate. On the other hand, he may be able to draw a beautiful teepee but when instructed to add a campfire at the left and a horse on the right, will have to guess at these juxtapositions.

Variations in Ability

What makes the language processing deficiency above so insidious is that it is so variable. If there are three students in the geography class who have learning disabilities, one of them might be entirely confused by the concept of "decolonialization" and miss everything else as a result. A second, unless there is a map right before him will be overwhelmed by all the verbal details of the countries mentioned. The third may understand the point perfectly, and even be able to hypothesize on it, but three days later on the examination, she may be entirely unable to put together the language that will explain what she thinks.

The English Language is a Factor

The subtleties of English may pose a barrier for the learning disabled. A teacher for example, who says to a student, "I don't see your answer" may mean a number of different things. She may mean the answer is simply not visibly apparent. Or that the answer was not completed, or possibly that she does not understand the answer, or that she disagrees with it. Because some learning disabled students not only have difficulty with language, but even further difficulty in reading between the lines of communication situations and social contexts, they may respond incorrectly to "I don't see your answer" or, respond undiplomatically, or just not respond at all.

Language that attempts to capture time and sequence is another of the many stumbling blocks, in part because the language itself can be very complicated, and in part because chronology and sequence are problems all their own. For example, in the sentence "Only after it first sprouts blossoms, can the tree bear fruit", the words and the syntax used to describe the sequence, set up real complications. The phrase "only after" is at the beginning of the sentence. Yet it sets up a condition and presents a time frame for the rest of the sentence, which then describes what in effect must happen *before* "only after"! Efficient language users can usually comprehend such a sentence. Students with learning disabilities often do not.

Still another barrier exists in the pronoun "it". Not only must "it" be held in short term memory until its referent ("tree") surfaces, the listener/reader must perceive that "it" refers to "tree" and not some other idea! (Research shows that the difficulty with pronouns normally experienced by young language learners, aged four and five, is experienced by the

For Discussion: the Case of Raghubar

Raghubar's mother is fully involved with the stress of learning to live in a new country and a new culture, but even though she has no other children on whom to base a comparison, she has not been too preoccupied to notice that her little boy does things differently. Not that he is hard to raise; and he definitely is not deaf, but somehow, he never seems to *hear* her. Well, not quite that way either. He hears her, but does perhaps half of what he's asked, or starts the task and then wanders away, or more often than not, does it backwards or leaves out a step. Raghubar almost never gets anything exactly right. Except in soccer. In soccer he is so good that older children in the community park stop to watch him. Still, that too is a mixed blessing. Raghubar is a natural athlete, a gifted one, probably. But he also has no fear. He puts himself at such risk that his mother is certain that one day he'll injure himself permanently. And that concern ties into another one. Raghubar never seems to learn from the experience of a bad fall or a banged shin or painful cut. The very next day, he'll go out and do the same thing that led to an accident the first time.

Although she has a fairly limited education herself, Raghubar's mom had the good sense to visit her son's teacher-to-be, well before his formal schooling began. As a result, the teacher was on the lookout for what sounded to him like a learning disability, a suspicion reinforced when Raghubar lagged behind the rest of the class when it began to learn letters. After six months now, in the first grade, it is clear the boy is not picking up what his classmates get. He recognizes only six letters, and in counting, gets to ten and becomes confused. Over half his class is already reading more or less independently.

When the teacher suggested to the principal that an IPRC might be in order, he got the two responses he expected: one, that Raghubar is far too young and undeveloped for such a major step; and two, that at this early stage the best strategy is to revise the boy's program. The teacher has now turned to his colleagues for help. Is a six year old too young and undeveloped to be called 'learning disabled', he wants to know? And, what program steps can he take right away, for a boy who does not count past ten, and recognizes only six letters?

learning disabled, well into their teenage and adult years.)

Difficulties like those above are compounded by learning disabled students' problems in relating one sentence to others in a passage, or in relating passages to passages, or even stories to stories, whether written or spoken.

Are We on the Same Wave Length?

One of the more unsettling aspects of the problem in processing language, for teachers, parents, and certainly for the students themselves, is the frustration of discovering that a communication which appeared to be successful, has been partly or even completely misunderstood or misinterpreted. (Admittedly, this is a common trait in all students, but what distinguishes the learning disabled is the consistency with which this occurs.) Because teachers, parents, and students often engage in a communication knowing that the potential for confusion is high, all parties often take extra care to be sure they are 'on the same wave length', that the communication has meshed in a way that what was *sent* is also what has been *received*. It is not difficult therefore, to imagine the stress that results when what appeared to be a successful interchange, was really two separate tracks of communication that overlapped from time to time but never bonded into that stage of information interchange we like to call *understanding*. The implications of this problem for life in general, and for the classroom especially, are significant. Whether it occurs solely because of faulty language processing, or because of memory problems, has yet to be clearly established. All that is known for sure is that it happens. Often.

In high school they put all us LDs in one class and that's the first time I ever felt comfortable. Nobody laughed if what I said made no sense because we were all in the same boat. See, if you're LD what you want to say isn't always what comes out. Sometimes only half comes out. Sometimes you even say the opposite of what you want to! Don't get me wrong, elementary was O.K., but there were times I thought I was on a different planet. So did the other kids! You see, I never understood anything first time. If two things came at me, I always missed the second one. (Still do!) Order is still a problem too. And jokes. I *never* got jokes! Pretended too, but... In high school, when we were all LD, then we could work on that stuff. Saved my life, I think. Still don't get jokes, though.

—Moira MacDonald (at her community college grad banquet)

Problems Remembering

An apparently poor memory for learning and for new information is another characteristic that distinguishes many students with a learning disability. They may, at the moment of instruction, learn a technique or an idea, or acquire information, or memorize a sequence or a formula at the same pace, and in the same depth, as their non-learning disabled colleagues. But unlike the latter, they will have difficulty retrieving it next day.

Accounting for this supposed memory problem has generated considerable speculation. One hypothesis is that the students forget because they cannot transfer learning and information from short term to long term memory, or at least, cannot do so easily. Another is that it is strictly a result of poor language processing: not a case of simple forgetting, but of not getting a correct grasp of the material in the first place. (More recently, there has been argument, particularly from audiologists, that the faulty processing results from imperfections in the central auditory nerve. See Chapter 11.) None of the explanations is entirely satisfactory. If the students cannot transfer from short to long term memory, then why can teachers and parents cite examples of phenomenal long term memory retention in learning disabled students? If the central auditory nerve is the culprit, why does the forgetting occur just as frequently with written language? And if language processing problems are the sole cause, why do learning disabled students so often make the same *social mistakes* time after time? (Learning disabled students frequently have difficult peer relations because of a seeming inability to gain from social experience.)

Some Day-to-Day School Problems of the Learning Disabled

Difficulty with Alphabet/Penmanship

- may confuse letters in writing and in recitation
- mixes upper and lower case letters
- mixes manuscript and cursive styles, or will continue to use manuscript long after age and grade peers use cursive
- frequently distorts letter size and shape, attempts at continuous text are scratchy, barely legible
- often mirrors or reverses letters
- awkward, even unnatural movement of the pen or pencil

Problems in Personal Organization

- forgets, misplaces things
- needs constant reminding (and often has successfully trained family/teacher/friends to do this)

Difficulty in Copying/Note-Making

- very careless, often reproduces inaccurately
- loses place often
- far-point copying very slow and inaccurate
- overprints, telescopes, omits
- may have difficulty reproducing a shape from memory
- ignores sub-headings and organization cues

Problems in Arithmetic

- reverses numbers (as well as letters)
- careless about columnar structure
- may not remember multiplication tables
- carries or borrows wrong digit
- skips or omits steps in problem solving

Problems in Reading

- loses place regularly
- makes many flying guesses
- does not "attack" a new or strange word, but tends to gaze at the teacher, or use other avoidance techniques
- ignores punctuation and other cues
- makes up words, telescopes
- reverses and transposes
- loses meaning of a sentence from beginning to end
- gets events out of sequence
- infers content that is not there
- forgets details

Slow Work Speed

- very often does not finish
- works slower than age and grade peers
- frustrated under time pressure

Problems with Time and Sequence

- poor notion of chronological order, sometimes confused about days of week, etc.
- tends not to see time in discrete units
- confuses a set of instructions, so that they are followed out of sequence (or partially ignored)
- often has difficulty starting a piece of work (doesn't know where, or how, or at what point)

Confusion in Spelling

- uses phonetic or invented spelling long past the age when more attention to correctness is expected
- does not seem to retain a basic stock of spelling words

They continue to repeat social gaffes, seemingly not remembering what happened when a similar situation cropped up previously.

Whatever the cause, it is essential to be aware that learning disabled students may well not have retained what everyone else thinks they have — or should have. It inevitably shapes how we relate to them.

Poor Executive Function

(Some prefer the term 'metacognition' over 'executive function': the understanding an individual has of the strategies available for learning a task, as well as an understanding of the regulatory mechanisms needed to complete it.) Usually a learning disabled student has great difficulty taking on a project or even a simple assignment, and organizing it through to completion. He or she finds it extremely difficult to know *how* to begin and *where* to begin. Finding information — the research component — is as problematic as is dealing with the information if it is found. And putting it together is overwhelming. Consequently, a student will almost invariably fail to complete an assignment without some very specific direction, not because he is avoiding or rejecting it (although by adolescence, avoidance does tend to be habituated) but because he simply does not know how to go about pulling it together. He needs *executive* help. (Parents particularly, are often frustrated observers of this characteristic in day-to-day living. Such matters as organizing one's own room, or hockey equipment, or toys, or hobby materials are managerial challenges for learning disabled children that go beyond "just being a kid".)

Difficulties With Sequence and Order

Learning disabled students miss steps in a sequence, get them out of sequence, reverse the sequence, and as often as not, may simply ignore a sequence. Research has not been able to demonstrate clearly whether this is a cognitive or an affective characteristic, but the weight of empirical evidence is in favour of the former interpretation.

Satisfaction With a Peripheral Understanding

An adolescent taking a credit in chemistry, when asked what is Boyle's Law, might typically answer "Oh, it's about pressure and that." The likelihood is he knows more: probably a definition of Boyle's Law, perhaps even an understanding of how to apply it in a problem. If this adolescent is learning disabled, the answer "Pressure and that" may well constitute the sum total of his knowledge of the law. *Yet he will quite likely believe he has a thorough grasp of it,* and proceed comfortably in that self-assurance until confronted by a request to apply Boyle's Law to a problem. This is the same student who in grade two, wrote three lines in his journal while the rest of the class averaged twenty. And who likely responded indignantly to a comment about such a slim output with something like, "I *did* my journal!" or, "That's all I have to say!"

The key feature is the student's satisfaction with a vague, incomplete, peripheral piece of work, *and* his conviction that it is adequate. This is a crucial behaviour for teachers to recognize. It's not defiance; it is not shirking; and it is not an utter lack of ability. It is a misinterpretation of what constitutes completeness.

Poor Time Management

It is not surprising that a student who rarely forwards plans, and even more rarely accommodates her activity to due dates and timetables, is frequently late, or in the wrong place, or in conflict with some time-specific requirement, or is just chronically off-task. Many learning disabled students seem to be unaware of time, or at least of time as a concept organized into sequentially discrete units. This page in the LD catalogue accounts for a significant portion of their trouble in school. Because schools are so time-driven, so inflexibly organized into chronological chunks — sequenced, hierarchical, chronological chunks — the student often feels entirely out of place. School bewilders her, not just because of its emphasis on language (and its commensurate de-emphasis of non-language elements where she may shine), but also because of its apparent obsession with time in specified units. Regrettably, the outside world is equally passionate about time, and learning to deal with that fact is a necessary prerequisite in all of education. It is not unusual for a student with learning disabilities to perform better, both generally and academically, in an environment where she is liberated somewhat from the demands of time.

Inconsistent and Episodic

What is at once tantalizing and frustrating for anyone who tries to view the field of learning disabilities objectively (viz., teachers, parents, academics, medical professionals, et al.), is the knowledge that a learning disabled student's profile is never the same day after day, and that a single characteristic of learning disability is never universal. A student with this disability may regularly write "on" for "no" and "b" for "d", yet in the same sentence use all four elements correctly. He may use "on" for "no" consistently for three weeks, and then suddenly and spontaneously use them correctly while simultaneously begin writing "was" for "saw", even though those had been correctly used hitherto. This is the adolescent who cannot remember a single irregular verb in French, or the formula for calculating the area of a circle, or the definition of alliteration, but who on a warm Saturday can strip down, clean, repair, and completely reassemble a mountain bike. This is the child who bumps into everyone in the queue, whose shoes are untied and whose

For over a century, 'dyslexia' has been a subject of research, theory, pedagogy — and controversy. In 1896, in the British medical journal *Lancet*, eye-surgeon James Hinshelwood and general practioner Pringle Morgan first used the term 'word-blindness' to describe a phenomenon whereby otherwise normal individuals seem unable to extract meaning from print. About the mid-twentieth century, educators slowly became involved, spurred by an American organization, the *Orton Dyslexia Society*, named after Samuel Orton, a neurologist. Orton was one of the first to claim a connection between reading problems and such "soft neurological signs' as mixed hand preference, finger agnosia, and letter reversals — which he called 'strephosymbolia'. His theories had wide appeal and the Society soon became gatekeeper of the term 'dyslexia', vaguely attributing its origin to an unknown writer from the 1930s, even though the term is found as early as 1887 — in German!

The 'soft sign' theory is discounted today, but Orton's work and that of the Dyslexia Society were instrumental in drawing attention to the fact that some individuals, hitherto presumed to be simply stupid, did indeed have a condition that made dealing with print exceedingly difficult. Unfortunately, 'dyslexia' also became very attractive to pop psychology and to the tabloid press. Together, these forces did much to generalize the term and fix it in the public consciousness as a partially understood substitute for learning disability. Once popularized, dyslexia quickly became the object of some quite strange research and bizarre pedagogy. (One of the more dramatic examples is a program developed on Orton's principles, which specifies, among other things, that for part of the program (two years) the student not be allowed to read or write!) Not that there haven't been real successes in what are often called "privately developed" methods. Some schools, private ones especially, claim major success in moderating the effects of dyslexia, and on the surface at least, the claims appear to have merit, notwithstanding the demurral of critics who wonder whether the precise reason for a successful turnaround can be demonstrated and proven.

After a century of speculation, however, there now seems to be a consensus that *sound* is the key to understanding the phenomenon. Interestingly, many educators have argued for years that dyslexics have problems with the sounds of language — letter/ sound correspondence, for example. (Which may explain why so many teachers of special education continued to rely — with success — on the teaching of phonics, even when the popularity of that method was in decline.) Now, research in neurology seems to confirm that view. Although the jury is still out, and may be for some time yet, and although the specifics of exactly how to address the problem of sound still eludes both education and neurology, it seems that after a hundred years, both fields are moving down the right, or at least the same, path.

shirttail is half out, but who is the first in his age group to earn Red Cross badges for swimming excellence. This is the student who forgets where he put his clothes, his books, and his lunch, who confuses his telephone number and his address, but can recite without error, a T.V. ad or the lyrics of a song.

It is an acknowledged fact by all associated with the learning disabled that no one student will be the same as another, and that no one student's own pattern will ever be consistent and regular. This phenomenon, among other things, makes learning disabled students almost completely resistant to positive identification by formal standardized tests. It bears equally important weight for the classroom teacher, who must be ever prepared to adjust to the episodic nature of their performance. And of course for parents, it is yet one more arrow in the quiver of confusion.

Difficulty Paying Attention

That learning disabled students do not attend as well in class as their more academically successful colleagues, is a given. What is less clear is the cause. Do they fail to attend because years of confusion have taught the value of avoidance? Or is this habit innate? The response to this question is a continuing debate in the field. Whether the characteristic is inherent or learned, the simple fact is that most learning disabled students do not concentrate in school (and often at home) in sufficient depth, or for sufficient time, to learn or acquire new information or receive instruction effectively. This attention deficit is expressed in forms that vary from simple daydreaming to pervasive, counter-productive physical activity.

Very Low Self-Esteem

Although there may be argument over whether other traits of the learning disabled are inherent or not, this one, clearly, is acquired. And the cause, at least as far as school is concerned, is fairly obvious. In a system, in a tradition, that not only rewards but celebrates academic achievement, it is easy to understand that a student who consistently, often dramatically, fails to achieve at anywhere near the expected standards, will develop serious doubts about his whole persona. What makes this characteristic so damaging is that it feeds a continuous loop. A student with a learning disability who has become accustomed to low achievement, also becomes accustomed to putting out minimal effort on the quite understandable premise that there is no point if there is no payoff. Therefore the achievement level decreases even further, both because it may have been affected in the first place by the learning disability, but also by lack of effort. As a result, neither teacher nor parent, nor the student, gets to see how good the results really could be. Even worse, both sides become so accustomed to poor achievement that on the rare occasions of success, they often look first for the fluke that brought it about!

The next link in this chain is invariably behavioural. Students develop personas to divert attention from their disability and their failure, and to attract attention to other matters. The class clown, the victim, the super-competent, the I-don't-care, the bad-guy — these are all popular masks that learning disabled students wear.

Assessment and Identification

By Standardized IQ and Achievement Tests

IQ tests and standardized achievement tests are too narrow to capture the complexity of a learning disability, at least in ways that benefit the student or his teachers. Most of the time, these instruments simply offer a number that reveals what everyone knows already. (But a number may have purpose if policy dictates that a cutoff level is necessary to pry loose funds, or to set the table for an administrative action.) Another drawback is in the episodic nature of a learning disability. A formal assessment might well produce different results on consecutive days, thus diminishing its reliability. Even more important, at least in the classroom, tests do not point to practical, helpful, strategies that classroom personnel can use.

Nevertheless, extensive formal testing to uncover learning disabilities continues in some boards, possibly because it is a long established practice (or perhaps because it offers at least a feeling that something is being done!). In situations where this type of instrument is used therefore, it is important that the results be seen as only one of several clues.

By Teacher-EA-Parent Teamwork

Experience shows that classroom personnel and parents of a learning disabled student, working cooperatively, often with the input of other professionals, are in the best position to establish the presence or absence of a learning disability with considerable certainty. In fact, this kind of teamwork, shaped by a few prerequisites, may be the only way to make a diagnosis with confidence. The prerequisites are disarmingly simple.

Terry, aged 10.1, grade four
*"My (School) Yard Rules
Let somebody else go first.
Watch what they do."*

- *Understanding the exceptionality:* To diagnose and identify a learning disability, one must be clearly aware of the characteristics that make up this special need. Because a learning disability does not yield to a definable set of criteria in the same way that a hearing loss, for example, does to an audiometric assessment, to uncover the presence a learning disability, one must first know what to look for empirically.

- *Careful observation:* Armed with the knowledge of what to look for (and sufficiently informed by that knowledge to go looking) it follows that an effective way of making the identification is to watch for clear evidence of some or all of the characteristics.

- *Over time:* Since a learning disability is episodic by nature, it is a given that observation must take place over a period of time. Learning disabilities are not revealed in a one-shot assessment.

- *Use of informal aids:* Rating scales, questionnaires, informal reading inventories and the like can be of assistance, especially in providing specific focus on a student's needs, and in collating the efforts of different observers.

- *Teamwork:* In the best interests of the student being assessed, everyone involved must share findings, and attempt to achieve a consensus. A team is more likely to impose caution on the identification process. Because the presence of a learning disability is difficult to pin down, and because every human being exhibits some LD characteristics some of the time, the broader view available to a team helps to keep things in perspective.

Some Issues in the Field

■ *A satisfactory official definition* of learning disabilities, one that is universally accepted not only inter-, but intra-jurisdictionally, is still being sought.

■ *Assessing* the presence and extent of a learning disability in a manner that produces clear, indisputable results, continues to confound educators.

■ *Integrating* learning disabled students into regular classes or educating them in self-contained classes, is always up for discussion. The principal advocacy group in the field, the Learning Disabilities Association (LDA) is generally supportive of the idea that schools should maintain the option of self-contained resource placement for some students. Because the trend toward integration continues, however, and given the numbers of students identified as learning disabled, teachers of regular classes in Ontario can be certain of having one or more — usually more — such students in their classes.

■ *Gender representation* has been a niggling concern for years and is no closer to being explained than it ever was. Data show that males outnumber females by at least two to one in the category of learning disability. Yet, examination of data from any typical Canadian jurisdiction will show that this phenomenon is equally true of almost every category of exceptionality, and these have never been explained either.

■ *Overidentification?* The data in Figures 3C/3D of Chapter 3, underline the fact that learning disabled students far outnumber their peers in any other category of special need. (This is not an Ontario phenomenon; these data are similar to those in other provinces and in the U.S.) Such numbers continue to provoke accusations of gross misidentification, and of excessive "dumping", viz., underperforming students are simply labelled learning disabled because that relieves the school system, the parents, and the students themselves of any blame for doing poorly. While there are few educators who would deny that this kind of escape indeed takes place, the accusation is very much unwarranted. Awareness of learning disabilities is relatively new in education and it follows that there may well have been a rush to identify students who fit so ideally into the category. Evidence that current numbers of identified learning disabled students are probably realistic, can be found by examining prevalence and incidence data over the past thirty years. The sharp rise in numbers over the late sixties and through the seventies began to slow in the mid-eighties, and numbers have remained quite consistent since.

■ *Quackery or experimental science?* Even before the term learning disability became popular, there had been a proliferation of teaching responses to the fact that certain students, despite apparently normal ability, spoke incomprehensibly, or wrote in most unusual ways, or generally performed in ways widely off the mark for their age. (See the writing examples in this chapter.) This unusual output generated equally unusual responses that often failed to find support after research into their effect. For example, it would have been fairly common practice at one time, to engage students like Terry and Vana (see pages 59 & 62) in extensive calisthenic exercises "to develop their visual-motor integration skills". The method did not hold up under scrutiny.

Yet it is unfair to dismiss unusual teaching methods out of hand, if only because, realistically, any response demands at least rational consideration. An interesting case in point is the recent confirmation of auditory factors in dyslexia (see page 58). The use of rhyme, singing, classical music, even nonsense sounds, has been touted for many years as a means to "unlocking" the reading barrier in some students, but tended to be dismissed as quackery.*

The ultimate resolution to this issue seems to rest in professionalism. Educators must, first of all, be open to examination of apparently unusual or even radical means to address a learning disability, an openness that presumes, and secondly, they will stay abreast of the literature.

---

*An example of an idea that met with derision is "scotopic sensitivity", first broached by the Irlen Institute in California, which advanced the theory that a type of visual flaw impairs some students' reading ability, and can be treated by having them wear coloured lenses. While the idea quite understandably challenges educators' common sense, evaluations reported in the *Journal of Learning Disabilities* (1990, 23,10) makes clear that the Irlen approach merits consideration in some cases.

(1) Empathy and understanding are prerequisite qualities in any person hoping to offer instruction to the learning disabled (although this point is likely redundant to an effective teacher). Once one "gets inside" the particular nature of learning disabled students, making the necessary steps of accommodation follows naturally. A teacher must set up a warm, supportive climate, without pandering to, or making excuses for, or drawing unnecessary attention to, the students' particular needs.

The older the students are, the more difficult this task tends to be, for they will likely have well-established and annoying avoidance behaviours, developed over years of practice. Yet, unless a teacher has an appreciation of what his or her students are contending with, and unless there is some sensitivity toward that, all efforts will eventually degenerate into despair and conflict. An environment of mutual trust is crucial for teaching all students with exceptionalities, but for the learning disabled there is an added, subtle layer, for these students usually do not appear at first to be handicapped in any way; in fact they often seem as though they should be especially successful. But they are not, and most of the time, they do not understand why, any more than the adults in their lives do. Such is the insidious nature of a learning disability. It is why empathy and understanding on the part of the teacher are so important.

Cameron, aged 15.3, grade nine — opening of a 95 word narrative . . .
"A black robe faced the window. When it turned around I saw it had a black hood. Snakes came out of the hood."

a BlaK roB FaS,d th< winddl wh
It trd a,r(sN ,sa, it had ~ BlaK
hod SnaKs Kam aut cF th hod

(2) Positive, frequent feedback as quickly as possible, especially on academic matters, is crucial. This helps practically, by keeping the student on task, and more abstractly, by reinforcing *momentum*, the component so necessary for continuing academic success and achievement. A learning disabled student, especially if he has had a history of failure, is not willing to defer gratification as successful students do. He needs reassurance and reinforcement to build self-esteem to a point where he'll put forth his best effort. Fortunately, this kind of feedback does not have to be dramatic (although an occasional "celebration" can work wonders). Simple attention to even modest achievement is often all that is necessary to develop self-esteem.

(3) A consistent, systematic approach will help the learning disabled student eventually learn to interpret and accommodate expectations. Part of this approach will be a firm insistence on on-task behaviour and thoroughness. Perhaps a more encompassing term would be structure. The very nature of the learning disabled student's day-to-day cognitive function means that not only classroom instruction, but such apparently simple things as classroom regulations and expectations must be clearly outlined, with the parameters firmly established. Teachers must remember that a learning disabled student not only does not learn or manage himself as effectively as he might, he usually does not know how. If his teacher establishes the boundaries and points out the steps, both self-management and learning become easier. (And once a structure is established, it is also easier for the teacher to be empathetic and supportive because an operating context has been established which both parties understand.)

(4) Graphic and visual support benefits learning disabled students significantly. Use of the blackboard, overhead transparencies, pictures, maps, and other concrete supports, helps them to comprehend what might otherwise be a mass of confusion. In fact, many successful teachers assert that it is impossible to teach otherwise. A positive note here is that while graphic and visual support are essential for the learning disabled, they are also helpful techniques for all students.

(5) Help in sequencing is important. Teachers must emphasize steps and stages in the proper order as a lesson progresses. The same applies to all assignments, projects, homework, or any

Vana, aged 8.6 (grade three)
"High Park
1. I liked the scavenger hunt
2. I liked feeding the ducks
3. I liked seeing the blue heron"
("I liked" was written on the chalkboard)

High Paa a r K
1 I lict the scmgrhnt
2 I lict feding the dcs
3 I lict seing the Blolrn harin

other item that requires independent and individual completion. Without guidance in where to begin, and what organization to follow, the learning disabled student will become confused and likely as not tune out or give up. Learning disabled students need 'maps'.

(6) Help in dealing with print is important for many learning disabled students. Reading, as well as producing legible and coherent text, can be a difficult and time-consuming procedure, so not only must a teacher recognize that challenge, and make allowances in time, he may well have to modify the challenge, by simplifying instructions, for example.

(7) Awareness of time constraints, one of the realities of school that regular students pick up quickly, is yet another factor that teachers must factor in for their learning disabled students. Many do not forward plan, and it may well take their entire school careers before they learn the responsibilities inherent in due dates, appointments and scheduling. Yet they can

and do eventually acquire these skills, however imperfectly, and for that reason it is essential that their teachers persist. (Both parents and teachers attest that this issue is one of the most frustrating, and one that offers the strongest temptation to simply give up.)

(8) "Staying-on-top of things", for lack of a more professional-sounding phrase, may be an apt way of describing all those apparently superficial, but in reality, fundamental behaviours, that a teacher must help her learning disabled students to exercise. Drawing the student's attention to signal words, counseling about sequence and about time, reminding him to bring and take, cueing things by saying "Watch for the change here." and "This is important" — all these seemingly small things go together to help the student cope with daily life in the classroom. It is part of developing his sense of 'executive function'. *Software programs are particularly useful here, and for suggestion #9 also.*

For Discussion: the Case of Tino

A multi media literacy program in the self-contained learning disability class at Tino's secondary school has had a major impact on him. The program uses video and audio tapes, and some single sheet print material, but its centrepieces are a software program, items downloaded from the internet, and a "chat line". Tino gives full credit to this program for the fact that he now can read the TV guide, and billboards, and can "get" the jokes that show up on the chat line. Two weeks ago, the second part of a standardized assessment instrument, administered in split-half form, showed that Tino has learned to note periods at the end of sentences; he can identify the correct spelling of previously learned words after three days (but does not yet write the words). And he can follow directions that tell him how to complete geometric figures. Tino could not do any of these things six months ago.

These are the first indications of progress for Tino in a very long time. He was identified 'learning disabled' seven years ago (he's now 15) and has been placed mostly in resource classes since that time. According to reading assessments, Tino has never been able to read above a grade three to four level. Prior to starting on this new program, Tino had been a regular visitor to both the vice-principal and the counseling office, but for the past while he has avoided demerit points.

Tino's situation comes up for annual review in a month, by the IPRC. Although reviews in the past have pretty much rubber stamped a continuation of his identification and placement, Tino's parents have served notice they want a "serious discussion" this time. The problem, they feel, is that the multi media program, while beneficial, is too much fun and too unrealistic. They argue that clicking responses on a screen to gradually produce a finished product of some sort (e.g., a math problem, a string of short, connected sentences, a drawing — the program also prints out a certificate of accomplishment each time) will achieve nothing in the long run. The parents want some evidence that Tino either can now, or will soon be able to, manage independently. The situation is not without irony, for Tino's teachers have also wondered about this. Yet they are more aware than most that for the first time, he seems to be getting somewhere.

The issue is how to wean him from the program, or perhaps even more basic: whether he should be.

Special education is rife with expansive instructional concepts, along with the impressive terminology that elevates them. Most of the time, these complex notions are recastings of time-honoured, sound classroom practice. When teachers take a moment to analyze techniques like 'scaffolded instruction', 'metacognitive training', and 'mnemonic keyword method', for example, they often recognize methods they already use instinctively, albeit with some modification. A benefit of this predisposition to embrace quasi-scientific models of instruction, is that they give classroom practices a focus (not to mention some lofty "insider" vocabulary). A drawback is that they tend to divert attention from the merit of simple ideas that experience has proven valuable. Two of these simple ideas, long known to be effective with the learning disabled, are *expanded instruction time* and *drill*.

Time

As any teacher or assistant will attest, everything with the learning disabled takes longer, and instructional time has to be adjusted to address this fact. Lessons take longer, and may have to be re-taught several times. Pacing of a lesson is crucial. So is the amount covered. Frequent reviews are essential. The *time spent* in teaching/learning must be expanded to equal the *time needed*. See the formula.

$$\text{quality of instruction} \times \left(\frac{\text{time spent}}{\text{time needed}}\right) = \text{degree of learning}$$

In the formula, let an (arbitrary) factor of <u>5</u> represent *quality of instruction*. Note the result when *time spent* (a factor of <u>1</u>) is less than the *time needed*.

$$5 \times (\tfrac{1}{5}) = 1$$

Adjusting the *instruction* improves the outcome. (Double the <u>5</u> to a <u>10</u>.)

$$10 \times (\tfrac{1}{5}) = 2$$

But note the degree of learning if the *time spent* is closer to the *time needed*.

$$5 \times (\tfrac{5}{5}) = 5$$

Like all learning formulas, the one above may be an oversimplification. But it illustrates the potential impact when an acknowledged need of the learning disabled is addressed. It is even more pertinent in light of the essence of special education: making special accommodations (like more time) to address special needs.

Drill

A logical correlate of time is *drill* (or "opportunity to reinforce by practice"). Both through research and empirically, teachers know that practice — drill — plays an important part in learning. Can it be less than reasonable to assume then that learning disabled students, who find learning difficult, require more opportunity to practice until they have something down pat? Granted, going over previously traveled ground is tedious for both teachers and students. Yet no procedure has yet been found, quasi-scientific or otherwise, that equals the effect of repeating something often enough until it becomes part of a student's repertoire.

The sentence by Cameron here is the fifth rewrite of the item that appears on page 61. A resource room EA assisted Cameron with rewrites 2, 3, and 4. This is an independent effort. Note the result of time and drill.

> a black note fas faced the window. When it turned around I saw it hada had a black hood. Snakes came out of the hood.

(9) Making allowances for those skills which the learning disabled never ever seem to master, is another part of the teacher's role. Correct spelling, for example, is an expectation many almost never meet, and to pursue it relentlessly is counter-productive. It is far more effective, both in short and long term, to teach them how to use a dictionary effectively, or to get help via computer software. Similarly, since they never seem to master the memorization of multiplication tables, it makes sense to forgo the memorization requirement.

Other matters, simple on the surface to most of us, frequently escape learning disabled students. Multiple choice questions for example, so time-honoured and so commonly used, often have a subtlety that totally confounds. So does convoluted syntax. An attempt to persuade, for example, by saying "Inasmuch as the field day is on Monday and the movie on Wednesday, wouldn't you be better to get the project done this week?" will not succeed like this will: "Finish the project this week, because next week we have a field day and a movie. There will be no time to do it next week".

(10) Simplifying the environment. Within the boundaries of what is practical and sensible, simply by removing distractions, a teacher can make a difference. Sometimes the seating arrangement in a room or the adjacent surroundings of a learning disabled student can be modified to his benefit.

Finally, as evanescent as *hope* and *optimism* may seem, they are the glue, along with *trust* and *encouragement*, that hold the relationship of teacher and student together. A learning disabled student, usually far more than his peers, will respond to a stimulus, not so much because of a vague awareness that it is part of his education, but rather, because his teacher, the one he trusts and respects, has asked him to. It is a reality that imposes a heavy responsibility on the teacher, but then, without that reality, the art of teaching would not be as exciting. Or as rewarding. It is trust and encouragement and hope and optimism that lead to the extra steps, the extra efforts, the one-more-times, and ultimately, to the breakthroughs. Realistically, breakthroughs are not all that common. What is far more common is plodding progress, but then progress of any kind is worth the effort.

Attention Deficit/Hyperactivity Disorder (AD/HD)

In only a few years, Attention Deficit/Hyperactivity Disorder (AD/HD) has become a very frequently applied diagnosis by psychiatrists and psychologists in North America. It has also attracted a great deal of attention in the popular press, and is a regular topic in the academic literature. However, most educational jurisdictions (including Ontario), even though they may acknowledge AD/HD, much in the same way as they acknowledge conditions like Tourette syndrome, do not list it as a distinct category of exceptionality. AD/HD, nevertheless, is a factor in special education today, irrespective of its legal or administrative position in education generally.

Is AD/HD a Type of Learning Disability?

AD/HD has been associated with learning disability almost from the time it first appeared in both medical and educational literature. The association lies in the inattentiveness factor that both LD and AD/HD share. They are *not*, however, the same thing. Nor does a student with a learning disability automatically have AD/HD, or vice versa. Estimates vary, but the literature generally suggests that about one-third of learning disabled students may have some degree of

AD/HD. Alternatively, the rate of learning disabilities is high in students who are diagnosed AD/HD, but one condition does not absolutely imply the other.

Is AD/HD a Real Exceptionality?

Those who acknowledge AD/HD as a genuine special need, argue that it has been around for a long time under other titles like 'hyperkinesis' and 'minimal brain dysfunction' and 'moral deficit'. They posit further, that what makes AD/HD a real disability is that it has a biological or psychological basis, or both. Biological factors arise from causes like neurochemical imbalances in the brain, and/or from genetic bases, and/or via environmental triggers. As for psychological cause, proponents argue that despite our culture's insistence that human will and self-control are managed from within, there are some individuals who, through no fault of their own, cannot do this.

Notwithstanding these arguments, most jurisdictions, including Ontario, have not established AD/HD as a separate category of special need, at least for legal purposes. Many school boards in the province, however, recognize and respond to AD/HD, even though the term itself may not be used for IPRC identification.

Is AD/HD Just Another "Modern Day" Phenomenon?

Not entirely, although it did not capture the public eye until the late twentieth century. A German doctor, Heinrich Hoffman, first described hyperactivity in 1845. In 1902, George Still, a British physician added the moral overlay idea which still dogs the field. (He described 'sick' children of average or higher intelligence who had an "abnormal deficit of moral control".) AD/HD was not classified clinically until 1968, and did not acquire its current designation until 1987.

How Does One Describe AD/HD?

Although attempts to clarify AD/HD, and to distinguish it from closely related behaviours, sometimes confuse the issue even further, there seems to be fairly substantial agreement that it is characterized by three primary behaviour features:

i) *Inability to sustain attention at age-appropriate level:* The student cannot screen out irrelevant stimuli, does not concentrate on tasks long enough to complete them, does not sustain the thought processes necessary to do school work.

ii) *Impulsivity:* The student does things without considering consequences, and often repeats the behaviour (does not learn from experience). Work patterns are erratic and "scatter-focused". Often perseverates with counter-productive behaviour.

iii) *Hyperactivity:* Student engages in non-purposeful movement and activity that is usually not age appropriate, and often at an accelerated level. Continues despite intervention.

Teachers often notice many of their students in a description like this, or members of their family, or even themselves! Key to the criteria however, are *frequency* and *severity*. The symptoms in a student who has AD/HD are high and wide. The symptoms are not situation specific, but are seen most if not all of the time. (And they are seen in boys over girls at a rate of about 4 to 1.)

What Makes AD/HD So Controversial?

There is intense, even vicious disagreement over whether AD/HD should be seen as a distinct clinical entity, or even stronger, whether it really exists! Critics contend that AD/HD has become a *label du jour* in North America, an invention of a culture that has cast aside its obligation to parent well, and to teach values, and now needs an excuse for the result. While such statements are unquestionably harsh, and probably offered more for effect than polemic, they have a powerful impact in the light of two very real factors. One is the accelerated rate of diagnosis. In 1997, the *Globe and Mail* newspaper reported that an estimated half million Canadians, mostly students, had been diagnosed, an extraordinary number for a condition that only got its name a decade before! The other is what has been called the failure of psychiatry to clarify the issue. It is difficult to have confidence in medical literature, and even in educational literature, when one can find, in addition to AD/HD, ADD (attention deficit disorder), ADD-WHO (without hyperactivity), AD/HD-HI (hyperactive-impulsive type), AD/HD-NOS (not otherwise specified), and other variations including classifications like ODD (oppositional defiance disorder).*

Yet another area of controversy, entirely separate but of major consequence, is the use (and possibly, abuse) of medication to control AD/HD.

---

*Refer to Diagnostic and Statistical Manual of Mental Disorders, 4th Ed. (1994) by the American Psychiatric Association.

How is AD/HD Managed?

Teachers and educational assistants have their own problems managing AD/HD, but initially, it is the parents who encounter the brunt. Although in a minority of cases, parents and their advisors look to altered diets for help, or to environmental control, in the belief that the behaviour may be triggered by reactions, the majority accept the recommendation that their child be medicated.

The most popular medication by far, is methylphenidate hydrochloride (brand name, Ritalin). Less frequently used are dextroamphetamines (e.g., Dexedrine) and magnesium pemoline (brand name, Cylert).

Although these medications have not been shown to improve scholastic achievement (even though some advocates make that claim) they have been shown to be effective in controlling behaviour in the majority of cases. The drawbacks of course, are side effects, both physical and psychological.

What does AD/HD Mean to To the Classroom?

Teachers and educational assistants have long been used to "antsy" students, particularly younger ones, who find it hard to sit still. And in most classrooms the behaviour is managed successfully most of the time. But where a true case of AD/HD is present, teachers can expect a high level of physical activity, inappropriate responses, low frustration tolerance — the list goes on. And every behaviour *repeats*, despite intervention. Whereas it is the student's parent who must bear the ultimate costs

For Discussion: the Case of Hannah

After only a month in nursery school, Hannah was being secretly called 'Beagle' by the staff, because of her penchant for running flat out until something or someone stopped her. It was a habit she continued over the next several years. Kindergarten passed fairly smoothly, for Hannah's teacher was a completely unruffled person, committed to letting her students express themselves as much as they wished. Grade one, however, was a disaster. Not entirely Hannah's fault; the grade one teacher was having a difficult year. She had two pre-school children of her own, one of whom was chronically ill, and a husband who worked shifts. But Hannah didn't help things. By this time, running about during story time, quiet time — *any* time — was an established habit. She regularly blurted out whatever was on her mind during instruction, and seemingly could not keep from interfering with others in the class when they teamed up for an activity. Hannah regularly "borrowed" material without asking, never returned it unless told to, and did not seem remotely aware of how annoying she was to others.

Grade two was marked by a field trip crisis when, because of Hannah, the class was asked to leave a petting zoo. Following this trip, Hannah's mother agreed to accompany excursions as one of the parent volunteers supervising a group. Nevertheless, because of some more incidents, and because of an extensive list of complaints from other parents, Hannah's mother eventually kept her daughter at home during all subsequent field trips. Unfortunately, the residue of this move carried into grade three, when several other parents used it — unsuccessfully — as a precedent for requesting that Hannah be removed from the class altogether.

In grade three, a pediatrician diagnosed AD/DH and prescribed medication (Ritalin), but Hannah turned out to be one of the minority for whom the side effects, especially sleeplessness, made it impossible to continue. Hannah's mother, a nurse, ruled out a second medication, Cylert, because she'd heard it may cause liver damage. Throughout grade three, Hannah's impulsive, annoying behaviours worsened. By then it was also evident that she was lagging behind her peers academically.

Hannah is now in grade four. Her mother reports that she had a "good summer" at a camp for children with AD/HD. Both mother and daughter have new hope because Hannah learned some self-control skills at camp, and because the grade four teacher has a reputation for competence in dealing with AD/HD. In spite of this, there has already been an incident. The class is forming groups to put together material for a 'time capsule' to be opened in June. Because no group would accept Hannah, she had a tantrum, and then for the first time any one can remember, she began to cry in a deeply heartfelt way. The teacher sees that as a sign the time is ripe for renewed effort to address Hannah's case. An In-School Team meeting has been called to come up with ideas.

emotionally and physically, teachers have a burden all their own, for a student with ADHD has a concentric effect. His lack of restraint and his acting out will invariably draw in his peers, or distract them, or cause conflict, or interrupt their work, or...

Regrettably, there is no sure remedy in the classroom. Certainly there is no universally accepted way to deal with AD/HD in school. Behaviour modification is often tried, but offers no guarantees. Isolating the student with AD/HD may be beneficial for her peers, but is not a solution for the student herself, at least not long term. Ultimately, the most effective management techniques usually turn out to be those that the teacher and educational assistant work out creatively, often with the parents' help, and these techniques, most of the time are uniquely successful for that particular student. Chances are slim the same methods will work with the next candidate. Nevertheless, most teachers do find through experience that there are a few common threads in successful management. One is flexibility. There is not much point in banging heads with a student who seems predisposed to repeat wrong behaviours in the first place. Another is setting modest goals, objectives the student has a realistic chance of attaining. Still another is diversion. And all of these must be supported by, for lack of a better phrase, "kind firmness".

<table>
<tr><td colspan="2">Classroom Strategies for
Students with Attention Problems</td></tr>
</table>

Environment: Seat the student away from sources of distracting stimuli like doorways and other traffic areas. Try to seat him so that stimulating peers are not in his natural line of sight; if possible, surround him with stable peer models. Provide a special, stimulus-reduced study area. Encourage parents to do the same. (Experiment with the effect of natural vs. fluorescent light. It *may* be a factor.)

While Instructing: Be simple and concise. Offer one instruction or task at a time. Limit your use of subordinate clauses. Welcome questions of clarification. Make the student feel secure. Stay nearby until she starts the work. While instructing a large group, stand near her often. If school policy permits, and if you and the student are comfortable with it, use frequent, BRIEF, physical contact (like a hand on the shoulder).

Managing the Day: Prepare him for shifts in topic, setting, schedule, etc. (Again, be physically nearby when these are about to happen.) Meet him and spend a few, positive, one-on-one seconds at crucial points (e.g., when he returns from somewhere, like lunch). When in-class work is assigned (homework too) help him get started, and then at first, check back frequently. Help the student organize and maintain (retain?) his work output so that he develops a visible, concrete, and cumulative record of achievement. Maybe try a daily assignment book.

Other Support: Enforce your classroom routines and procedures consistently. (And have only a very few!) Always give enough time. DO NOT debate or argue; you can't win. Reinforce "good" chunks of time with just-for-her, positive eye contact/expressions. Use antiseptic bouncing; i.e., when she is stirred up, send her on an important errand out of the room, or, provide an important-task-that-needs-doing-now.

Think Momentum: Not motivation but *momentum*. A teacher who motivates is always pushing from behind. Eventually, she wears out — or runs out of patience, ideas, or most likely, desire. On the other hand, a teacher who tries to build momentum in her students, who works at developing in the student, a sense of responsibility for his own fate (and his own behaviour) and a sense of desire within, will not only last longer herself, but make a far greater impact on the student. One way to do this is to help the student focus and manage his own behaviour by establishing a contract or agreement that aims at two, and only two, behaviours so that the objectives are clear (and realistically attainable) and the hope of success thereby increased. Reinforce these with a progress record in chart or other form so that you and the student can point to accumulating proof of improvement.

For Further Investigation

Barabasz, M., & Barabasz, A. (1996). Attention deficit disorder: diagnosis, etiology and treatment. *Child Study Journal, 26*, 1-38.

Cantwell, D.P. &Baker, L. (1991). Association between attention deficit hyperactivity and learning disorders. *Journal of Learning Disabilities, 24*(2), 88-95.

Gersten, R. (1998). Recent advances in instructional research for students with learning disabilities: An overview. *Learning Disabilities Research and Practice, 13*(3), 153-172.

Higgins, E. L., & Raskind, M. H. (1995). Compensatory effectiveness of speech recognition on the written composition performance of post secondary students with learning disabilities. *Learning Disability Quarterly, 18,* 159-176.

Hinchelwood, J. (1917). *Congenital word blindness.* H.K.Lewis.

Huntington, D. D., & Bender, W. N. (1993). Adolescents with learning disabilities at risk? Emotional well being, depression, suicide. *Journal of Learning Disabilities, 26,* 159-166.

Maag, J. W., & Reid, R. (1994). Attention deficit hyperactivity disorder: A functional approach to assessment and treatment. *Behavioral Disorders, 20*(1), 5-23.

McKenzie, R. G. (1991). Content area instruction delivered by secondary learning disabilities teachers: A national survey. *Learning Disabilities Quarterly, 14,* 115-122.

Raskind, M. H., Herman, K. L., & Torgeson, J. K. (1995). Technology for persons with learning disabilities: Report on an international symposium. *Learning Disability Quarterly, 18,* 175-184.

Richardson, S. (1992). Historical perspectives of dyslexia. *Journal of Learning Disabilities, 25*(1), 40-47.

Seigel, L. S. (1992). An evaluation of the discrepancy definition of dyslexia. *Journal of Learning Disabilities, 25,* (10).

Swanson, H.L. (1993). Executive processing in learning disabled readers. *Intelligence, 17*(2), 117.

For the Classroom Teacher

Aust, P. (1994). When the problem is not the problem: Understanding attention deficit disorder with and without hyperactivity. *Child Welfare,* 73, 215-227.

Barkley, R. A. (1990*). Attention deficit hyperactivity disorder: A handbook for diagnosis and treatment.* New York: Guilford.

Deshler, D.D., Ellis, E.S., & Lenz, B.K. (1996). *Teaching adolescents with learning disabilities: Strategies and methods.* Denver: Love Publishing Inc.

Ferretti, R. P., & Okolo, C. M. (1996). Authenticity in learning: Multimedia design projects in the social studies for students with disabilities. *Journal of Learning Disabilities, 29,* 450-459.

Garnett, K. (1992). Developing fluency with basic number facts: Intervention for students with learning disabilities. *Learning Disability Research and Practice, 7,* 210-216.

Hallowell, E.M., & Ratey, J.J. (1995). *Driven to distraction.* New York: Simon and Schuster.

Hughes, C.A. (1996). Memory and test-taking strategies. In D. D. Deshler, E. S. Ellis, & B. K. Lenz (Eds.), *Teaching adolescents with learning disabilities* (2nd ed.). Denver: Love.

Landau, S., & McAnich, C. (1993, May). Young children with attention deficits. *Young Children,* pp. 49-57.

Levy, N.R. (1996). Teaching analytical writing: Help for general education middle school teachers. *Intervention in School and Clinic, 33*(2), 95-103.

Salend, S.J., & Hofsetter, E. (1996). Adapting a problem-solving approach to teaching mathematics to students with mild disabilities. *Intervention in School and Clinic, 31*(4), 209-207.

Sherman, G.F. (1995). Dyslexia: Is it all in your mind? *Perspectives,* 21(4), 1.

Welch, M. (1992). The PLEASE strategy. A metacognitive learning strategy for improving the paragraph writing of students with mild learning disabilities. *Learning Disability Quarterly, 15,* 119-128.

(See also materials available from Learning Disabilities Association of Ontario.)

7

Students With Behaviour Disorders

" Don't ask why I did it. I don't know. Look. If it's
there, I take it. If I want to, I do it. That's the way it is."
—Alvin K., aged 16.5

Misconceptions About Behaviour Disorders

1. Only mental health professionals are equipped to deal with behaviour disorders.

People with little or no professional training can be very helpful, especially to students.

2. A permissive atmosphere that allows students to develop understanding and acceptance of the self, is the most effective way to change inappropriate behaviour.

Evidence suggests that a highly structured, ordered, and predictable environment brings about the greatest change in students with a behaviour disorder.

3. Behaviour disorders are neither age nor gender related.

Most studies show identified cases of males outnumber females by ratios of 3.5-5 to 1. Incidence rates are highest in the upper grades of

elementary school and first grades of secondary school, and lowest in the primary grades. In the last decade of the twentieth century, however, new data began to show significant *rate* increases for girls over boys, in identified behaviour and in crime.

4. There is no relationship between single-parent families and behaviour problems.

Statistics Canada reports (1998) that children in single-parent families have behavioural, emotional, academic or social problems at a rate 1.5 - 2 times greater than children in two-parent families.

5. Behaviour disorders generally are patterns of aggression and frustration.

There is no doubt that outward-directed behaviour is noticeable and may well be disordered. However, symptoms of behaviour disorder can also be expressed by reticence and withdrawal. The latter is not as easily noticed, particularly in large classroom groupings.

5. Very often a behaviour disorder indicates a student who is bright but frustrated.

Available data suggest a correlation between behaviour disorders and average to low IQ test scores, with the more severe cases even lower.

6. Difficult behaviour is usually an external manifestation of something deeprooted.

There is no sound evidence that all the causes of behaviour are rooted deep in a student's psyche, or even necessarily connected to emotional disturbance. Especially in school, inappropriate behaviour is often spontaneous and temporary.

What is a Behaviour Disorder?

To most people, disordered behaviour is behaviour that varies markedly and chronically from accepted norms. In a general way then, the notion is quite widely accepted and understood, much in the same way that a general notion of *normal* behaviour is widely accepted and understood. It is from this point that differences develop. Therefore, in order to create a common ground of understanding, professionals concerned with behaviour disorders, particularly mental health professionals, have attempted to organize behaviour disorders by classification. Unfortunately, the consensus in these classifications varies from limited to non-existent. Interestingly, professionals in education seem to have less difficulty with this issue, probably because they have a more unified perspective. Immediately following is a brief description of the more popular views held by mental health professionals, and of the general view held by educators.

> Six school behaviours linked to *hunger*, are fighting, blaming others, defying teacher, disobeying rules, stealing, clinging to parent. (Kleinman, et al., in *Pediatrics*, Jan.,1998).

A Mental Health View of Behaviour Disorders

Mental health professionals tend to view behaviour disorders from a particular perspective or theory or enveloping concept. It's a tendency that affects research, treatment, and to a lesser extent, education. These are some of the more widely held perspectives.

- *Environmental.* Factors in the environment like diet, air pollution, metals, etc. lead to behaviour problems.
- *Psychodynamic.* People with behaviour problems are experiencing deep-rooted inner turmoil. Their deviations are a manifestation of this.
- *Psychosocial.* An individual's relationship with family and peers may bring on inappropriate or unacceptable behaviour.
- *Psychoeducational.* A student's behaviour may be owing to a combination of circumstances that are brought about in school.
- *Behavioural.* Deviation from "normal" is the result of learning the wrong things. That is, the individual's behaviour has been taught him, either directly or by example.
- *Biophysical.* Deficiencies in genetics, neurology, biochemistry, along with disease and malnutrition cause an individual's behaviour.
- *Combinations.* Some or all of the above theories apply in combination.

An Education View of Behaviour Disorders

Most teachers, educational assistants, child care workers and others responsible for the education and treatment of students with behaviour disorders, accept the value of classifications for mental health purposes, but do not find them very practical on the front lines. Thus, while the classifications used by mental health professionals may be informative to educators, or may have some administrative value, or may possibly be used by a multidisciplinary team, the prevailing style in education is to approach the notion of behaviour disorder without terminology. In determining whether or not a student might be behaviour disordered, an assessment team will almost always consider exclusionary factors as well: whether or not the behaviour can be traced to specific sensory, social or health-related causes. Nevertheless, even if a student's inappropriate behaviour can be explained as a direct outcome of some specific, explainable factor, he or she might still be identified as simply behaviour disordered, because, no matter what the cause, it is still the behaviour — the effect—that the educators must deal with.

When educators identify a student as having a behaviour disorder, they generally do so on the basis that the student

- deviates in a significant manner from the behaviour normally expected in the situation;
- breaks social or cultural norms that are usually quite well established for the age level;
- shows a tendency toward compulsive and impulsive behaviour that negatively affects learning;
- has poor interpersonal relationships, and low self-esteem;
- demonstrates very low academic achievement for reasons that can best be explained by his or her conduct;
- manifests any or all of the above characteristics *regularly* and *consistently* over a period of time so special education is likely required.

Causes of Behaviour Disorders

Biological

The majority of students who have behaviour disorders appear to be physically healthy. Nevertheless, theory and research in the latter years of the twentieth century suggest possible links between biological makeup and behaviour. Sometimes the connection is clearly, if also distressingly, apparent. Children born with fetal alcohol syndrome or fetal alcohol effects are a case in point (see page 103). The causes of pervasive development disorder (autism) have become an area of extensive research — and speculation — inasmuch as biology is concerned. Research in genetics is provoking a continuing reassessment of disorders like schizophrenia. In short, biology is now being considered in cases of behaviour disorder, almost as a matter of course.

Allergies

Allergies, too, are being re-evaluated as long-ignored causes of disordered behaviour. While the physical effects of allergies on some students are readily acknowledged, a more recent conception of allergies incorporates the thesis that allergenic reactions can generate learning and behaviour problems in a far deeper and more subtle way than the very obvious physical reactions. A widely accepted notion now, is 'total load' : the idea that an individual has a capacity to tolerate only so much substance in the environment. In some individuals, say, a student

in a classroom, a combination of stale air, chalk dust, moulds and fungi in the carpet, and perfume or shaving lotion on the teacher, may exceed that student's tolerance (total load) and cause an allergic reaction expressed both in a physical way (e.g., a rash or watery eyes or sneezing) and in her behaviour. These reactions are often far more profound than may be immediately apparent.

Speech and Language

There is a higher prevalence of behaviour disorders among students with speech and language impairments than is found in the general population. Cohen et al. (1993) for example, in a study of young psychiatric outpatients, found a significantly higher number of language impairments in the outpatients than had been suspected at intake. While there is some debate in the field over whether language impairment is a cause or an effect of behaviour disorder, it seems logical to conclude that a student who has difficulty expressing his needs — or his frustrations — may choose to act them out. Either way, it is certainly a point which classroom personnel must heed.

Psychological

In the Home

Explanations for behaviour that are found in psychology will vary by perspective (e.g., a psychoanalyst will see things differently from a behaviourist) and by setting (e.g., the home, the community, the school, etc.). For educators, two very powerful influences on a child's behaviour are the home and the school itself. A child's relationship with parents is crucial to development, particularly in the early years. In homes, for example, where discipline is inconsistent and sometimes harsh, and where there is little reinforcement for affection, children often learn to be aggressive. Empirical evidence, supported by research, has consistently shown that the style of child rearing used by parents will have an impact on the behaviour of their children. One of the more recent and interesting releases of data by Statistics Canada (1998) suggests that immigrant children are two to three times less likely to manifest the most common behaviour disorders of childhood. Whether this outcome is a product of the closeness that is presumed to prevail in the homes of newcomers to Canada, is still being examined.

Teachers, especially those who are parents, realize that the causes of a child's behaviour may well be a two-way street, with parents responding to the behaviour originated by the child, rather than the latter simply becoming a product of what she is taught. Unfortunately for teachers, assistants, and others working directly with a student, the cause of the disordered behaviour is less of an immediate issue than the effects, and is in any case, something they are somewhat powerless to modify: one reason why the multi-disciplinary team, which usually has a member working with the family, can be effective.

In the School

There are still a few mental health professionals who maintain that schools are the major cause of behaviour disorders, but there is no clear evidence to support this. Still, since schools are where students spend a major portion of their wakeful day, it is logical to conclude that what goes on in the classroom, under the direction of the adults there, can have a major influence on behaviour. The relationship therefore, between a student and a teacher, between the student and peers, and between the student and the school at large, can have a significant impact. A key issue for teachers is to give this impact an appropriate and sensible weight, for just as children must share some responsibility for their behaviour in the home, so must they in school. Many an attempt by school personnel to resolve a behaviour situation has undermined itself by too obsessive a concern with the dynamism of intra-school relationships.

Assessment of Behaviour Disorders

Identification of a student with behaviour disorders usually begins with a feeling in the mind of a teacher or parent that something is not right. As subjective as this might seem, and

For Discussion: the Case of Logan

On just her second day in office, the (acting) principal spotted Logan under her secretary's empty chair after morning recess. He was pale, and shaking, and appeared to have been crying. Logan is a month away from his seventh birthday and is in grade two. The principal, suspecting a playground incident, deliberately ignored Logan for a few minutes, but intervened fifteen minutes later, when he had not moved and began crying hard. In her office, Logan said his grade two teacher "touched me here and here and put his hand inside my pants", adding that it had happened several times. When the principal moved to follow board policy by notifying authorities, the school secretary, who had only just returned from an errand, suggested she call both of Logan's parents first. The parents are divorced and have joint custody of Logan. Last year, he told each of them, on consecutive days, that the other was abusing him sexually. Before the accusations were exposed as completely false, Logan's mother was asked by her professional association to voluntarily suspend her practice (she practices pediatric psychiatry). His father, an attorney with a prominent firm, was asked to take a leave of absence, although the firm denied the request was connected to an interview that Logan gave — on his own initiative — to the tabloid press. In this most recent crisis, both parents independently advised the principal that the teacher was almost surely innocent, and after an intense flurry of questioning, she agreed. Nevertheless, the teacher was under a cloud of suspicion for several weeks.

During her investigation, the principal learned that in grade one, Logan had convinced a girl in the class that her parents were separating. She is now in a different school, but according to her parents, still has anxiety attacks even if the two of them leave for work at different times. Also in grade one, until the teacher discovered it, Logan was quietly talking classmates into destroying their work because it was no good. The same teacher suspects, but cannot prove, that Logan is responsible for a spate of missing materials, and that it was he who ruined the controls of an electric wheelchair used by a disabled boy in the class. At the same time, she acknowledges that Logan is academically superior, that she has never actually seen him do anything remotely improper (the second grade teacher agrees) and that in terms of completing work, obeying routines, and in helping others, Logan appears to be a model student. The acting principal's instinct is to call for an IPRC which would likely identify Logan 'behavioural'. Still, she wonders what that would accomplish.

despite the concern that classroom teachers, especially teachers of a regular classroom, tend to identify a very high proportion of students as behaviour disordered, informal screening by teachers and educational assistants has been established as a fairly reliable first measure.

In most jurisdictions, what follows formally after this initial phase is usually governed by a board's particular plans and procedures for behaviour disordered students. These include the types of assessment used (which in turn may also be governed by the availability and the expertise of personnel) and the conceptual model for dealing with behaviour disorders.

Typically, to provide a somewhat more objective overview of the student in question, the teacher, and assistant, and often the parents and possibly a social worker or other community service worker, will be asked to complete some form of observation instrument like a behaviour checklist or rating scale. A declining practice in the assessment of behaviour disorders, although it is still used in some jurisdictions that favor the psycho-dynamic approach, is the administration of projective tests, instruments that purport to reveal the intra-psychic life of the subject. (These tests have come under fairly heavy criticism not just for their questionable validity and potential for entirely subjective interpretation, but also because an evaluation of this type can tap only an extremely limited sample of the subject's life.)

Since there is fairly convincing evidence that students who have serious behaviour problems

in the later grades often had difficulties in kindergarten, there is usually some pressure to identify behaviour disorders early. This is not always possible, however, since disorders often do not emerge until the later grades when personal responsibilities and social and academic demands increase in complexity. Ultimately, the identification of a student as "behaviour disordered" is best accomplished by teamwork, by the collaboration of classroom personnel, parents, and where available and helpful, mental health professionals, operating in an atmosphere of mutual respect and understanding

Some Issues in the Field

■ *Agreement on an acceptable term* for this exceptionality has been an abiding concern. Among the more popular identifiers, some of which are still current, are: *socially maladjusted, emotionally disturbed, mentally ill, predelinquent, delinquent, emotionally handicapped, socially handicapped,* and of course, most frequently used in education: *behaviour disordered.* In the past, labels appeared at what seemed to be the discretion of whomever was writing on the subject. *Emotionally disturbed,* for example, first appeared (without precise definition) at the beginning of this century. Other terms have cropped up at other times. Education has not always been helpful either, for one jurisdiction will choose whatever term suits it, often without reference to any other jurisdiction, so that across

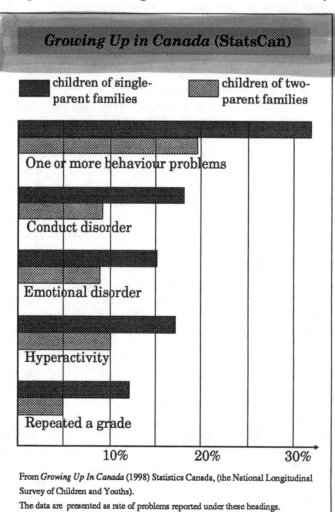

Growing Up in Canada (StatsCan)

■ children of single-parent families
▨ children of two-parent families

One or more behaviour problems

Conduct disorder

Emotional disorder

Hyperactivity

Repeated a grade

10%   20%   30%

From *Growing Up In Canada* (1998) Statistics Canada, (the National Longitudinal Survey of Children and Youths).

The data are presented as rate of problems reported under these headings.

Survey covered 4.67 million Canadian children & youths.

Canada there can be found a variety of descriptors all more or less the same in intent but sometimes markedly different in substance.

The term *behaviour disordered* has acquired a steadily strengthening credibility among educators because it is conceptually inclusive of a variety of problems that warrant professional attention; it is less negative and stigmatizing than many of the other terms in use; and it tends to circumvent the suggestion of legal identification. Above all, it is sufficiently comprehensive to have wide applicability.

■ *Developing a useful definition* has proven just as difficult, for it follows that if the names for an exceptionality are elastic and capricious, describing it would be just as problematic. Definitions are very vulnerable to the theoretical perspective of their authors: behavioural? psychodynamic?; to the discipline: teacher? psychiatrist? lawyer?; and to the purpose for writing a definition: for research? for education? These differences are a serious block to practical communication, especially in light of the fact that a multi-disciplinary approach is often necessary, especially in the more serious cases.

On the other hand, there may be merit in the argument that this exceptionality, more than any other, should perhaps not be defined at all, that rather, a statement of needs should suffice. Inasmuch as there is no definition of normal behaviour — which would therefore be the referent for behaviour that is not — it is only reasonable that behavioural exceptionality cannot be defined either. Even though behavioural disorders are distinguished by frequency and degree rather than by their nature, disorders cannot be measured quantitatively. There is no system analogous to the IQ test. And people who exhibit disordered behaviour also behave normally! Most of all, behavioural anomalies are usually exclusive to an individual. There is really no set of symptoms common enough to permit a description, much less a definition, that will be applicable to all cases, and be helpful to those who work with the individuals in question. The likelihood, therefore, is that the lack of a useful definition will prevail.

■ *Are needs being met?* An area of concern is the discrepancy between the percentage of the school population that is behaviour disordered and the percentage that is actually being served. A Canada-wide study by Dworet and Rathgeber (1990) found that not only are the needs of large numbers of behaviour disordered students going unserved, this population is getting even less attention than it did in 1981! Hallahan and Kauffman (1994) conclude that over two per cent of the school population exhibits disordered behaviour. Yet data show that typically, less than one per cent is being served. Ontario MET data show a fairly consistent rate of 'behaviour' identifications by IPRCs at around .53 to .56 percent of the school population. Recent U.S. Office of Education data show about 1% identified as 'seriously emotionally disturbed'.

■ *School standards too high?* There is some evidence that schools illuminate behaviour as unacceptable because they have unrealistic and unnatural standards. Some theorists refer to this as *iatrogenic disorder*: i.e., the behaviour arises as a consequence of the way the student is treated, and not out of a natural predisposition at all. Other theorists advance the idea of *psychonoxious* behaviours or attention-getting styles that, over time, accumulate a large pool of resentment in peers and teachers so that the student in question is treated as behaviour disordered, whether he or she actually is so or not.

■ *Socioeconomics* come into play in this exceptionality. Particularly among adolescents, students from lower income families report a greater number and variety of penalties for their behaviour. Moreover, certain behaviours by lower income students are more likely to be regarded as disordered, whereas similar behaviours by students from high-income families are more likely to be seen as legitimate responses to some stimulus. A study by Brantlinger (1991) suggests that this phenomenon may be owing to inequities in the school conditions for lower income students. Her study was conducted in the U.S., however. In Canada, there is ample reason to argue that poor school conditions for lower SES areas are not typical, and that in fact extensive resources are committed to preventing such inequities. Nevertheless, this is not to deny that different *attitudes* toward the behaviour of students from lower social classes may well prevail here.

■ *The stigma* of behaviour disorder creates a lasting impression. It affects the opinion of teachers and peers, and it can contaminate matters for the student identified. Once placed in the 'behavioural' category, exceptional

With the cooperation of the school board, an arrangement worked out by Scott's social worker, the crown attorney, and the family court, will keep Scott in custody for the remainder of June, and for July and August. In September, he will go to a different school from the one he attended for the past two years. The school will be in a different neighbourhood, for Scott will live in a secure group home until it is decided he can be placed with foster parents. Scott is thirteen.

The board has two possible schools for him. One school has a full rotary timetable and a behaviour resource class called the 'drop-in room', where students may or may not be counseled, depending on need, or work on their academic program, or just relax. If Scott goes to this school, he will be enrolled in a regular grade six class. An IPRC has confirmed his 'behavioural' identification, and he will be eligible to go to the drop-in room when he feels the need, or, he can be sent there by any of the teachers. The principal of this school, and the staff, openly espouse a "nurturing and personal development" philosophy. The second school does not have a drop-in room; in fact, it has no designated class for behaviour, and has only a very limited rotary timetable. If Scott goes here, he will be enrolled in a regular grade six class and spend most of his time with the teacher of that class. Whereas the three educational assistants in the other school are assigned to specific classes full time, the three in this school move as needed. The principal here believes strongly in academic achievement and the development of self-reliance, and she too, has attracted a staff with similar beliefs. Neither of the two schools has ever objected to the placement of a student.

Because of the Young Offenders Act, no one knows why Scott is presently in custody. However, it is known in the school board, that he has a history of aggressive behaviour, especially toward girls, and that the current brush with the courts is the latest in a string. What is known is that Scott's full scale IQ score is Average; there is no evidence that he has a learning disability, and that on a standardized achievement test, he was one grade below the age-appropriate level in math and three grades below in language skills. The director of the board has asked for a recommendation as to which school should receive Scott.

students often find their history hard to escape, and must contend with an atmosphere where expectations govern the way others respond. As a consequence, administrators are often reluctant to apply a behavioural identification, so that genuine cases of behaviour disorder may not be getting the appropriate intervention.

■ *Legal requirements* regularly complicate the education of a behaviour disordered student who has become involved in crime. One of the more significant issues is the disruption of a student's education if he or she is moved through a variety of settings while a case is being decided and a sentence is being served. It is not unusual, for an adolescent particularly, to experience a variety of custodial settings through both the court hearing procedures and subsequent serving of a sentence. These settings will invariably have different educational approaches — if any — and usually, little effort is made to coordinate them. Another complication is the rigorous privacy stipulations of the Young Offenders Act which in some cases preclude a teacher's being informed of circum-

stances surrounding a student's involvement in crime, or even of being informed about a transgression at all. While this law may have no immediate bearing on educational planning, it may require the withholding of information that in some cases could be important not just to the student's program, but also to the well-being of the teacher and other members of the class.

Models of Treatment and Their Educational Implications

Academics and mental health professionals tend to subscribe to a particular school of thought when it comes to treating behaviour disorders. As 'behaviourists' or 'environmentalists', for example, they generally approach matters from a unified perspective. In the classroom, such emphasis on a single view of behaviour is far less common. However, it behooves teachers and educational assistants to be aware of some of the perspectives that prevail.

Psychodynamic Perspective

Although this approach is a declining force among educators, it continues to attract a lot of attention in television shows and popular literature. This perspective views behaviour disorders as being within the individual. In the classroom, when this treatment approach is taken, the teacher is part of a mental health team that seeks to develop a warm supportive atmosphere in which the student will hopefully overcome his or her inner turmoil. Emphasis is placed on acceptance and tolerance, somewhat at the expense of direct instruction and acquisition of academic skills. A variation of this style is called the *psychoeducational approach*, in which more effort is directed to practical classroom outcomes. One of the reasons for the decline of the psychodynamic approach is evidence that it does not improve academic achievement, while there is only limited evidence that it helps to improve behaviour.

> Sigmund Freud established the practice of sitting out of his patients' sight during therapy sessions. Although this practice has its own justifying literature today, Freud said he did it for the simple reason that he couldn't stand looking at human faces for eight hours a day!

Biophysical Perspective

This approach emphasizes the organic origins of behaviour, and postulates a direct relationship between behaviour and such things as physical defects, illnesses, diet, and allergies. Advocates of this view have generated a multiplicity of causation theories each with a responsive therapy. Some examples include megavitamin therapy, diet control, symptom control medication, and removal of offending substances (like carpets). In the classroom, this perspective is often combined with a structured, behaviour-based approach that emphasizes routine, daily scheduling, frequent repetition of tasks presented in careful sequence, and the elimination of environmental stimuli that are perceived to be extraneous. Available data on the results of this treatment have difficulty separating which aspect, the therapies or the style of instruction, has the most impact.

Environmental Perspective

Supporters hold that individuals are a particular collective in a particular space and time, and as such, must be regarded as the product of an ecological unit made up of themselves, their family, school, neighbourhood, and community.

Educational response to behaviour disorder therefore must necessarily involve the whole of the ecological unit. Where this theory is followed in schools, teachers are expected to instruct the student in social and interpersonal environment skills. At the same time, attempts are made to modify the school's environment to meet the needs of the individual. Family counseling, and in some cases, counselling of the student's classmates may be part of the program. The key element is to create, in all parts of the unit, an awareness of its reciprocal relationships, and an impetus toward monitoring these relationships to the ultimate benefit of the behaviour disordered student. Classroom teachers and educational assistants with experience in this approach, while they attest to its efficacy, at least initially, also point out that the amount of coordination necessary to make it work well, is almost impossible to bring about.

Behavioural Perspective

Still seen as the dominant theory from an educational point of view, this approach follows the assumption that all behaviour is observable and modifiable by principles of reinforcement. (The dominance is at least partly owing to the vast amount of published material it spawns, much of it from American colleges and universities where the theory does indeed prevail. The Canadian view, and especially Canadian educational practice, does not favour behaviourism quite as heavily.) Educators who adhere to this approach believe that behaviour is controlled by impinging stimuli and that it is possible to:

i) create behaviours that presently do not exist;

ii) maintain and generalize behaviours already established; and,

iii) eliminate inappropriate behaviours.

What happens practically is that, first, a desirable behaviour or set of behaviours is established. Then, using a potent reinforcer at the appropriate time, teachers and assistants intervene when these behaviours appear. Educators who use behaviour modification — and many do to a degree, even those who would deny being 'behaviourist' — regard every student as a candidate for learning, irrespective of whatever psychopathology may be at the root of behaviour.

Classroom Perspective

Teachers and educational assistants who study behaviour theory often find it difficult to be entirely faithful to only one of the perspectives above when they apply it in the cold (or hot!) reality of the classroom. Therefore, while academics tend to attach themselves to a set of opinions or to a theoretical perspective, and do research or offer lectures from that viewpoint, educators tend to be quite a bit more eclectic. Most classroom professionals combine a variety of approaches and apply them on a by-case basis. All teachers of all students, for example, not just the behaviour disordered, espouse the value of a warm, supportive atmosphere. All teachers recognize the interplay of environmental stimuli, and all are aware of the importance of these phenomena in both learning and social development. Teachers and assistants universally modify behaviour in their students but

only some will call it behaviour modification. And the view of each student as a dynamic, individual entity is at the very heart of teaching as a profession. Taken together, the practices followed by most educators most of the time, could best be collected under the expression: flexible common sense. While the term may not have definitive intellectual reverberations in the field of behaviour theory, it describes pretty much the route followed in the classroom.

Managing Behaviour with Medication

An increasingly popular means of managing the behaviour of students today, is through the use of medication. Tranquilizers form part of the catalogue of drugs being used, but far more common are stimulant medications prescribed to control hyperactive behaviour. Because these medications may have side effects, both physical and psychological, that can have an impact on students, teachers and educational assistants often find it necessary to learn more about these medications than customarily appears in the popular press. (See also page 67.)

For Discussion: the Case of Suzette

Although the school board that expelled Suzette six weeks ago has a zero tolerance policy on violence, she was given several chances before the expulsion occurred. On one occasion she pushed and then slapped a teacher. Action on this incident was shelved by mutual agreement, when Suzette insisted she had reacted "when he grabbed me". Three student witnesses and one teacher utterly contradict that claim but the teacher asked the principal to drop the matter because, innocent or not, he refused to be "dragged through media mud". On another occasion, Suzette scratched another student seriously enough to cause a permanent scar, but an investigation of the incident gave Suzette the benefit of the doubt on the basis of self-defence. The precipitating event for the expulsion was another fight. This time Suzette beat up another girl very badly.

Suzette's exasperated parents have prevailed upon a personal friend, the principal of a secondary school in a neighbouring board, to accept Suzette, but now he has a dilemma: whether or not to place her in the school's behavioural resource class. This is an exceptionally successful unit with a highly competent teacher who places almost all her emphasis on academic achievement. There is no scheduled counseling in the class, and despite the fact that all but one of the students has a social worker, she has banned every one of them. The students work hard on a full program, go on field trips, and participate in school events, but their entire program is delivered in this class.

Suzette is sixteen and was designated 'behavioural' four years ago. She had been an excellent, high achieving student until, as her mother said to an IPRC, "she went teenage-nuts!" Suzette is articulate and has a very powerful personality. At one of her several court hearings, a judge remarked, "After five minutes with you, no one would ever say 'Suzette who?' the next day."

What the principal is worried about is a struggle for power if Suzette goes to the behavioural class. He knows her potential for success is very high there, and if a power struggle erupts, he has little doubt the teacher will win it. But victory may well be at the expense of the students already placed there.

Teachers and educational assistants who work with the behaviour disordered are the first to acknowledge that there is no pedagogical magic, no secret formula for teaching success in this area of exceptionality. And those who think there is one and go looking for it are bound to be disappointed. Still, there is one truth, an abiding one that all educators recognize, as do students, parents, and anyone else who bothers to take a second look at classrooms. This is the truth that the teacher who is effective (albeit, not perfect) with 'regular' students, is usually more effective (albeit, not perfect) with 'behavioural' students. It follows then, that to *emulate what effective teachers do* is at the very least, a practical beginning point for all classroom professionals.

What Effective Teachers Do

- They establish and then maintain consistent routines for matters like entering the classroom and beginning the session (the point at which much of the tone for what follows is established). E.g., an effective teacher is *always* at the doorway to greet, manage, and intervene if necessary.

- They set up and insist on specific seating arrangements (which are then altered as deemed useful in order to reduce or increase opportunities).

- Make sure they are visible. Interact with students outside the classroom. Try to attend anything in the school in which a behavioural student is involved.

- Use 'antiseptic bouncing' when a student is worked up or aggressive. They give him an errand to run outside the class, or some activity that may let off steam.

- If demerits are used in the school or class, then they allow for merits to be earned too.

- They use proximity control and stand nearby when it appears a situation may develop. Proximity also works in the sense of being available to help and being available to interact. Effective teachers never spend their whole day at the front of a classroom.

- Effective teachers rarely, if ever, make the dread mistake of being sarcastic, and avoid yelling (a profoundly counter-productive behaviour if it's used more than once a term) or other behaviours that shred their dignity.

- They do not use corrosive discipline techniques, e.g., writing out lines, class detentions, using curriculum content like math or spelling drills as a punishment.

- Effective teachers do not confront behaviour disordered students in front of their peers, and do not get into arguments.

- They use diversions. Younger students especially, can be distracted from a counter-productive path by giving them alternate activities and goals.

- Effective teachers let students know they have high expectations. In the case of a behaviour disordered student, or one who is learning disabled or developmentally disabled, an effective teacher will quite willingly manipulate the components of a task to ensure a positive outcome.

- They set short term goals for students who have not yet learned to defer gratification.

- Effective teachers use visible reward systems like progress charts, and ensure that students accumulate notes and other visible, physical evidence that the time spent in school is producing something of consequence.

An Effective Teacher's Attitude

There are many human strengths needed to teach effectively. Traits like patience, flexibility, creativity, a sense of humour, a capacity to see all sides of an issue — these are elements that, in the heat of a teaching moment, outweigh intelligence and scholarship. Effective teachers manifest these characteristics *most* of the time. However, what they manifest *all* of the time is not a characteristic at all, but an attitude, a perspective, namely: <u>respect</u>. When a teacher's, or an educational assistant's abiding view is built on respect for students — and on self-respect — the atmosphere in their classroom immediately reflects that attitude in a variety of ways. A place where students feel respected is a safe place to make a mistake, and therefore, an ideal place to learn and grow. Where respect prevails, students recognize that in the eyes of the significant adults there, they have value. Once students feel respected themselves, they are far more likely to show it toward others. And respect for others is fundamental if students are ever to modify their behaviour.

From the instructional end of things, respect, quite simply, infuses everything a teacher does. It smoothes rapport, supports flexibility and patience, and fuels the vitality of faith and hope. A teacher who respects students, plans better, prepares better and instructs better. A teacher who respects students instinctively avoids spontaneous but regrettable and damaging management errors, from which recovery is so difficult. Above all, if a teacher establishes genuine respect as the central idiom in a classroom, then everyone shares a behavioural reference point. Mutual respect offers both a stage from which to begin, and an objective to keep in sight.

An Effective Teacher's Classroom Style

(1) Recognizing where students are 'at'. Students with a behaviour problem are often burdened by a history which, as they know all too well, shapes the expectations that others have of them. A second burden, one that reinforces the first, is a kind of in-the-classroom helplessness which increases the probability that their behaviour problems and their academic achievement will only get worse. So many of them do not know how to set about academic tasks, or, how to conduct themselves socially in any way other than in the manner that brought on their problems in the first place. An effective teacher is very much aware of this fact, and begins much of his or her work from "inside" the student's view. It is a delicate undertaking, for one must empathetically go to where the student is 'at', while at the same time continuing to be a separate, adult mentor, with all that the role implies. For a teacher or educational assistant to become "one of the boys' is a deadly mistake. Students don't want that. What they want is an adult who is open, who listens, and who will attempt to understand what they know and do not know, and who will then help them in a face-saving way that produces results, however modest.

(2) Realizing the importance of personal conduct. The manner in which teachers and assistants present their professionalism is a crucial factor in preventing inappropriate behaviour in the classroom. Ideally, adults who deal with behaviour disordered students are role models who don't react defensively to challenge, who have the skills to divert a troublesome situation until stability is restored (and then deal with it) and who employ fair and realistic consequences in a consistent way. These are also the people who get to class ahead of time, who are present and visible, responsible and proactive. They are role models of adulthood that communicate to students the possibility that the world does have some sense to it.

Naturally, things do not always work out this way, but even the students (or perhaps especially the students, unfortunately) don't expect things to work right every time. Nevertheless classroom professionals must strive to model this type of conduct if there is to be any hope of modifying their students' behaviour.

"Some teachers, they don't get much work ready for us 'cause they think we don't care about nothin' right? And they think we don't notice. But how many crossword puzzles do you gotta do before you figure it out, right? Don't know why they do that. I mean, we're in school, so why not give us schoolwork? But that's not everybody, now. You take Mrs. P.... Now in her class do we ever have to put out. I mean, she's got work and everything every day! Like there's always stuff on the board for us, and then we get a lesson-thing. And then more work. And we got this ton of notes.

What's cool is nobody messes around in Mrs. P.'s class. And like, it not's just that she's OK and all that. She really is but she teaches math! Who wants to do math? But I mean — like — it's like you're really doin' something in that class, man. It's — it's like you're learning something!"

— Fergie V., aged 15 (identified 'behavioural')
(Mrs. P. was in her first year of teaching.)

(3) Establishing a realistic, <u>consistent and predictable</u> learning environment. This is the *sine qua non* of an effective teacher's style. Students with a behaviour disorder already have trouble making sense of the world, not to mention school. And they are notoriously poor at reading between the lines to determine what is expected of them. These are not students who

know how to, much less want to, play the 'game of school'. Teachers and assistants can make things much easier for them — make it more possible for them to behave appropriately — if procedures and expectations are clear, uncomplicated and predictable. Particularly in the beginning, and until the students develop some confidence in themselves and in their teachers, a predictable pattern is crucial.

This sense of stability and consistency in the classroom develops naturally out of the behaviour of the teacher, but also out of the day to day organization. Effective classrooms are not hamstrung by a long list of ironclad rules that students will invariably break, and for which some disciplinary response then becomes necessary. Structure, organization, sequence: these are essential features, and a minimum number of simple, reasonable *procedures and routines*, not rules, for ensuring that these obtain, makes sense even to students with behavioural problems. There will be some bona fide rules, of course, but most of these are the ones established by the school or the board or other more global entity. And what distinguishes them from classroom procedures and routines is that consequences are applied for breaking them. In the classroom, however, teachers and assistants who organize from a perspective of respect, and who model that attitude themselves, not only have a standard to refer to, but have some room for flexibility when a student pushes against it.

(4) "Catching a kid doing something good." It may be a very challenging task sometimes, but looking for positives and discreetly praising them will pay dividends. "Discreet" is an operative word here. Behaviour disordered students, especially older ones, often harbour a profound cynicism that walls them in and protects them from positive reinforcement that they are convinced is insincere. Many of them have had unsatisfactory experiences with so-called 'positive reinforcement programs' and as a result they have well-developed detectors. Praise is important, but it must be proportionate to the accomplishment, sincere, and utterly free of excess. Effusiveness will only embarrass the students and may provoke them into negative behaviour just to restore the balance.

(5) Treating democracy as a very fine line. If given the opportunity, students quite naturally wish to contribute to the classroom's plans,

procedures, and even curriculum. Understandably, this is more often the case with older students. The issue is a difficult one for teachers. Any one who has ever experienced the oft-repeated dialogue ["What do you want to do?" "Nuthin!"] is naturally wary of a suggestion that students should be consulted. And it is a healthy wariness. To expect students who have been identified behaviour disordered to involve themselves in productive interchange about procedures and curriculum is something that happens more often in movie scripts than in special education classrooms. Still, for many teachers, it's worth a try. Most effective teachers would never begin a term or a relationship this way, if only because students with a behavioural problem are looking for leadership and order, whether they realize it or not. After some time has passed, however, and once an atmosphere of respect is established, eliciting and then acting upon a behaviour disordered student's suggestions can produce real benefits, if only because he has thereby taken on some responsibility. At bottom, teachers and assistants must keep in mind that they are dealing with an exceptionality where almost always, chaos in various forms has prevailed. That reality must infuse all democratic decisions.

(6) Establishing <u>momentum</u> is more important than motivating. A teacher who constantly seeks to motivate is soon exhausted by the effort it takes to be always pushing from behind. A teacher who feels obligated to motivate, simply runs out of ideas over a long school term because the responsibility is always his or hers. Not that motivating is counter-productive, or a waste of time, but it is only superficial, and while it may pay temporary dividends, motivation rarely has a lasting impact because it is always the teacher's responsibility (a fact which doubles the risk of an all too common teaching trap: the teacher becomes an entertainer).

More effective is to plan, organize, and teach with a view to getting students "rolling on their own". Each teacher will accomplish this in different, personal ways, but establishing momentum has a few absolutes. One is beginning where the student is 'at' and then setting achievable goals so that he can have the delightful (and hitherto unusual) experience of success. Part and parcel is making those goals short term so the success can come soon. Another is designing the goal — especially at first

— to make certain the student does succeed. Then, as soon as there is a success, set up opportunity immediately for another, so that the first one can be reinforced and momentum can begin. Still another absolute, a very simple one on the surface, is arranging one's planning and teaching so that students accumulate visible products, like notes, every day. Most behaviour disordered students have never had the sense of accomplishment that comes from accumulating a set of notes, or of accumulating anything. (Worth pointing out here, is that teachers who are successful in establishing 'momentum' in their students, report that they are then much easier to 'motivate'!)

(7) Keeping academics front and centre. With the possible exception of cases where the mental health of a student is a serious issue (even then the exception should be only 'possible') the premier classroom focus should be on academic learning. Even if the development of social skills is a vital feature of a student's educational plan, the perception of the student should always be that he or she is "here for education". A student with behaviour disorder already feels singled out. To devote the major part of a program to the development of social skills in a transparent, obvious way, only reinforces the distinction. Social skill development can continue to be a principal objective, but its realization should be achieved not just by direct social skill instruction itself, but by learning it during the process of studying what all the other kids are studying.

(8) Working hard is better than sitting around. Fergie, a fifteen year old student in a regular grade nine class with a "reputation", and in which five (sic!) students were identified 'behavioural' (including Fergie) presents this argument much better than we can. (See the sidebar on page 80.)

READINGS & RESOURCES

For Further Investigation

American Psychiatric Association. (1994). *Diagnostic and statistical manual of mental disorders: DSM-IV* (4th ed.). Washington, DC. Author.

Bratlinger, E. (1991). Social Class distinctions in adolescents' reports of problems and punishments in schools, *Behavioral Disorders, 17*(1) 36-46.

Brendtro, L.K., Brokenleg, M., & Van Bockern, S. (1990). *Reclaiming Youth at risk: Our hope for the future.* Bloomington IN. National Education Service.

Caseau, D., Luckasson, R., & Kroth, R. L. (1994). Special education services for girls with serious emotional disturbance: A case of gender bias? *Behavioral Disorders, 20*(1), 51-60.

Csapo, M. (1981). The emotionally disturbed child in Canada's schools, *Behavioral Disorders, 6*, 139-149.

Clarke, S., Dunlap, G., Foster-Johnson, L., Childs, K.E., Wilson D., White, R., & Vera A. (1995). Improving the conduct of students with behavioral disorders by incorporating student interests into curricular areas. *Behavioral Disorders, 20*(4), 221-237.

Coleman, M. (1992). *Behavior disorders: Theory and practice* (2nd ed.). Englewood Cliffs, NJ: Prentice-Hall.

Coutinho, M. (1986). Reading achievement of students identified as behaviourally disordered at the secondary level. *Behavioural Disorders, 14*, 157-165.

Cullinan, D., Epstein, M.H., & Lloyd, J.W. (1991). Evaluation of cinceptual models of behaviour disorders, *Behavioural Disorders, 16*, 148-157.

DePaepe, P.A., Shores, R.E., Jack, S.L. & Denny, R.K. (1996). Effects of task difficulty on the disruptive and on-task behavior of students with severe behavior disorders. *Behavioral Disorders, 21*(3), 216-225.

Dworet, D.H. & Rathgerber, A.J. (1990). Provincial and territorial government responses to behaviorally disordered students in Canada. *Behavioural Disorders, 15*(4), 201-209.

Hoge, R.D., Smit, E.K., & Andrews, E.A. (1992). Assessing conduct problems in the classroom. *Canadian Psychology Review*, 1-20.

Kauffman, M. (1997). *Characteristics of emotional and behavioral disorders of children and youth* (5th ed.) New York: Macmillan.

Kauffman, J.M. & Wong, K.L.H. (1991). Forum: Effective teachers of students with behaviour disorders: Are generic teaching skills enough. *Behavioural Disorders, 16* 225-237.

Koyanagi, C., & Gaines, S. (1993). *All systems failure: An examination of the results of neglecting the needs of children with serious emotional disturbance.* Alendria, VA: National Mental Health Association.

Knitzer, J., Steinberg, Z., & Fleisch, B. (1990). *At the schoolhouse door: An examination of programs and policies for children with behavioral and emotional problems.* New York: Bank Street College of Education.

Newcomer, P.L. (1993). *Understanding and teaching emotionally disturbed children and adolescents* (2nd ed.) Austin, TX.: Pro-Ed.

Peterson, K.L. (1992). Helping student teachers understand conflict among preschool children. *Journal of Early Childhood Teacher Education. 13,* 15-18.

Rapp, L.H. (1991). *Is this your child? Discovering and treating unrecognized allergies.* Morrow.

Rosenberg, M.S., Wilson, R., Maheady, L., & Sindelar, P.T. (1992). *Educating students with behavior disorders.* Boston, MA: Allyn & Bacon.

Zigler, E., Taussig, C. & Black, K. (1992). Early childhood intervention: A promising preventive for juvenile delinquency. *American Psychology, 47*(8), 997-1006.

For the Classroom Teacher

Cole, E. (1995). Responding to school violence: Understanding today for tomorrow. *Canadian Journal of School Psychology, 11,* 108-116.

Colucci, S. (1993, May). Peer mediation: Creating opportunities for conflict resolution. *Communiqué,* pp. 25-27.

Faber, A., & Mazlish, E. (1996). *How to talk so kids can learn.* New York: Fireside.

Furr, D.L. (1996), Now I understand the rage. *Reaching Today's Youth, 1*(1), 9-12.

Henley, M.. (1997). *Teaching self-control: A curriculum for responsible behavior.* Bloomington, IN: National Education Service.

Jensen, W. R., Rhode., & Reavis. (1994).. *The tough kids toolbox.* Longmont, CO: Sopris West.

Johnson, D., Johnson, R., Dudley., & Burnett, R. (1992). Teaching students to be peer mediators. *Educational leadership, 50*(1), 10-13.

Jones, F. (1994). *Positive classroom discipline.* Santa Cruz, CA: Fredric H. Jones and Associates, Inc.

Koplewicz, H.S. (1996*). It's nobody's fault: New hope and help for difficult children and their parents.* New York: Times Books.

Lantieri, L., & Patti, J. (1996). Waging peace in our schools. *Reaching Today's Youth, 1*(1), 43-47.

Lewis, T.J., Heflin, J., & DiGaugi, S. (1991). *Teaching students with behavior disorders. Basic questions and answers.* Reston, VA: Council for Exceptional Children.

MacDonald, I.M. (1997). Violence in schools: Multiple realities. *Alberta Jounal of Educational Research, 43,* 142-156.

Mendler, A.N. (1992). *How to achieve discipline with dignity in the schools.* Bloomington, IN: National Education Service.

Murray, F.R. (1996). You think you have animals in your class? *Beyond Behavior, 7*(3), 10-13.

Rhode, G., Jenson, W.R.., & Reavvis, H.K. (1992). *The tough kid book: Practical classroom management strategies.* Longmont, CO: Sopris West.

Wright-Strawderman, C., Lindsay, P., Bavarette, L., & Flippo, J.R. (1996). Depression in students with disablilities: recognition and intervention strategies. *Intervention in School and Clinic, 31*(5), 261-275.

8

Students Who Are Gifted

❝ Truly, the most serious misconception I have to cope with is that people think I'm weird, that maybe I've got two heads. Or — this is worse — that I don't want to play at recess or don't want to share social confidences. Look. I watch Seinfeld. I cheer for the Leafs. I get into disputes with my sisters. O.K., I can speak three languages. That's because we speak two at home and the third I acquired here at school, just like my classmates. But I'm no John Stuart Mill. He learned Greek at three. Yes, things come easily. But I'm still a person.❞

— Davey Trace (at age 10)

Misconceptions About Giftedness

1. Giftedness is a stable characteristic.

The remarkable abilities that some people demonstrate appear to come and go in many cases. Some talents develop early in life and continue. Others are not noticed until the person matures. Some abilities appear early and then seem to fade. Giftedness is not always evident consistently.

2. Gifted students are superhuman.

Gifted people may have extraordinary abilities in some areas, but like all human beings, they may have faults and weaknesses as well.

3. Gifted students always outdistance their peers academically.

It does not always happen that a gifted student's achievement reflects his or her ability. Perhaps for this reason as much as any other, giftedness is included in the special

education corpus. Another factor is that some students' gifts are expressed in non-academic ways. (Some educators distinguish this as 'talent'; whether or not they imply a hierarchy by this distinction is moot.)

4. Gifted students work harder than other students.

Strong task commitment has come to be one of the accepted markers of giftedness, especially among educators, but a student's task commitment may not become evident until he or she is identified and working in an environment that stimulates the commitment.

5. Gifted students do not need the expense of special education.

Some gifted students do indeed excel without any particular assistance or incentive. Most require effort and support just like any other exceptional students, and may not come anywhere near reaching their potential unless their special abilities are fostered by appropriate conditions.

6. Gifted students are bored with school, disruptive, and antagonistic.

Usually they enjoy school, are well adjusted and get on easily with peers and teachers. But like any other student, they will react to neglect or inequity, or other issues they regard as important.

7. It is common for emotional instability to accompany giftedness.

Gifted students are usually in good mental health and tend to have fewer emotional problems than the norm. Empirical evidence suggests they may be exceptionally sensitive to matters like injustice, world issues, etc.

8. Gifted students are physically inept, self-absorbed and narrow-minded.

For the most part, they look and act like any other students, although teachers generally report them as above average in health, moral responsibility, and social adeptness.

9. Gifted students are easy to identify.

They do not necessarily stand out in a group of age peers. Theoretically, a gifted student performing at age level is underachieving. Although IQ tests are a frequent means of identifying gifted students (and they may often score very high) these instruments are far too narrow as a sole criterion, for they are unable to measure or even highlight characteristics like artistic ability or creativity, for example.

10. Normally a school system will find 3 to 5 per cent of the population gifted.

The percentage identified usually depends on the jurisdiction's definition of the gifted, and on its conception of giftedness. (Many Ontario boards interpret giftedness quite generously, as the data in Chapter 3 imply.)

Defining Giftedness

How an education system defines students who are gifted not only influences how they are identified and taught, but also how the environments and organizational models for instruction are then designed. Unfortunately, a reasonably stable, universally accepted definition of giftedness has always eluded educators. At the research level, the use of "gifted" prevails in spite of a strong push by a U.S. Department of Education task force report in 1993, to delete the word and substitute "exceptionally talented" and "outstandingly talented". Provincial policy in Ontario has stuck with "gifted". The dominant parent advocacy group, ABC, (Association for Bright Children) has long maintained a distinction between "gifted", a conception oriented toward intellectual ability, and "bright", a wider conception that encompasses intellectual, creative, musical, artistic, athletic and leadership abilities.

No matter what approach one takes, any attempt to describe the characteristics of gifted students reveals just how interwoven are matters like ability and desire in the human psyche, and how crucial are the matters of opportunity, environment and circumstance. Every classroom teacher, for example, will notice in many of her students, from time to time, any or all of the characteristics that follow in the list below. But then she will inevitably be compelled to reflect on whether the characteristics are situation-related and temporary; or whether they have always been present and genuine in the student, just waiting for exposure by the circumstance. There are other concerns too, like distinguishing high verbal ability (a commonly accepted characteristic) from mere artfulness and facility; or, distinguishing genuine, inherent abilities from those that may well be manifested in school as a consequence of the student's life at home. The end result is a large body of literature and a wide range of views on just what constitutes giftedness.

Defining by 'Characteristics'

Gifted students appear to have characteristics or abilities that stand out from the general run of things. What follows here is a list of those that continue to be used by both educators and parents. Note that this is only *one* way of defining gifted students, a method that prevails more out of tradition perhaps, than scientific method. However, it is at the very least a beginning point. The challenge, for educators especially, is to determine not just the presence and the stability of these characteristics in a student, but to decide on their relative importance as standards that qualify a student for specialized instruction.

- wide range of abilities both academic and otherwise;
- well developed attention span, and a deep curiosity;

- ability to grasp, retain, synthesize, and act upon information;
- ability to work independently, and to take responsibility;
- capacity to adjust easily to new situations and demands;
- able to offer innovative responses;
- superior vocabulary and reading ability;
- considerable energy and above-average health;
- well-developed capacity for abstracting and conceptualizing;
- more interested in questions than answers;
- highly developed sense of consequence and forward planning;
- able to see unusual diverse relationships;
- persistent in meeting goals;
- advanced sense of moral/ethical judgment;
- trusts, and will defer to, intuition;
- thought processes accelerated.

Defining by 'Interactions'

Most educators recognize that giftedness is a dynamic exceptionality, really too complex to be confined to a list of static, observable characteristics. Consequently, it has become regular practice now, to define giftedness in terms of fluid, overlapping constellations. According to this approach, giftedness is the result of a number of characteristics *interacting* to achieve a purpose, rather than being present in the individual in a kind of parallel isolation. One of the first and still very much accepted presentations of this style of identification was offered by Renzulli (1977) which he called the *Enrichment Triad Model**.

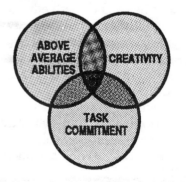

*Renzulli, J.S. (1977) *Enrichment Triad Model: A guide for developing defensible programs for the gifted and talented*, Creative Learning Press. (The model has been embellished slightly in subsequent editions.)

Enrichment Triad Model

Sometimes called the "three-ring model" because it is often presented as three overlapping circles, giftedness in this schema is seen as an interaction among

- a high level of general ability;
- a high level of task commitment;
- a high level of creativity.

Students who are gifted, according to Renzulli, are those capable of developing this composite set of traits and applying the composite to any potentially valuable area of human performance.

What is significant in this approach is the recognition of both human dynamism and the interplay of key qualities. There are times, quite naturally, when the degree of task commitment glows and fades in an individual. Everyone is more (or less) creative at some moments than at others. And abilities may well be relative to the nature of a task. The Enrichment Triad Model accommodates all of this, which probably explains why it gained very rapid acceptance among educators. Yet it has not led gifted education entirely out of the woods. Renzulli himself, in subsequent publications, argued that general ability is less important than specific performance in an operational definition of giftedness. (Which means, of course, that everyone can be gifted at some time: another major consideration for educators who must take responsibility for definitions.)

Defining by 'Multiples'

An increasingly popular way of looking at giftedness is to recognize that enriched abilities in a human being not only take many inherent forms, but can be expressed in a variety of ways. Such a point of view is eminently satisfying to those educators who accept that academic achievement by itself, along with the traditional view of intelligence as measured by an IQ number, are entirely inadequate representations of giftedness. (Which may be one reason for the increasingly broad appeal of this type of theory.)

Triarchic Theory of Intellectual Giftedness

Robert Sternberg (1997) who has published extensively on the nature of creativity has offered special education two multiple views of what giftedness means. In the first, his "triarchic theory", Sternberg posits three kinds of intelligence as necessary for giftedness:

analytic: particularly analytic reasoning and reading comprehension (the intelligence more likely to be measured by traditional IQ tests);

synthetic: creativity, intuition; responding to invention, novelty and coincidence;

practical: applying one or both of the above pragmatically.

Most people incorporate all three of these in their makeup, but a central part of giftedness in this theory, is the act of coordinating the abilities and knowing when to use which one. A gifted person then, is a competent self-manager. Such an individual not only knows *what* and *how* better than most, she also knows better *where* and *when* to use the what and how. One reason for the positive reception of Sternberg's position among teachers is its appeal to the notion that creativity, adaptiveness and old-fashioned common sense and shrewdness must play a major role in gifted behaviour.

Pentagonal Implicit Theory of Giftedness

Sternberg, with Zhang (1995) presents another theory of giftedness which offers criteria that they say are held as implicitly valuable in a culture. The five characteristics are excellence, rarity, productivity, demonstrability, and value. (See Figure 8A.) Educators who give credence to this theory are led to consider first what their culture holds dear, before they propose to set out a definition of giftedness. If nothing else, this is a theory that goes a long way toward answering a frequent criticism of gifted education: namely, that it ignores gifted potential in minorities because of a prejudice in favour of the dominant culture. It also adds background light to the charge that most people interested in gifted education, both implicitly and explicitly limit that interest to elements our society values most. That is to say: in our education system, to be gifted as a writer of poetry, or to be a virtuoso violinist, has more value than to be a gifted cabinetmaker, because that reflects the dominant cultural view.

For Discussion: the Case of Kyle

Kyle is an only child of professional parents, both very successful lawyers, and both very caring and nurturing to their son. A nanny brings Kyle to the school's day care when it opens, but one or sometimes both parents pick him up (at varying times) from day care after school. Their home and their life style is very much intellectually and culturally enriched. That influence was very obvious when Kyle entered grade one with a vocabulary and linguistic ability very much beyond the norm for his age. His identification as gifted was immediately and smoothly effected. (The parents had requested an IPRC prior to his enrolment.)

Throughout grades one and two, Kyle's school performance was equal to that of his also-identified-as-gifted classmates, although there was a glitch in grade one. Kyle began the year in French immersion, but it became obvious immediately, that it was a most unsuitable program for him. The parents demurred at first, but after extensive consultation with a psychologist they retained privately, they accepted the school's recommendation and Kyle was withdrawn. Early in grade three, a more serious problem developed. The gifted group, although nominally in regular class, was doing more and more study on a self-contained basis and Kyle had trouble keeping up. By the end of grade three, the gap between him and his classmates had widened.

It is now June, and the crunch has come. The regular IPRC review requested a full assessment of all students in the gifted primary group, because board policy shifts placements at grade four to either full time special class or full time regular with enrichment. Kyle and one classmate are below criterion for special class on all markers but one (parent nomination). Board policy gives the IPRC latitude to withdraw Kyle's identification as gifted. The committee declined to do that but did place him in a regular class. His parents are appealing now, on two bases: one that assessments of children Kyle's age (7.9) are unreliable; and two, that separating him from his peers of the past two years is not in his best interests, especially since it was the board that grouped him thus in the first place. The school board says that by its widely accepted standards, Kyle's abilities do not merit special placement. The Appeal Board must now make its recommendations.

A Summary Adaptation of the Pentagonal Implicit Theory		
Criterion	Explanation	Example
Excellence	superior in some way to age peers	writes narrative fiction much better than peers with same schooling
Rarity	ability infrequent at age/peer level	not just better fiction but usually superior
Product-ivity	individual produces	other writers recognize superior skill
Demon-strability	proven in a public way	wins awards of consequence
Value	ability is valued by society	recognized by the culture in public ways

Figure 8A

A Summary Adaptation of Multiple Intelligences (Gardner Theory)	
Type	Manifestation
1. Linguistic	exceptional ability to use words, often prolific
2. Musical	uncommon senitivity to pitch, rhythm, timbre, often without training
3. Logical/ mathematical	rapid problem solving; grasp of underlying principles of casual systems; extraordinary ability to handle long chains of data
4. Spatial	transforms easily among elements, superb mental imagery, very highly developed perception of pattern
5. Bodily/ kinesthetic	poise and control of body and movement evident even before training
6. Interpersonal	capacity to 'read' people even without language
7. Intrapersonal	very mature sense of self
8. Naturalist*	sensitivity to nature and ability to recognize and classify natural things

*A recent addition. It has not been accepted as enthusiastically as the initial seven.

Figure 8B

Multiple Intelligences: The 'Gardner Theory'

In *Frames of Mind*, Howard Gardner (1983, 1993) proposes a theory of multiple intelligences: linguistic, musical, logical-mathematical, spatial, bodily-kinesthetic, interpersonal, intrapersonal and naturalist. (See Figure 8B.) The theory holds that each of these intelligences is independent in function, and that if one intelligence is more powerfully developed than another, it will take over for a weaker or less developed one. (He originally developed the theory while studying stroke patients.) Gardner's very persuasive writings, supported by interesting research, emphasize the multifold aspect of human intelligence (illuminating yet again the inadequacy of IQ testing with its implied notion of intelligence as a single, internal construct). His work has been instrumental in expanding the view that there is considerable development and plasticity in human growth. Further, even though this plasticity may be modulated by genetic constraints, humans are predisposed to certain intellectual operations and styles of operation, all of which can be addressed by education.

The Gardner theory has particular appeal to teachers, perhaps because it reflects much more than other notions, the wide variety of abilities they see in a classroom full of students. Not only that, a theory of multiple intelligences reinforces the natural disposition of teachers to promote self-esteem in their students by recognizing that the world has room for many kinds of talent. On the other hand, the theory has also been criticized as a first step in the demise of gifted education for, as the definition becomes broader and more all-encompassing, it has the effect of eliminating any distinction giftedness may have.

Emotional Intelligence

A view advanced by Daniel Goleman (1995, 1997) concludes that star performers owe their superiority to what he calls *emotional intelligence*. According to Goleman, this intelligence is found in "people skills", social radar, political sensitivity, trustworthiness, empathy in personal relationships, and team-building ability to create opportunity out of diversity. The theory was developed out of a survey of personnel in over 500 organizations world-wide. Although Goleman's theory enjoys an exceptionally enthusiastic reception in business and industry, it does not have the same appeal to education. Supporters have argued that educators' reticence is owing to the fact that the theory appeared first in the popular press instead of acquiring official sanction by exposure first, in academic publications.

> All of us do not have equal talent, but all of us should have an equal opportunity to develop our talents.
> — *John F. Kennedy*

The Importance of a Balanced View

The varied explanations of giftedness (there are others beyond those summarized above) both plague and enrich the attempts of educators and parents to define giftedness and properly identify its candidates. Nevertheless, because these views tend to lead away from the notion of giftedness as a single construct (the IQ notion) toward a view of giftedness as an expression of several contributing factors, students are being more fairly identified. Above all, the idea of giftedness as a construct standing on a number of foundations, gives more credence and importance to creativity, to commitment, and to the expression of ability in ways other than the narrow confines allowed by academic achievement alone.

Some Issues In The Field

■ *Separate Classes?* How to deal with students once they have been identified as gifted, is a continuing debate. At one time, the heat arose primarily over whether or not the students should be congregated in separate schools. Proponents of this approach argue that a totally separated (but not totally isolated) environment can offer a much more enriched experience where the students are challenged by interchange with others like themselves, by special teachers, by an atmosphere of intellectual ferment, and by the momentum of exclusivity where elevated goals will obtain. The argument goes further to posit that a congregated environment will offer an intensity of role modeling less likely to be available in the mainstream. There are reasons to accept the validity of this position. Empirical evidence particularly, has long demonstrated the stimulating power of high expectations in a specialized, highly-charged, intellectual environment.

On the other hand, there are also strong arguments in favor of integration. A principal tenet holds that although segregated environments may be successful, they are so specialized as to be unrealistic, and therefore counter-productive. By extension, experience in a rarified environment may mean the gifted student will be ill-prepared to perform effectively in the real world.

Ultimately, like most arguments over this issue, whether to congregate gifted students in special schools, or integrate them, is probably unresolvable on a universal basis, not least because of the politics involved.

■ *How to program?* When decisions have been taken to maintain gifted students in an integrated environment, a next stage of issues inevitably arises over concerns like the following:

enrichment: providing special activities in regular classes for selected students. Proponents say that this keeps the gifted student rooted in reality, and that given the premise that everyone exhibits giftedness from time to time, there is less risk that potential giftedness will be ignored. Detractors state that enrichment really does not qualify as gifted education.

ability grouping: In an integrated environment, the gifted are selected out for differentiated instruction in more or less homogeneous groups within a regular class, or in congregations outside the class on a regular, part-time basis. Supporters of this style usually advance the congregation argument described above, while detractors say the procedure fosters elitism.

acceleration: Although a great deal of uniformly supportive evidence can be found in favour of this technique, it is one of the least used programming methods, usually because of the fear of negative social and emotional consequences for the accelerated student.

Most school boards tackle the issues above, by offering a variety of programming styles for students identified as gifted, on the quite reasonable premise that a variety of programs is necessary to be effective in educating a variety of superior abilities.

■ *Limits to the category?* Advocates of gifted education wince at the irony in the fact that no matter how generalized — some may say *realistic* — the view of genuine giftedness has become over time, programming for *talent*, unusual ability in, say, music, or athletics, or drama, or the visual arts, continues to be a poor relative in most school boards. Because these abilities are not necessarily accompanied by superior academic achievement, the issue is first: whether to classify them as examples of giftedness; second, and likely far more important: how — even whether — to offer programs aimed at developing these talents. An increasing practice in larger jurisdictions now is to develop 'arts schools' for the talents that come under that rubric. However, admission to these excellent academies is often tied very strongly to prior demonstration of superior academic achievement. (It is an interesting comment too, on our culture — Sternberg's implicit thoery notwithstanding — that exceptional ability in areas like carpentry or design or other *trades* receive little or no accommodation under the title of giftedness.)

■ *Survival?* Almost every program for the gifted endures the accusation of meritocracy and elitism at one time or another, no matter how egalitarian its admission prerequisites may appear to be. For this very important, if somewhat insidious reason, special education for gifted students is often in jeopardy. It is not unusual therefore, for the mere existence of specialized programming for the gifted to be dependent on the vigour and determination of parent advocacy groups, acting in support of determined educators who feel this kind of special education is not just a practical but a moral obligation. On the other hand, it is impossible

Gifted Underachievers?

These are students whose potential is implied by significant achievement, or by high IQ test scores, but whose apparent abilities are not realized. Not that they are failures, necessarily. They may well work at grade. However, if an individual is truly gifted, yet produces at an average level, then it may be reasonable to conclude he is an underachiever. On the other hand, lest students who are thought to be superior become tarred with the brush of underachievement, it is important for their parents and teachers to evaluate a number of factors before making a judgement.

Has he learned to learn? Many very able students 'coast' in the early grades because they master classrooms demands effortlessly. Then, as the level of challenge increases and more is required, they may not rise to the occasion, either because their confidence is eroded, or more likely, because they have not learned consistent, effective work habits.

Do the social factors permit success? Some children deliberately underplay their potential because they do not wish to be singled out.

Are expectations realistic? Learning is not automatically easy for children who are bright. Sometimes the expectations of the adults in their lives, especially parents, do not match what the children are capable of doing at particular points in their development.

Is there a good 'fit' between the child and the classroom? Some gifted children do not fare well in structured environments. Others find it difficult to conform even to the simple demands that are necessary to make a school run efficiently. Such students may well underperform as a result.

to ignore conclusions implicit in the high number of students identified as gifted. Many educators note with bitter irony, the fact there is far less outside pressure to identify students as behavioural or developmentally disabled, than there is to identify them gifted.

■ *Gifted education for primary?* An enduring argument in the field thrives over the issue of offering programs for the very young. Many boards of education are very reluctant to formally identify students in the primary grades as gifted, and equally reluctant to authorize congregated classes, or formal, differentiated programs for them. This attitude has taken hold, first of all, because the developmental elasticity so typical at ages 4-5 to 8-9 can make confident identification difficult. Secondly, since primary education is usually very adaptive and flexible, and more individualized, the gifted can be easily accommodated in the mainstream. Further, in primary education there is an importance attached to social skills that in some schools takes precedence even over the development of academic and cognitive skills.

■ *Gender?* More males are identified for gifted programs than females, and both educators and parents have had difficulty finding concrete and agreeable explanations for this. There is no conclusive research that points to biological difference as an explanation. Yet, explanations that point to traditions of male dominance in our culture have equally sparse research support. Evidence in the data issued by the Ontario Ministry of Education and Training (see Figures 3B and 3C in Chapter 3) suggest that this gender differential continues.

■ *Building a labyrinth?* The field of the gifted is regularly accused of burying itself in complexity, with inordinately interwoven and complicated models for identification, equally intricate models for program, and constant, involved requisites of review. There is considerable empirical evidence to support this. Some

For Discussion: the Case of Lydia

At a professional development day, one of Lydia's former primary teachers (grades one and two) met the girl's present eighth grade teacher, and naturally, inquired about her progress. The primary teacher was surprised to hear her former prize pupil was just "getting by".

"Lydia can certainly handle the curriculum, " the grade eight teacher said. "and she's truly a pleasant young person — wonderful with the little kids in our tutoring program; one of those naturals that can teach as well as we do! — but yes, getting by. The work's always done. On time. And adequate. But not a lot more than that."

"I've got a big class," the grade eight teacher continued. "I've always suspected she could do more, but I just can't get around to her. Especially with some of the demanding ones I've got."

The conversation proved to be a watershed in Lydia's case. With his curiosity piqued, the grade eight teacher eventually uncovered the fact that Lydia had been identified gifted in grade four, before he had come to the school, but neither her placement nor her program had changed. Lydia's family had emigrated to urban Ontario directly from a mountain village in southern Europe when she was a young child. Her parents still do not speak English. Their parish priest does all the inter-acting with the school on their behalf. Lydia's older sister had caused a mild conflict at the board office when she left school after grade six to marry the man to whom she had been betrothed by her parents. And Lydia's grade four teacher, an active feminist who defiantly enriched the girl's program, had been transferred to another school at Christmas when the parish priest threatened to invoke a human rights confrontation.

Without authorization, the grade eight teacher had Lydia complete a standardized achievement test and discovered she could — according to the test — work at the grade 11-12 level in language, and, notwithstanding the fact she had not yet been exposed to high school math, she was just as accomplished in that area.

"A waste," he said on the telephone the following day to the primary teacher. "A shame and a waste. She belongs in a gifted class, or at the very least, she deserves enrichment. And I can't do it! Something should be done but I'm not sure whether logic outweighs ethics here."

jurisdictions in Ontario, for example, while recognized for their commitment to educating the gifted, have such amazingly intricate and time-consuming patterns of identification — and the programs to match — that it is conceivable that some students may not be receiving appropriate programs for the simple reason that they (or their parents) lack the will or the means or the stamina to crawl through the web of bureaucracy.

How Students are Nominated for Gifted Programs

1. Despite the acknowledged weaknesses of the IQ test, it continues to be a main screening device.

What is administratively significant about IQ tests, is that they produce a quantified statement, a *number*, irrespective of whatever else they offer, and in most jurisdictions this number becomes an entry level border for admission to programs. The established figure varies from one jurisdiction to another (Figures of 140 and 130 Full Scale score on the Wechsler Intelligence Scale for Children are typical). The work of such people as Sternberg and Gardner notwithstanding, the use of numbers it seems, and faith in tradition, has not yet been seriously shaken.

2. Tests of creativity are sometimes used to identify gifted especially in jurisdictions where creative behaviours are given credence as a major cluster. However, because the validity of these tests is so much in question, their use has less impact, generally, than IQ test scores, and teacher, parent and peer nominations.

3. Achievement tests are used as initial screening mechanisms for giftedness much in the same way as in the assessment of retarded performance. In typical practice, the student who scores significantly above his or her age level (usually two or more grades) is a potential candidate for gifted programming.

4. Teacher nomination is a principal method of screening for the very early grades. Many boards require teachers to use a clearly defined rating scale, or inventory checklist to substantiate the nomination. One problem with this method is that scales usually correlate the academic behaviour of students with what is expected of them academically in the succeeding years (inevitably raising the concern that students who "play the game" are most likely to have an advantage).

5. Parent nomination is used by many school boards, on the quite reasonable premise that parents have the best knowledge of their child's development, and this knowledge can be crucial. This feature is not without its own difficulty, however. Parents from lower socio-economic groups seem more likely to report giftedness than parents from higher socio-economic areas. As well, parents often lack opportunity for comparison in being able to predict their child's future success in school.

6. Peer nomination is yet another method for initiating referral. Although experts in the field have been favourable in their attitude to this style, there is still a serious lack of research to support it. That may be, however, because truly helpful research on a matter of this nature is extremely difficult to design.

7. Self nomination has developed as a recent practice. In this case, the student nominates himself or herself in the initiating stage of the identification process. Very often a self-nomination accompanies a nomination by teacher or parent, and more often than not is presented because the student has been asked to do so by one or both of the latter.

All school boards in the province, whatever their respective policies regarding the nomination of candidates for gifted education, use a number of different methods for making final determinations. Usually, a board relies on a combination of elements like the ones listed above.

Organizational Models

Organizing the Students

It is quite common practice for boards to organize students identified as candidates for gifted education into levels, most commonly three levels. Given names like 'mode' or 'plateau' or 'level', these groups are usually differentiated by ability so that the majority will likely be identified as 'Gifted: Level I (or Mode or Plateau I). A smaller number will be designated Level II and even fewer will be in Level III.

By the end of the second grade, Colin's pranks had already made him a legend in his school. At first, most of the staff were willing to see the funny side. The upset he caused with his first major foray, for example, by putting what appeared to be soiled facial tissues (he used camembert cheese) on the tables at the school bake sale, was forgiven with chuckles. So was the time he upped the ante with seemingly-used toilet tissue in his classmate's lunch boxes. However, everyone was less than amused when, during the return from a fire drill, Colin somehow convinced the entire junior kindergarten class to hide in the janitor's storeroom. Nor was the principal too pleased when Colin attached an inflated condom to the parents' notice board in the entrance hall.

Inevitably, the litany of mischief gradually became more serious. Colin discovered he could bring police to the school by activating the overnight security system with a handheld laser pointer. On one occasion he pulled the fire alarm at dismissal time and in the ensuing chaos, disabled two school buses by plugging their tail pipes with styrofoam. It was a carefully planned endeavour, for the plugs were precut to size and the chosen vehicles were at the very front and very back of the bus lineup. When a large order of pizza arrived at the school during the first week of school in grade three, it was widely concluded that Colin was warming up for another year, and something would have to be done.

Serendipity intervened at this point, in the combination of an educational assistant with three year's experience in a class for the gifted, and a teacher with a passion for Renaissance art. In response to a group project they devised for the class, Colin produced a mural which duplicated Da Vinci's *The Last Supper*, but from a ground level perspective. Thirteen very large pairs of feet exactly paralleled the positioning in Da Vinci's famous work! Among the reactions to this mural was the educational assistant's strong push to have Colin assessed as a candidate for gifted class. The outcome confirmed her intuition. He was found to be "off the scale" in creativity and very superior in IQ test results. As well, Colin became caught up in the "Renaissance passion", and the pranks stopped, or at least went on hold.

Where things stand now, Colin qualifies for the highest level of gifted placement in the board's Special Education Plan. That would mean a transfer to a nearby school, but both Colin and his foster parents (Colin is a ward of Children's Aid) object to any placement that would take him away from this grade three teacher and educational assistant. Unfortunately, his present school is not designated for in-class gifted resource. And the educational assistant is soon to be fully involved at the other end of the grade three pod, with two students who have severe multiple disabilities including profound chronic health problems. Everyone is concerned that if Colin is unchallenged, the ever more serious pranks will return.

The largest group, Level I, will likely spend most of its time in the regular classroom, but will receive some enriched or differentiated curriculum. This may be in the form of a theme study undertaken independent of (but in addition to) the regular curriculum. The classroom teacher may be helped by a resource teacher, or the latter may have responsibility for the venture entirely on her own. (Many schools encourage the teacher and resource teacher to cooperate, and to involve all the students in the class as much as possible, whether they are designated Level I or not.)

Level II students may also be assigned to a regular class, but may be withdrawn more frequently for independent pursuits under the guidance of a resource teacher. These students may also be somewhat more involved in projects that involve several schools at once, and that culminate in special presentations, workshops, etc. Level III students are more likely to be in congregated classes where the entire curriculum is differentiated.

Organizing the Programs

School boards invest considerable time and effort in developing organizational models to fulfill programming requirements for the gifted. One immediate outcome is that the programs are thus established on a broad basis, so that there can be a good deal of interaction among schools, with sharing of resources, expenses, etc. To a greater extent too, than in most other areas of special education, there tends to be more board-wide excursions, cooperative projects, and involvement with what the community at large has to offer. Whether or not a board formally divides its gifted students among levels as described above, it usually designs the delivery of program service around a particular style or model. Following is a list of some of the models that continue in popular use in Ontario. Almost without exception, however, they are implemented with local variations to suit local conditions and values.

> The most gifted members of the
> human species are at their creative
> best when they cannot have their way.
> — Eric Hoffer

The Enrichment Triad

With modifications, the Enrichment Triad (Renzulli, 1977) is very widely used in the province, indeed throughout Canada. It proposes three levels of activity:

General Exploratory Activities, designed to expose pupils to exciting topics, ideas, and fields of knowledge not ordinarily covered by the regular curriculum. They include such items as visiting speakers, field trips, demonstrations, interest development centres.

Group Training Activities, of methods, materials, and instructional techniques designed to develop thinking processes, research and reference skills, and personal and social skills.

Individual or Small-Group Investigations in which students investigate real problems and topics using appropriate methods of inquiry.

An important modification of the Enrichment Triad is the *Revolving Door Identification Model* (Renzulli, et al., 1981)) which is designed to deal with problems in identification, motivation and curriculum. In this model, the resource room teacher is a consultant and the classroom teacher is directly involved in the students' special projects. Students are not permanently in or out of the program, but can apply for special consideration to work on projects of their own choosing. The resource teacher helps the student to focus or frame the area of interest into a researchable problem; suggests where he can find appropriate methodologies for pursuing the problem like a professional enquirer; helps him to obtain appropriate resources, provides assistance and encouragement, and helps find appropriate outlets and audiences for the creative work.

Both styles above enjoy more popular use than a third notion developed by the same author called the *Multiple Menu Model* (Renzulli, 1988) which focuses on ways to teach content in efficient and interesting ways.

The Autonomous Learner Model

This is a program developed by Betts (1985)* principally for the secondary school. It adapts to the departmentalized structure of high schools, and anticipates that students will be withdrawn for single periods at specified times of the week. The student progresses through five stages:

i) orientation;

ii) individual development: learning the attitudes and concepts necessary for life-long learning;

iii) enrichment activities: exploring outside the curriculum and become aware of resources;

iv) seminars: presenting results of personal pursuits and findings to larger groups for evaluation;

v) in-depth study: opportunity to pursue an area of interest on a longer term basis.

The Purdue Three-Stage Enrichment Model

This is a half-day or full day withdrawal program (Feldhausen & Koffoff, 1986) used mostly in elementary schools. There are three basic components:

i) divergent and convergent thinking abilities, in which the program concentrates on problem solving, decision making, forward planning, etc.;

ii) creative problem solving abilities, which offer strategies and techniques in creative problem solving of real problems;

iii) development of independent learning abilities, which requires the student to engage in the development of a product through learning and investigation and then share it with an audience.

---

*Note that almost all of the models listed here continue to undergo modest revisions (with later publication dates) but in all cases their basic structures are the same. As it is, very few schools or school boards adopt a model without making further adaptations.

The Purdue type of program is quite popular (under names like "Challenge", "Upward Bound", etc.) because it offers enrichment and opportunity without taxing the already scanty resources that typify so many elementary schools. Needless to say the quality of these programs varies dramatically according to the teacher in charge.

Other Styles

Other responses to the need for educating the gifted use more time-honoured approaches.

❖ Enrichment in the classroom: A differentiated program of study offering experiences beyond the regular curriculum. This model is delivered by the regular classroom teacher, with or without assistance from a consultant or resource teacher.

❖ Consultant teacher program: Differentiated instruction is provided within the regular classroom by the classroom teacher with the assistance of an educational consultant or specialist. (Occasionally delivered by the specialist.)

❖ Community mentor program: Students interact on an individual basis with selected members of the community to study topics of special interest.

❖ Independent study program: projects supervised by a qualified adult.

❖ Learning enrichment service: Generally, this is a networking system that combines many of the above ideas in an organized way.

Although the content and methods in the styles immediately above do not differ widely from those of the more formal models (assuming they are well-run) they are not as well-received, principally because, their defenders say, they lack the aura that attaches to a program with an impressive title and a more apparently formal design. Critics, on the other hand, say that less formalized structures are much more susceptible to casual, ad hoc programming, and are at greater risk of arbitrary cancellation.

✔STRATEGIES FOR THE CLASSROOM

"Achieving potential" is admittedly a buzzword in all of special education, but its use requires no apology for it identifies what special education is all about. The phrase has extraordinary personal and societal significance in the case of the gifted. A program for gifted students must be based on the idea of achieving potential, and from that premise alone proceed to accommodate their unique needs. Part of that program — in some cases perhaps all of it — will be met in the role played by the classroom teacher. Each individual teacher of the gifted brings to a program, or a class, or a student, his own unique nature, as well as his own unique talents and interests and skills and background, all of which in the right circumstances, go a long way toward fulfilling the notion of achieving potential. In other words, as with any teaching-learning situation the teacher is the key.

There are however, certain absolutes to which teachers should subscribe, irrespective of their own preferences, styles, and areas of interest. These are planning goals which include the following:

(1) Establish an environment which shows clearly that intelligent thought, analysis, and creativity are valued.

(2) Encourage students to discover and develop their special abilities. Provide the time, space, materials and opportunities for them to do this at the sacrifice, if necessary, of the laid-on curriculum. (In this sense the teacher is much more of a facilitator than an instructor.)

Arrange learning experiences that go beyond the normal acquisition-of-knowledge level. Gifted students need to go higher, deeper, and wider in their pursuit of a subject, pushing past the usual limits. Very often the teacher acts as a consultant, using her maturity and experience to help the student find a productive critical path, or a method of investigation.

(3) Provide opportunities for students to interact with adults, other students, and with various experts so that they will be challenged, not just to know about *things*, but about *people*, and so that they will learn to see their own place and their responsibility in the human connection.

(4) Create an atmosphere where risk-taking, speculation, and conjecture can be undertaken safely. The teacher recognizes that trial and error are part of learning and that the only real failures in a classroom are those which erode self-esteem. If the teacher herself takes risks, and fails, the student invariably will learn from this too.

The Characteristics of the Teacher

More than in any other area of special education, the literature on the gifted goes on at great length on the ideal teacher. Most texts spin out lists of desireable characteristics that, viewed cynically, could only force the conclusion that truly effective teachers of the gifted are a composite of genius, encyclopaedic information-storage, intuitive splendour, and sainthood. Realistically, truly effective teachers are effective no matter what their responsibilities. And one would hope that all teachers are effective. Yet common sense dictates that the gifted and talented will naturally respond better to teachers with broad interests, extensive information and

> Creative minds always have been known to survive any kind of bad training.
>
> — *Anna Freud*

abundant creative energy. Not that students who are — say — learning disabled or behaviour disordered would not benefit from such teachers as well. The difference may lie in the horizons implied by achieving potential. The needs of a student with a learning disability or a behaviour disorder, for example, are usually more immediate and more focussed. But for the gifted, achieving potential provokes images of more distant horizons.

The "miles to go before I sleep" of Robert Frost's famous poem, *Stopping By Woods On a Snowy Evening*, simply seem more numerous, and more significant in the case of the gifted, and therefore generate more concern about the teachers who will show the way.

READINGS & RESOURCES

For Further Investigation

Bain, D.A. (1980). Gifted and enriched education in Canada. In M.Csapo & Goguen (Eds.) *Special education across Canada: Issues and concerns for the '80's.* Vancouver: Center for Human Development and Research.

Betts, G.T. (1986). *Autonomous learner model for the gifted and talented.* Autonomous Learning Publications and Specialists.

Borthwick, B., Dow, I., Levesque, D., & Banks, R. (1980). *The gifted and talented students in Canada: results of a CEA study.* Toronto: The Canadian Education Association.

Collangelo, N., & Davis, G.A. (Eds.) (1997). *Handbook of gifted education (2nd edition).* Boston: Allyn & Bacon.

Feldhausen, J.F., & Kolloff, P.B. (1986), The Purdue three-stage enrichment model for gifted education at the elementary level. In J. S. Renzulli (Ed.) *Systems and models for developing programs for gifted and talented.* Mansfield Centre, CT:Creative Learning Press.

Gardner, H. (1983). *Frames of mind: theory of multiple intelligences.* Basic Books.

Gardner, H. (1993). *Multiple intelligences.* Basic Books.

Heller, K.A., Monks, F.S., & Passow, A.H. (Eds.) (1993). *International Handbook of Research and Development of Giftedness and Talent.* New York: Pergamon.

Milan, C.P., & Schwartz, B. (1992). The mentorship connection. *Gifted Child Today, 15* (3), 9-13.

Renzulli, J.S., & Reis, S.M. (1986). The enrichment triad/revolving door model: A schoolwide plan for the development of creative productivity. In J. Renzulli (Ed.) *Systems and models for developing programs for gifted and talented.* Mansfield Centre, CT: Creative Learning Press.

Silverman, L. K. (1994/1995). To be gifted or feminine: The forced choice of adolescence. *Journal of Secondary Gifted Education, 6*(2), 141-156.

Sternberg, R.J. (1997). A triarchic view of giftedness: Theory and practice. In Colanelo, N. & Davis, G. (Eds.) *Handbook of Gifted education (2nd ed.).* Toronto: Allyn & Bacon.

Sternberg, R.J., & Zhang, L.(1996). What do we mean by giftedness: A pentagonal implicit theory. *Gifted Child Quarterly, 39*(2), 88-94.

For the Classroom Teacher

Allen, D. (1995). Encouraging success in female students: Helping girls develop math and science skills. *Gifted Children Today Magazine, 18*(2), 44-45.

Ambrose, D., Allen, J., & Huntly, S.B. (1994). Mentorship of the highly creative. *Roeper Review, 17*(2), 131-133.

Archambault, Jr., F.X., Westberg, K.L., Brown, S.W., Hallmark, B.W., Zhang, W., & Emmons, C.L. (1993). Classroom practices used with gifted third and fourth grade students. *Journal for the Education of the Gifted, 16*, 103-119.

Clarke, B. (1988). *Growing up gifted: Developing the potential of children at home and at school.* New York: Merrill-Macmillan.

Davis, G.A., & Rimm, S.B. (1994). *Education of the gifted and talented (3ʳᵈ ed.)* Boston MA: Allyn & Bacon.

Del Prete, T. (1996). Asset or albatross? The education and socialization of gifted students. *Gifted Child Today, 19*(2), 24-25, 44-50.

Dorry, G. (1994). The perplexed perfectionist. *Understanding Our Gifted, 6*(5),1, 10-12.

Friesen, J.W. (1997). The concept of giftedness in First Nations context. *Multicultural Educational Journal, 15*, 26-35.

Goleman, D. (1995, 1997). *Emotional Intelligence: Why it can matter more than IQ.* Toronto: Bantam Books.

Louis, B. & Lewis, M. (1992). Parental beliefs about giftedness in young children and their relationship to actual ability level. *Gifted Child Quarterly, 36*, 27-31.

Maker, J.C., Nielson, A.B., & Rogers, J.A. (1994). Giftedness, diversity and problem solving. *Teaching Exceptional Children, 27*, 4-19.

Parke, B.N. (1989). *Gifted students in regular classrooms.* Boston, MA: Allyn & Bacon.

Reis, S.M., & Westberg, K.L. (1994). The impact of staff development on teachers' ability to modify curriculum for gifted and talented students. *Gifted Child Quarterly, 38*, 127-135.

Renzulli, J.S. (1988). The multiple menu model for developing differentiated curriculum for the gifted and talented. *Gifted Child Quarterly, 32*, 298-309.

Shore, B. M. , Cornell, D.G., Robinson, A., & Ward, V.S. (1991). *Recommended practices in gifted education.* New York: Teachers College Press.

Smutny, J.F., Veenkner, K., & Veenkner, S. (1989). *Your gifted child.* New York: Ballentine.

Toil, M.F. (1991). Full-time gifted programs. *Gifted Children Today, 14*(6), 12-13.

Van Tassel–Baska, J. (1994). *Comprehensive curriculum for gifted learners.* Boston, MA: Allyn & Bacon.

Van Tassel – Baska, J., Patton, J.M., & Prilliman, D. (1991). *Gifted youth at risk: A report of a national study.* Reston, VA: Council for Exceptional Children.

Waldron , K.A. (1991). Teaching techniques for the learning disabled gifted student. *Learning Disabilities Research and Practice, 6*, 40-43.

Winner, E. (1996). *Gifted children: Myths and realities.* New York: Basic Books.

9

Students With Developmental Disabilities

*" I like school.
I have friends. I
like Mrs. Smyth.*
— *Becky*

*" If you think these kids don't belong
in school just come see her face in the
morning when that little yellow bus
comes. You'll be a believer.*
— *Pauline T., Becky's mother*

*" Is it hard with a kid
like that in your class?
Of course it's hard!
But it's worth it.*
— *Mrs. Smyth*

Misconceptions About Developmental Disabilities

1. An intellectual limitation is life long.

Intellectual functioning is not a static thing. (If it were, the role of education would be much different!) Especially for a person with mild developmental disabilities, intensive instruction can make a major difference for the future.

2. There are limitations to what a person can learn.

There is no hard evidence to confirm the existence of a ceiling of learning or of a limit to an individual's developmental capacity. Learning and development can be life long for everyone.

3. Developmentally disabled students appear physically different.

Certain groups of students, including many with Down syndrome, do appear physically different from their peers, but the vast majority of students with developmental disabilities look just like any other students.

4. Most developmentally disabled persons are identified in infancy.

In a significant number of cases, it is not until the demands of school make it apparent, that some developmental disabilities become evident.

5. Students with intellectual problems always learn more and learn better when they are integrated with regular students.

It is not possible to lump all special students into a learning environment classification. If these students learn much like everyone else as the evidence suggests, it must be granted that — just as with everyone else — no one environment is consistently and universally superior.

6. A low IQ test score is usually evidence of at least borderline disability, and means the subject's adaptive skills are below normal.

An IQ test may be an indicator of mental ability, particularly as it pertains to academic or school matters. However an individual's adaptive skills can be largely independent of his IQ test score, because they are often more a factor of training, motivation, and social environment.

7. Developmentally disabled people develop in very different learning stages from that of so-called normal people.

They develop through the same stages but often at a slower rate and with smaller gains.

8. Students with Down syndrome are invariably pleasant and compliant.

Many individuals with Down syndrome are pleasant, compliant and happy, but like all people with or without a disability, they experience emotional stresses and react accordingly.

9. Certain racial groups have a higher incidence of mental disabilities.

This particular misconception has developed in part because a severe, genetically based condition, Tay-Sachs disease, occurs almost exclusively among Eastern European Jews. However, other causes are no more frequent among Eastern European Jews than among other racial groups, nor do other causes have the peculiar racial exclusivity of Tay-Sachs disease.

Definition And Classification

Like blindness, deafness, and physical disability, a developmental disability is recognized as an identifiable, exceptional condition, but unlike the others, it has no universally accepted, standardized definition. One reason is that various disciplines — education, medicine, psychology, for example — all approach this exceptionality from their own perspectives. Another reason is that public perception is constantly changing. The once common view of this exceptionality as a genetically determined, terminal condition (reflected in differentiating classifications like 'idiot', 'imbecile' and 'moron') has been replaced by a much more flexible and realistic view that acknowledges the dynamic interplay between an individual's natural abilities and the environment.

The most widely accepted definition in use today is that proposed by the American Association on Mental Retardation (AAMR) formerly known as the American Association on Mental Deficiency. While the parameters of the definition are under constant review, there seems to be stable acceptance that a developmental disability is defined by the presence of three interrelated factors:

- sub-average intellectual functioning, resulting in or associated with
- problems in adaptive behaviour,
- manifested during the developmental period.

Sub-average Intellectual Functioning

This part of the definition is usually addressed by the use of IQ test scores to indicate different levels of intellectual function. Whereas it was once common practice to use a single number as a plateau or cutoff point, the AAMR now recommends the use of *ranges* of scores for that implies flexibility, and acknowledges the possible imperfections in IQ tests for identifying the presence of a mental handicap. The practice reflects a significant evolution in attitude. Prior to 1973, the AAMR recommended a cutoff IQ score of 85 for identification as 'mentally retarded', only one standard deviation below the mean, or norm, of 100. The change to approximately 70 to 75 (note the range rather than single number) or approximately *two* standard deviations below the mean, indicates a recognition of the importance of adaptive behaviour relative to so-called measured intelligence.

Adaptive Behaviour

Generally, adaptive behaviour refers to how well an individual is able to meet — *to adapt to* — demands made by the environment. It is a dynamic construct, necessarily affected by cultural norms and age-related expectations. The inclusion of this factor in the definition is another important step away from the use of IQ score results as the sole criterion for definition. The fact is that many students who obtain a low IQ test score can live and learn quite well in a variety of environments.

Developmental Period

According to the AAMR, this is the period from conception to an individual's 18ᵗʰ birthday.

Classification in Education

There are considerable variations in the jurisdictions across Canada. Some areas use no classifications at all; usually, these jurisdictions describe themselves as inclusive ones, integrating all students at all levels. Others, whether or not they have an inclusive policy, or a variation of this, use the mild-moderate-severe-profound ranges* of the AAMR. Still others use variations of the three descriptors below that suggest attainable levels of performance for educational purposes.

- *Educable:* Capable of basic academic subjects up to advanced elementary levels. General achievement ranges from second to fifth grade.
- *Trainable:* Capable of attaining self-help skills, self-protection, and social adjustment. Very limited achievement in areas considered academic.
- *Custodial:* With intensive and extensive training may learn some basic self-help and communicative skills. Will almost certainly require regular supervision and support.

The 'Mild' Distinction

Most boards in Ontario now follow the practice of identifying students as being *developmentally disabled,* or, as having *mild intellectual disability.* These distinctions are not necessarily tied to IQ test scores, although test results may be a factor. What is far more common is to apply the distinction on the basis of the students' observable achievements and abilities, thus making classifications that are far more sensitive to an individual's educational needs. The practice is more accommodating of a radical policy departure first advocated by the AAMR in 1992, namely that an individual be classified by the degree of *support* needed to function as competently as possible. The four recommended support levels, *pervasive, extensive, limited,* and *intermittent,* although not yet fully adopted in the field, nevertheless reinforce even more, a philosophy of flexibility and individualization.

---

* Very much in decline in Ontario, this classification uses IQ test score ranges as follows: *mild* (55-69), *moderate* (40-55), *severe* (25-40), *profound* (-25).

Some Issues in the Field

■ *Identification.* An abiding concern among educators, health professionals, and particularly advocates and parents, is what to call a developmental disability — or whether to call it anything at all! Part of the tension arises out of the desire of administrators, researchers, clinicians and academics to have a practical and efficient means of identifying a consonant group for their various purposes. The wish is to have a neutral, scientific, and widely accepted term. Balanced against this is the far less scientific but equally important desire of parents and advocates to expunge terminology from the field, for the simple reason that descriptive terms for this exceptionality, no matter how carefully they are chosen, invariably seem to imply limitations, and very rapidly are adopted for pejorative use in popular parlance.

There appears to be no simple way out of this dilemma. Terminology is not just useful to professionals, it is part and parcel of scientific, educational practice. Yet what terms are appropriate, and how can they be kept from degenerating into insult? No serious professional today would dream of using discarded terms like 'feeble-minded', a once widely accepted and scientific term. Yet so much of the new, semantically gentler terminology seems only to generate its own black humor. This is made especially ironic in light of the fact that 'mentally retarded', the long-accepted term, seemed to have successfully shed its pejorative connotations as society at large developed a more enlightened and balanced view of intelligence, ability, and individual worth. Yet, at least in Ontario, advocates were generally successful in arguing for its removal from the special education lexicon.*

■ *Normalization.* The argument that people should be seen for their similarities to, rather than their differences from, the population at large, and that they should be allowed to thrive in the larger society to the maximum possible

---

*During our preparation of the Fourth Edition of *Special Education in Ontario Schools*, we examined over two dozen textbooks in current use in North America and found the prevailing term continues to be 'mentally retarded' (as it is in most of the literature). In this text, however, we use *developmental disability* to be consistent with both the Ministry of Education and Training, and what appears to be unanimous practice in the province.
—*K.W. & S.B.*

extent, has provocative implications. In the nineteenth century, the gradual development of institutions to care for the developmentally disabled was regarded as a major step forward in the attitude toward exceptional people. And no doubt it was, for institutions which offered care when the alternative was often abandonment, reflected a degree of social and moral responsibility hitherto unknown. But institutions have a potentially insidious nature. For reasons of economy, ease of management, and sometimes ignorance, the residents of an institution are often kept in an environment that is impoverished in terms of stimulation and opportunity. Given what special educators now know about human development, it is apparent that many of the behaviours historically associated with a mental handicap are consequences of institutional life, or perhaps more specifically, lack of stimulation and direct instruction.

The overwhelming impetus in the field therefore, has been toward de-institutionalization, and integration with mainstreamed society. The impetus has been driven more by advocacy groups than by governments and educators, but the response of the latter, although late, has been very positive. The reality today therefore, is that very large numbers of developmentally disabled people are living in the mainstream, many of them on their own, or with some supervision, many with gainful employment, and acquiring and enjoying the benefits of education.

> I think we accepted early on, my wife and I, that this was a lifetime commitment. Our Sammy's retarded, but he's ours and we don't love him any less. Probably a bit more. Still it's scary when we wonder what will happen to him when we're not around any more. The schools . . . they've done a good job. Really, they have. But he won't be in school forever. And if his mother and I aren't here, what then?
>
> — *Hank Sovano*

■ *Inclusion* (Although *integration* is the term adopted by the Ministry of Education, and therefore the one used in this text, the term *inclusion* is most strongly endorsed in this particular area of special education.) Including developmentally disabled persons without reservation in mainstream society is a high profile issue, in large part because of conflict that seems to arise out of the impatience of its supporters, and the guarded hesitancy of parts of the larger society. At the most liberal end of the spectrum are those who argue that all persons should be fully integrated into society — and most especially into schools — immediately.

These supporters tend to see the matter in absolute terms and brook no modification of a person's environment whatever. Their view is that total integration at once is the only possible position that a society can morally and ethically adopt. The intensity with which this position is presented often forces an adversarial context, particularly when educators respond that integration is a relative matter, and that for some students, a modified school environment may be more beneficial.

It is not that the educators reject inclusion but rather that some prefer a cautious approach, arguing that students should be considered on an individual basis, that not all cases are ideal for total inclusion immediately, and that the consequences of forcing immediate change can be potentially disastrous for everyone involved. But often, instead of being able to recommend this position, these educators are made to defend it, and find themselves using arguments — and taking positions as a result — that can be interpreted as pro-segregation, whether or not this is indeed what they believe. The risk for students with developmental disabilities in this controversy, is that the significant maturing of society's attitude, especially in the past few decades, may be put in jeopardy by hasty decisions, emotion, polemics and blanket policies. What is especially distressing to classroom teachers and parents is that empirical evidence shows that generally, children who begin their school lives in integrated classrooms treat that environment as natural. And most of the time, this integration is successful and continues to succeed for all children as they grow. Where success is not as universal is in those situations where the integration does not start until later grades, and where it is arbitrary.

■ *Time to learn.* Early theory held that a developmental disability implied an absolute limit to potential. This notion was handily reinforced by supposed empirical evidence (especially bizarre behaviours which often turned out to be institutional behaviours) and by notions of incurability. Particularly since the success of the normalization movement, it has become evident that with stimulation, support, and direct instruction, there is literally no limit to students' learning capacity. However, the process for some takes longer. Developmentally disabled students are learners but they are slower learners. This fact should not make much difference in a modern education context, especially in light of individualized learning principles. However, the time factor becomes an issue because many jurisdictions make school enrolment terminal (usually tied to chronological ages of students) either through funding limitations or simply by decree. While continuing education programs go a long way toward circumventing this problem, it is still an issue that has not yet been satisfactorily resolved by school boards and governments.

■ *Employment and vocational training.* Some developmentally disabled adults have paid employment in industries known by such descriptions as 'sheltered workshops', where they are paid for relatively simple and repetitive industrial tasks. On one side of this issue is the thought that they are thus given opportunity to contribute to their own support by gainful activity that is within their capacity under supervision. On the other side, there is opinion that such employment is exploitation, and simply an unsubtle extension of institutionalization. The issue is an awkward and difficult one to resolve in a free economy, and proponents of both sides are able to refer to many practical examples that support their respective arguments. For educators, the disagreement is uncomfortable, since they must resolve for themselves the importance of this potential employment when determining learning objectives for their students.

■ *Modern medicine.* Techniques in medical science have introduced whole new areas of uneasiness and controversy. One such, developed in Europe, involves surgery that may alleviate the respiratory complications often suffered by children with Down syndrome. It has become fairly common practice to include facial surgery in the procedure — some argue it is necessary — in order to enhance speech abilities, and to

For Discussion: the Case of Blaine

Blaine has just completed his first year at secondary school. He is 18. Although the school is committed to inclusion, three self-contained classes are available on an ad hoc basis. No one is officially placed in these classes full time; however, during the past year, four students have spent their entire school time there. For the final quarter of the year, Blaine became the fifth, mostly because of his overwhelming moroseness and melancholy, and his apparent unwillingness to do anything whatever on his own behalf.

In Blaine's medical report, *fetal alcohol syndrome* is noted as a primary cause of his disability. He also has chronic health problems and spent three years in a hospital school. Academically, Blaine works at approximately a 9-10 year old level, but every teacher who has had responsibility for him, insists that he is significantly more capable than his output indicates. They are unanimous in the belief that the academic performance gap is a product of attitude, which — also unanimously — they call 'learned helplessness'.

The school's physical education department has proposed to the In-School Team (IST) that next year, the senior football team make Blaine one of the school's 'inclusion pals'. He would be made an honorary lineman, attend all practices, and be at all games, dressed in equipment and uniform. Although he would not actually compete, he would be part of every other activity. Football team members would also be expected to invite Blaine to their social events and involve him after school. The coach has done this type of thing once before with a special student, Mel, and the project was so successful it attracted enthusiastic reviews from the media. Blaine's parents, however, are aware of a dark side. When most of the football team graduated and scattered to universities, colleges, and employment, Mel was, in effect, suddenly abandoned. So traumatic was the experience that he has still not recovered. Mel was then 22 years of age and he too left the school but now his guardian (a grandmother) reports that "for nigh on a year now he sits, and eats, and stares. Won't talk. Won't look at me. Won't do anything."

Blaine's parents are willing to do anything for their son but want some assurance from the IST that the football team's undertaking will not end up the way Mel's case did.

alter the mongoloidal appearance of the children so that they will look "normal". Its advocates support it largely on the premise that if the children appear normal, they will be treated normally, and grow into a better life as a result. Its detractors hold that normal appearance will raise false and unattainable expectations.

Causes of Developmental Disability: A Concern For Educators?

For educators, knowing the cause of a particular student's disability satisfies both intellectual curiosity and a natural desire to know as much as possible about a student in order to support him or her effectively. However, the value to educators of knowing the causes of mental handicaps is somewhat diminished by three factors.

❖ The amount of hard science, theory, speculation, and yet-to-be confirmed knowledge, is both extensive and bewildering, even to medical specialists in the field. Causes range from trauma (such as anoxia at birth) through chromosomal abnormality (e.g., Down syndrome, tuberous sclerosis, Klinefelter's syndrome) to metabolic (e.g., phenylketonuria, Prader-Willi syndrome) and infectious/toxic in the pregnant mother (e.g., rubella, syphilis, alcohol, cocaine). As well, more than one name is used for some conditions (e.g., *epiloia* for tuberous sclerosis), and very often the conditions are very poorly or incompletely described, or presented in language that is comprehensible only to the thoroughly initiated. Not only does this lead to confusion, it is also rare in any case, that a practical educational response can be inferred from a description of cause. Even worse, it is not unknown for a child's case to be given up as educationally hopeless on the basis of a scientific description of cause. For these reasons, some educators argue that causes, therefore, should be tendered only for very compelling reasons.

❖ It is usually only in the more profound cases that clear physiological cause can be established. Since the causes are pretty much irreversible, they are irrelevant for decisions involving educational placement, curriculum, and style of instruction, unless immediate issues of health and safety are involved.

Fetal Alcohol Syndrome ✍

The combination of physical, behavioural and intellectual deficits that may develop when an expectant mother uses alcohol during pregnancy, leads to an organic disorder called *fetal alcohol syndrome* (FAS). (Awareness of the issue, as well as research and discussion, is relatively recent, and information about FAS is still somewhat elastic. For example, some educators distinguish FAS from FAE, *fetal alcohol effects*, which they contend is less intense.)

Whether to classify FAS as a developmental disability or a physical/health matter, or a behavioural problem is still being debated. Most educators, even though FAS does not always result in intellectual retardation, tend to classify it as developmental because of the cognitive problems that often result. Very often a student with FAS manifests physical characteristics not unlike Down syndrome (smaller stature, noticeable facial anomalies, etc.) and has significant behavioural problems such as hyperactivity, indiscriminate forming and severing of bonds or attachments, difficulty expressing emotions, poor inner control, low rate of task completion, etc. These are usually compounded by poor motor control and by significant learning problems typically found in students readily classified as developmentally disabled (poor visual scanning, reading problems, inattentive to or unable to absorb detail, difficulty generalizing and deducing, etc.).

Although conclusive data on the subject of FAS are still being developed, there is a consensus that the incidence is rising and that it has become an issue of concern for the classroom. Even more irritating to teachers and educational assistants is the fact that FAS is not a genetic accident but an entirely preventable condition. For the most part, practical classroom response is similar to the methods applied in the case of other students with developmental disabilities (See *Strategies for the Classroom*).

❖ For a significant percentage of the students, particularly those whose disability is mild, or possibly only suspected, it is often difficult to determine whether they are genuinely slower intellectually, or whether their performance is a temporary outcome of limited learning opportunities, or repression, or poor nutrition, or other external conditions. Of all the causes of mental handicaps, this one can be very important to education, since if deprivation in one form or another is in fact a cause of retarded performance, it at least is potentially reversible.

For the reasons above, most boards of education in Ontario, as a matter of practice if not official policy, do not state the cause of a student's developmental disability on his or her record unless the cause has treatment implications that are important to teachers and caregivers.

The Special Case of Down syndrome

One area of developmental disability in which cause may have significance for educators is the chromosomal abnormality called Down syndrome, estimated to account for 5-6 per cent of all cases of intellectual retardation. Students with Down syndrome are often recognizable because of certain characteristics like a generally smaller stature, thick epicanthal folds in the corners of the eyes, and a smaller oral cavity that results in a protruding tongue. (Less easily noticed but typical, are speckling of the iris, a wide gap between the first and second toes, and a single palmar crease on short, broad hands.)

These physical factors provoke an issue of importance when they are juxtaposed with a typical factor that is non-physical. Most persons with Down syndrome are in the mild to moderate range of retardation, and experience increasingly shows that intensive instruction will often result in their making lasting academic gains. Thus, because the physical aspects of Down syndrome are quite recognizable, it would be a mistake to assume automatically, as many uninformed people do, that a student with the syndrome is intellectually retarded and *ipso facto* incapable.

A second issue accruing to Down syndrome is the physical health factor of which teachers especially, should be aware. Persons with Down syndrome are at greater risk for congenital heart defects and upper respiratory infections.

Many have hyperflexible joints with a high potential for orthopedic injury. Taken together or singly, these characteristics have implications for what goes on in a classroom or schoolyard.

Educational Implications of Mental Handicaps

The effects of developmental disabilities are usually seen in a relatively slower attainment of life achievements than would be expected in the norm.

Physical

Milestones like learning to walk, toilet, etc., tend to be attained up to nine months or a year later than the norm. There is also a tendency to perform below age-related standards in motor areas, and frequently, features of height, weight and skeletal development are often at the extreme ends of age norms. Persons with moderate (as opposed to mild) disabilities often show even more complex physical differences, and tend to be markedly less able motorically. Very often severe mental handicaps are part of a multiple set of disabilities with the consequence that locomotion and other simple activities become an issue.

Learning and Memory

Problems here, as with other areas, become more marked and more easily observable from 'mild' to 'severe', but in almost all students with a developmental disability, learning and memory problems are usually significant. Specific areas of difficulty include ability to pay attention, verbal communication, motivation, ability to generalize, and the ability to understand similarities and differences. Quite typical is difficulty with short term memory. The students do not tend to use memory strategies spontaneously, although they will learn to use mnemonic strategies if explicitly taught to do so. It is important to point out that once a thing is learned and filed in long term memory, developmentally disabled students will recall it as well as anyone else when conditions are appropriate.

The combination of apparent lack of motivation, tendency to be off-task, and poor short term memory often leads to passivity and a pattern of *learned helplessness* where the student allows a significant adult to manage everything. Viewed from the other side, so to speak, the student sometimes actually manages, subconsciously, to train a significant adult to do everything for him, simply by being universally passive. Educational assistants in particular, report this as a recurring problem.

Speech and Language Problems

Speech defects are considerably above the norm in frequency. Mutism and primitive speech are quite common in the more severely disabled. Typically, the language level, both oral and written but especially the latter, is below commonly accepted age norms.

Social Adjustment

Many of the students experience difficulty in social interaction for a variety of reasons. Because they do not find it easy to 'read' a social setting, it is not uncommon for them to participate in it inappropriately, perhaps by being too loud, or too ebullient for example. Some students in an integrated setting may at first function in what is called "parallel existence". That is, because they do not know how to naturally ingratiate themselves with their peers, they simply go along in their own world, without really becoming a part of the general social environment. This will occur most frequently when developmentally disabled students and so-called normal students interact with one another for the first time, especially if there has been no preparation. (It is very encouraging however, to observe a class of very young children. The uncritical, mutual acceptance one invariably sees, forces the conclusion that interaction like this is entirely natural when inclusion begins early.)

Some students develop behaviours that the rest of the world may look upon as bizarre, and they often tend to indulge in these behaviours repetitively (known as *perseveration*) especially in times of stress or discomfort. As a consequence, a large part of educational planning is sometimes devoted to teaching self control of these behaviours. Proponents of inclusion argue — with considerable empirical evidence to support them — that inappropriate behaviours are eliminated more easily and quickly in the mainstream.

For Discussion: the Case of Christina

The annual IPRC review of Christina's case took longer to complete this year because she is in grade eight and the committee requested a full psychometric assessment. It was the first such undertaking since she was in grade three, five years ago, and confirmed the assertions of the special education resource teacher in the school: that Christina is not only an improved but an improving student. Her IQ test score (both verbal and performance) on the Wechsler scale is Low Average to Borderline (as it was in grade three). But her scores on standardized achievement instruments confirm the grade eight teacher's report that there have been significant gains in academic skills. Christina reads grade four/five material comfortably. (She has had a particularly rewarding experience this year as a "reader" in the kindergarten class.) Creative writing is still a challenge, although this may be a physically related issue. Christina has a disabled right arm but is naturally left-handed. Yet even with the classroom's several computer programs to help her, she seems to have trouble writing even minimally coherent prose. Math gains are significant and measurable. Five years ago, she could not do any basic arithmetic. This year she is working (albeit one-on-one) out of the fourth grade textbook.

All the adults who have immediate contact with and responsibility for Christina — her mother, the grade eight teacher, and the educational assistant who has known her since grade six — each confirm independently that she has had "a very happy year". As well, everyone agrees that the happiness is very much a result of the efforts by the teacher and assistant to manage her occasional bursts of unusual behaviour, and the fact that Christina's classmates accept her so completely and without reservation.

In light of this knowledge, and given that next year's placement must be decided, the IPRC has offered two options: one that Christina be promoted to grade nine and go with her classmates to the neighbourhood secondary school (She would have an integrated program as in grade eight), or two, that she spend another year with the grade eight teacher and educational assistant. Christina's mother has mixed feelings on the matter. Christina herself is quite passive and expresses no opinion at all. The IPRC has asked the teacher and assistant to indicate which placement, in their opinion, would work best.

Academic Achievement

It requires little insight to deduce that academic achievement is an issue. Achievement deficits seem to be most pronounced in reading comprehension, in arithmetical reasoning, and in problem-solving. A steadily growing body of research evidence suggests that time is an important factor. Developmentally disabled students pass through the same phases of cognitive development as everyone else, particularly the childhood phases, but they pass through more slowly and often attain lower levels of achievement. Accordingly, it's safe to infer that many developmentally disabled students can indeed learn much of a standard school curriculum, but they will do it a great deal more slowly, and likely with less efficiency. This makes *time* and *regular practice* crucial items in the educational planning process.

The Importance of Self-Help Skills

For obvious reasons, the most immediate of which is physical health, an important part of an education program deals with items like hygiene, eating and dressing, use of the toilet, physical appearance, etc. While this aspect will be part of an educational plan only to the extent necessary, and that necessity will vary according to the degree of need, learning these culturally significant skills is nevertheless crucial to a student's sense of well-being and sense of self. Teachers of developmentally disabled students find much truth in the old adages that connect "feeling good" to "looking good".

Self-Esteem

Self-esteem tends to be low. A combination of discouraging social experience and of repeated failure often leads to self-expectations of poor performance. When this is overlaid with what seems to be a ready willingness to give over control to someone else, either peers or an authority figure, it is easy to understand why the developmentally disabled students often avoid or ignore challenging tasks. The 'if-at-first-you-don't-succeed: quit' syndrome is often a tempting and comfortable one. Teachers must avoid the trap of becoming a controller — the easy route — and instead, by judicious encouragement and behaviour modification, demonstrate to the student that she can do the assigned task and should feel proud because of it.

Genetic Research and the Future

Research in the field of developmental disabilities may one day yield vastly important information for educators. The work being done by geneticists on *Williams' syndrome* is one example. Persons with Williams' syndrome are usually mildly to moderately retarded intellectually (Typical IQ test scores are about 60), and have profound difficulties with spatial relationships, abstractions and logical sequences. They typically have elfin-like facial structure, an above-average incidence of heart problems and very often, hyper-sensitive hearing. At the same time, persons with Williams' syndrome have strikingly developed vocabularies, are often warm, compassionate and outgoing, and — what intrigues researchers most — many have what is clearly prodigy-level talent in music. What is believed to be the cause of the syndrome was discovered in 1993: the loss of some genetic material on Chromosome 7. Researchers believe this is the same collection of genes that aid in the human ability to concentrate, and is also the seat of visual and spatial skills.

Assessment and Placement

Although IQ tests continue to play a role in this area of exceptionality, their use has declined significantly, along with the amelioration of public attitude toward, and insight into, developmental disability. Thus, in practice, a student with this special need may only be assessed with an IQ instrument should an unique situation arise (e.g., the need to settle an issue of degree of disability for funding, or perhaps, a legal purpose.)

Anecdotal reports by parents and classroom personnel play a far more important part in completing a picture of needs. So do a range of instruments known as Rating Scales, Achievement Inventories, Personal Checklists, etc. These vary in length and in nature of information sought, but are similar in principle. They are completed by adults who have been able to observe the developmentally delayed student in different situations and are able to judge the student's skills in a number of areas. Usually, the skills are judged on a comparative basis (fair, good, excellent, etc.). And most often, the questions deal with areas of general performance like family, community and peer relations, self-care skills, cognitive abilities, and so on. Although these instruments are usually quite informal, and are often constructed locally to meet local needs, there are published adaptive behaviour scales available (e.g. Vineland Adaptive Behaviour Scales, 1984, American Guidance Service). In practice, an IPRC will quite regularly accept any informed comment about a student with developmental disabilities when it is making determinations regarding identification and placement.

As the tables in Chapter 4 indicate, relatively more students in this area of special need are placed in full time and part time self-contained classes, despite the vigor of advocates who favour inclusion. Nevertheless, compared to the days before the passing of Bill 82 (see Chapter

---

Prerequisites to Successful Inclusion ✎

A lucid and comprehensive article in the *American Educational Research Journal,* by Scruggs and Mastropieri (1994) offers both a summary of useful research and their own findings on this issue, concluding that seven factors are crucial to successfully integrating students with special needs.

1. Administrative Support
2. Support from Special Education Personnel
3. Accepting, Positive Classroom Atmosphere
4. Appropriate Curriculum
5. Effective General Teaching Skills
6. Peer Assistance
7. Disability-Specific Teaching Skills

For Discussion: the Case of Robyn

At age seven, Robyn spent several months in a day program at a development centre, but then became ill (she has severe respiratory problems) and remained at home where she was visited daily by a Special Services At Home worker. At age eight she attended her neighbourhood school in a regular grade one for three weeks, but with the agreement of her parents, was transferred to a special resource class, full time. This placement continued until grade four, when she was gradually integrated into a regular class. Robyn moved with her classmates to Grade five and spent that year with them. She is now in grade six.

Robyn is identified as severely developmentally disabled. Her language abilities are below age norms. Her speech is babyish and mostly in the third person "E.g., *Teacher:* Hi, Robyn! How are you today?" *Robyn:* "Robyn O.K." She does not seem to be able to read, but very much enjoys being read to. She does not participate in any meaningful way in the curriculum; however, she likes to be part of a group when it pursues a task, and very much enjoys being paired with other students when "seat work" or other individualized tasks are assigned. Any attempts at "parallel curriculum" have been singular failures. Since grade four, Robyn has never once worked on her own. She seems content only when she is part of others' endeavours. One occasional exception to this behaviour is her willingness to spend time at an art table, colouring in designs with crayons and magic markers. But she tends to have temper tantrums when tired of this activity if she is not immediately diverted. (Robyn destroyed a keyboard when she became bored with a program on the class's only computer with a colour monitor.)

Until now (February of grade six) the fact that there is no assistant available to this class (and will not be) has been blunted by the willingness of two different girls to befriend, guide, and patiently assist Robyn. But almost simultaneously, the two girls — in the words of their teacher — "have just discovered boys!" and now actively avoid Robyn, not just inside the classroom but outside too. Robyn's tantrums are now frequent and severe, and her skills have regressed. Motivated at least in part by complaints from two parents of other children, the principal has called for an IPRC review. At the committee's first meeting, Robyn's mother made it clear she will not agree to a special class placement. The committee has asked the school, as a first step, to prepare a new IEP for Robyn, working within the present resources available.

1) when it was rare for a developmentally disabled student to attend a regular school, there have been very great changes. Specially dedicated schools for the mentally retarded, where these students were enrolled — if they went to school at all — have almost all been closed and reopened as regular neighbourhood schools. Developmentally disabled students, even though some may be placed in special classes, are part of those neighbourhood schools now, and the majority of students by far, are placed in classes on the basis of what their teachers and their parents together believe is in their best interests.

> My first year of teaching and I get not one, but *two* developmental kids in my class! I have to be honest; at the end of September I was going to quit. Sure glad I didn't though. Now that I've had some time, well . . . It's no different from having any other kids in your class. Not really. But then, these two were pretty good kids. One thing. I sure could have used more time on special kids in my teacher training. We never talked about them enough, and well . . . They're the *real* challenge.
>
> — *Alexandra Page*

the popularity of the practice is that time and again, the assistants have proven their value. However, doubling the number of adults in a room does not double the achievements automatically. Whether an assistant is assigned to a whole class or specifically to a student (this latter option has come in for serious criticism as a form of de facto segregation) it is crucial that both teacher and assistant work together in an atmosphere of mutual respect and appropriately shared responsibility.

✔STRATEGIES FOR THE CLASSROOM

(1) For teachers and educational assistants in this area of special need, there is a prerequisite to individual education plans, instructional strategies, curriculum — all the trappings that gather nominally under "education". The prerequisite, quite simply, is a positive attitude: recognition and acceptance that these are students like any other, with strengths and needs and likes and dislikes and ideosyncratic behaviours *and a capacity to learn*. What distinguishes them, perhaps more than any other trait, is that they tend to learn more slowly. The implications of that learning speed (perhaps learning *rate* is better) are significant, but the students *can and do* learn. Classroom professionals, by nature, accept this, but when they have such students in a class, they need just a bit more of that faith: that quality reflected in the patience, the effort, the flexibility, and the sense of humour that together with enlightened instruction, make classrooms successful. Without these intangibles — in liberal quantities — no amount of tactic or technique can be effective. The teacher, as always, is the key.

(2) It is common administrative practice to arrange for educational assistants in classrooms where one or more developmentally disabled students are enrolled. A principal reason for

(3) In a similar vein, teachers recognize that when students with special needs are in their classes, they are expected to cooperate extensively with other professionals, other significant persons, and certainly with parents. In the case of students with developmental disabilities, this support circle often widens considerably. Very active involvement by groups such as the Association for Community Living for example, often leads to the development of a team of key players in a student's life, who share information, ideas and concerns about that student and then take some wider responsibility for promoting his integration in the life of the community. Since school is a major part of a student's community, it is only natural that such a team will often involve and overlap the teacher's role. Thus in addition to their responsibility for individual instruction, teachers often find themselves part of a larger circle of action that includes other students, parents, and interested members of the community.

Sometimes the teams are organized under relatively formal structures (one such is MAPS*); at other times the situation is informal, often the result of the will and dynamism of a key player in the student's life. Either way,

---

*Known variously as Multi-action Planning System and McGill Action Planning System. MAPS asks specific key questions about a student's life and develops a coordinated plan (e.g., 'What are our dreams for...?' 'How can they be fulfilled?'). See Forest, M., & Lustaus, E. (1990) "Everybody belongs with the MAPS action planning system", *Exceptional Children*, 22, 4 (36-39).

teachers of a student with a mental handicap should expect involvement that often goes way beyond the walls of the classroom.

(4) Careful attention to structure both in direct individual instruction and in the general learning environment is another important factor for teachers to consider. Experience in both integrated and modified environments suggests that the students are much more comfortable when classroom routines and expectations are regularized. In this case, familiarity breeds not contempt, but comfort, and in the security engendered by this comfort, a teacher can usually assure more effective learning. Establishing a structured environment may mean that the teacher arranges for and continually repeats certain sequences until they are fully assimilated by the students. It may mean temporarily reducing the number of choices a student is expected to make.

Very often a great deal of effort is expended by the teacher on what, in the grand scheme of things, may seem relatively trivial: colour-coded notebooks, for example, with red for one purpose, green for another, etc. Yet these are precisely the kind of arrangements that protect the students from confusing and overlapping demands, and allow them to bring their available cognitive strength to bear on a learning task. Without a carefully established structure in which to learn, students tend to expend a prohibitive amount of energy trying to establish it on their own. Some permit the perceived disorganization of an unstructured environment to carry them away into helplessness or counterproductive behaviour.

The challenge for the teacher is finding the right balance of structure and flexibility so that organization does not become more important than learning. An additional challenge is finding this balance in an inclusive classroom, where there are many students whose need for a structured and carefully sequenced instruction may not be the same. Teachers in this type of classroom can argue with considerable authority that such a placement for a student with developmental disabilities, with all its benefits, also means having to forgo a degree of the learning support that arises from a carefully arranged structure.

(5) Interestingly, just as advocates have tried to find a more palatable term for 'mental retardation', educators have tried to upgrade the vocabulary for a time-honoured *and effective* practice for all students and especially for those with mental handicaps: namely, 'drill' and 'repetition'. Whatever the currency of suggested replacements, the simple fact is that all students seem to need the opportunity to go over material a certain number of times until it is taken in, and students with this disability perhaps more so.

(6) Momentum, or commitment within the individual is another concern. Students with a mental handicap regularly and successfully invite others to do their work for them, and equally regularly, back away from challenge and opportunity. Encouragement by significant adults is very important therefore. In fact, a teacher who establishes a sense of commitment in a student has usually led him or her through one of the most important steps of development.

---

(7) Particularly for students whose developmental disability is fairly extensive, the task analysis method has been found to be very successful. It is based on sequencing and operant conditioning, and because the procedure involves breaking down complex tasks into simpler components, it offers the student an opportunity not just for learning but for a sense of accumulating success. An example of task analysis follows.

Using the Task Analysis Method

Task analysis is a method of breaking down a general concept or skill into its component parts. The component parts are then arranged in a logical teaching sequence.

Teaching begins at *baseline:* the level where the student is functioning prior to instruction (or, one step below, where success is assured). Each step is taught in a variety of ways until 'overlearning' has taken place. Overlearning means practising the concept beyond the point of original mastery because the teacher cannot assume the student has mastered the concept on the basis of a single correct response. Instead the teacher should present the concept on numerous occasions, over a time period, expecting the student to respond correctly most of the time before being satisfied the concept has been mastered. Some teachers set criteria for mastery, e.g., four correct responses out of five consecutive trials.

The Task Analysis method makes it easier for students to experience a sense of achievement at each step along the way.

Illustration:

1st step: state *behavioural* objective; e.g. :

1. tell time to 1/4 hour
2. order an item from catalogue
3. correctly address envelope
4. measure length of room

2nd step: list all steps, operations and prerequisite skills necessary to do step 1.

3rd step: order these in hierarchy or logical teaching sequence.

4th step: find out where in this sequence the student is functioning (baseline). By simply testing the performance of each step, the teacher can quickly find out what steps in the sequence have been mastered.

An Example of Task Analysis: Steps 1-3

Objective: Student can count a handful of coins correctly (pennies and nickels only)

Task Analysis:

1. verbally identifies penny and nickel
2. states nickel = 5 pennies
3. counts rows of pennies — straight line
4. counts pennies scattered on desk
5. counts one nickel and several pennies — placed in straight line
6. counts, when arranged in a straight line, one nickel and several pennies when nickel is not first
7. same — scattered fashion
8. counts by 5's
9. counts rows of nickels (straight line)
10. counts nickels (scattered)
11. counts rows of several nickels and pennies when all nickels are placed first
12. counts (same as 11) but all nickels are not first
13. counts nickels and pennies scattered (the stated behaviour objective).

READINGS & RESOURCES

For Further Investigation

Beck, J., Brores, J., Hogue, E., Shipstead, J., & Knowlton, E. (1994). Strategies for functional community-based instruction and inclusion for children with mental retardation. *Teaching Exceptional Children*, (Winter) pp. 44-48.

Clark, G.M., Carlson, B.J. (1991 Winter). Is a functional curriculum approach compatible with an inclusive educational model? *Teaching Exceptional Children*, (Winter) pp. 36-39.

Drew, C.J., Hardman, M.L., & Logan, D.R. (1996). *Mental retardation a life cycle approach* (6th ed.), Upper Saddle River NJ: Merrill/Prentice Hall.

Eyman, R.F., Call, T.E., & White, J.F. (1991). Life Expectancy of people with Down syndrome. *American Journal of Mental Retardation, 95*, 603-612.

Glidden, L.M. & Zetlin, A.G. (1992). Adolescent and community adjustment. In L. Rowitz (Ed.), *Mental retardation in the year 2000* (pp. 101-114). New York: Springer-Verlag.

Greenspan, S., & Granfield, J.M. (1992). Reconsidering the construct of mental retardation: Implications of a model of social competence. *American Journal of Mental Retardation, 96*, 442-453.

Grossman, H.J. (1992). *Special education in a diverse society*. Boston: Allyn & Bacon.

Haldy, M.B., & Hanzlik, J.R. (1990). A comparison of perceived competence in child rearing between mothers of children with Down syndrome and mothers of children without delays. *Education and Training in Mental Retardation, 25*(2), 132-141.

Kozma, C. & Stock, J. S. (1993). What is mental retardation? In R. Smith (Ed.), *Children with mental retardation* (pp.1-49). Rockville, MD: Woodbine House.

Meyer, L.H., Peck, C.A., & Brown L. (1991). *Critical issues in the lives of people with severe disabilities.* Baltimore, MD: Paul H. Brookes.

National Prevention committee, Canadian Association for the Mentally Retarded. (1982). *Final report to the Minister of National Health and Welfare on the five regional symposia on the prevention of mental retardation in Canada.* Ottawa: Health and Welfare.

Reiss, S. (1994). Issues in defining mental retardation. *American Journal of Mental Retardation, 99,* 1-7.

Sands, D.J., & Wehmeyer, M.L. (Eds.). (1996). *Self-determination across the life span: Theory and practice.* Baltimore: Brookes.

Scruggs, T., & Mastropieri, M. (1994). Successful mainstreaming: A qualitative analysis of three reputational cases. *American Educational Research Journal, 31*(4), 785-811.

Smith, T.E.C., & Dowdy, C. (1992, September). Future based assessment and intervention for students with mental retardation. *Education and Training in Mental Retardation,* pp. 255-260.

Vernon-Levett, P. (1991). Head injuries in children. *Pediatric Trauma, 3,* 411-421.

For the Classroom Teacher

Bergman, T. (1989). *We laugh, we love, we cry: Children living with mental retardation.* Milwaukee, WI: Gareth Stevens.

Bricker, D. & Cripe, J.J. (1992). *An activity based approach to early intervention.* Baltimore, Brookes.

Brigance, A.H. (1995). *Life Skills Inventory. North Billerica,* MA: Curriculum Associates.

Carnevale, A.P., Gainer, L.J., & Meltzer, A.S. (1990). *Workplace basics, The essential skills employers want.* San Francisco: Jossey-Bass.

Cipanni, E., & Spooner, F. (1994). *Curricular and Instructional approaches for persons with severe disabilities.* Needham Heights, MA: Allyn & Bacon.

Craig, D.E., & Boyd, W.E. (1990). Characteristics of employers of handicapped individuals. *American Journal of Mental Retardation, 94*(1), 40-43.

Crealock, C., & Bachor, D. (1995). *Instructional strategies for students with special needs.* (2nd Ed.). Scarborough, ON: Allyn & Bacon Canada.

Cronin, M.E., & Parron, J.R. (1993). *Life skills instruction for all students with special needs: A practical guide for integrating real life content into the curriculum.* Austin TX: Pro-Ed.

Connections: A planning guide for parents of sons and daughters with a mental handicap. 34 Church Street Brampton, Ont. L6X 1H3.

Flavey, M.A., Forest, M., Pearpoint, J., & Rosenberg, R.L. (1994). Building connections. In J.S. Thousand, R.A. Villa & A.I. Nevin (Eds.) *Creativity and collaborative learning: A practical guide to empowering students and teachers.* (pp. 347-368). Baltimore Brookes.

Harrison, P.L., Kaufman, N.L., Bruininks, R.H., Ryndeers, J., Ilmer, S., Sparrow, S.S., & Cicchetti, D. (1990). *AGS Early Screening Profiles.* Circle Pines, MN: American guidance Service.

Helmke, L.M., Havekost, D.M., Patton, J.R., & Polloway E.A. (1994, Winter). Life skills programming: Development of a high school science course. *Teaching Exceptional Children,* pp. 49-53.

Noonan, M.J., & McCormick, L. (1993). *Early intervention in natural environments.* Pacific Grove, CA: Brooks/Cole.

Safe and Secure: Six steps to creating a personal future plan for people with disabilities. 3790, Canada Way, Burnaby BC, V5G 1G4.

Snell, M.E. (1993). *Instruction of students with severe disabilities* (4th ed.). New York: Macmillan.

10

Students with Physical Disabilities

Neurological Disabilities • Chronic Health Needs • Multiple Disabilities

" My whole world is two-three feet lower now. That's what happens when you can't stand up. And I plan. Not just plan my day but plan my minutes. Do I drink that Coke, for example? If I do, then where will I be in half an hour when it works its way through and I have to go to the bathroom? Things like that. I never thought just going to the can would become an event. "

— Terry Nain (who became physically disabled in grade twelve)

Misconceptions About Physical and Other Health Needs

1. When a student has a condition such as Tourette syndrome or spina bifida or asthma, he or she is automatically a candidate for special education.

Physical or neurological or health needs do not automatically make a student educationally exceptional. Where conditions like spina bifida or asthma or Tourettes are primary or sole conditions, the distribution of intelligence, and distribution of other abilities like hearing or vision are similar to that in the rest of the population. It is possible, in some situations, that the medication used for treatment may have side effects that could make an adjusted program beneficial for a student, and it may be best to deliver such a program through special education services.

Another matter is that students with chronic needs often miss a great deal of school because of hospitalization or illness cared for at home, and may need a remedial program which special education is best equipped to deliver.

2. The physical condition of students with cerebral palsy cannot be remediated or improved.*

Although cerebral palsy is considered irreversible, therapy, prosthetic devices, and sometimes surgical procedures, can make a positive change. This is most especially the case if intervention is begun early.

3. The most challenging issue in this area of special need is developing strategies for special instruction.

*Recent research in England has demonstrated positive effects with the use of oxygen.

Students with these special needs, and their advocates, insist that the principal issue continues to be the task of making non-disabled peers, adults, and others understand and be sensitive to their needs.

4. When disabling conditions are neurologically based, there is always a consequent diminishing of intellectual capacity.

There is a higher incidence of intellectual delay among people with cerebral palsy, but the connection is not absolute. Other conditions such as spina bifida, muscular dystrophy, or convulsive disorders, generally have no connection with levels of intelligence.

5. Conditions like epilepsy and Tourette syndrome indicate a predisposition toward mental illness.

People with these conditions are no more or no less disposed to mental illness than people who do not have them.

6. People with spina bifida are invariably incontinent.

Lack of bowel and bladder control is a genuine problem which accompanies the severer cases of spina bifida, but milder cases generally do not have this effect.

7. Arthritis is found only in adults, especially the elderly.

It is found in all ages.

8. Advances in medicine are reducing the incidence of physical disabilities and chronic conditions.

The number of children with these conditions is increasing because medical advances, particularly in post-natal care, have increased the birth and early year survival rate.

Describing the Needs

The primary distinguishing characteristics of students with a physical disability or other neurological or health need, are the proper concern of the health professions. Still, because these students attend schools — more and more of them regular, neighbourhood schools — it follows that teachers and educational assistants should therefore have some information about them. From an educational perspective, some bio-medical knowledge can be useful for developing an appropriate program. Certainly the knowledge can be very helpful in understanding a student's emotional needs and learning patterns. In the vast majority of cases (with the occasional exception of some neurologically-based conditions, like Tourette syndrome, for example, and some forms of pervasive development disorder) a student with a special physical or health need will arrive in class already defined and classified by health personnel, and will have been presented to an IPRC. Thus, classroom personnel should get a fair amount of information in advance.

It is very important to recognize that a physical or health or neurological condition will manifest itself in a variety of ways, but even more important, when it does, the student who has it is still, first and foremost, a *student*. Thus it is important that teachers approach medical information principally from an educational and co-operative perspective, and not from a diagnostic or treatment point of view. In addition to learning about a particular condition, it is also wise to seek out the peculiarities of the individual student's case, since epilepsy, for example, or Tourette syndrome or brain injury, will manifest itself in a variety of ways across a population, and with widely varying degrees of difference.

The descriptions that follow below are quite brief and offer preliminary information only. (The authors have also scrupulously avoided presenting a catalogue of conditions encountered in the schools of the province. A glance at the data in Chapter 3 will verify that despite the drama implied by the conditions, the number of students is small.)

Cerebral Palsy

This is a condition caused by injury to the brain before, during, or after birth. It is chiefly characterized by motor disorder. It is not progressive but is not considered curable although therapy can be helpful in improving comfort and mobility.

Approximately fifty per cent of people with cerebral palsy have what is called *pyramidal (also called spastic)* palsy, characterized by slow, laborious, poorly coordinated voluntary movement, stiff, tense muscles, and in some cases a degree of involuntary movement. About twenty-five per cent have *extrapyramidal (also called choreoathetoid, and atonic)* cerebral palsy, characterized by regular, involuntary, writhing movements, difficulty maintaining posture, and floppy muscle tone. *Ataxic* cerebral palsy, characterized by poor coordination, balance and posture, affects approximately fifteen per cent. People with ataxia may be ambulatory; most others generally require a wheelchair. Some people with cerebral palsy have a combination of these symptoms.

Other matters associated with cerebral palsy are developmental delays (not an absolute connection but the incidence is significantly higher than in the general population) speech and language problems, sensory loss, especially visual and auditory difficulties, and seizures. An ongoing debate over cerebral palsy arises from the fact that average IQ test scores for children with this condition are lower than the general average. However, appropriateness of IQ tests, their administration and interpretation are often suspect in these situations.

For educators, a profound reality is that students who have cerebral palsy often present multifaceted educational problems. Not only do the students frequently require special equipment and procedures, the fact that other conditions often accompany the case means that classroom personnel need competence in a variety of areas.

Spina Bifida

Spina bifida occurs in the spinal column when one or more vertebrae do not close during pre-natal development. The resulting condition varies from minor to serious. The most severe condition is spina bifida with *mylemeningocele* which usually results in irreversible (so far) disability, the most obvious being lower body paralysis. Less severe conditions such as *spina bifida occulta* and *meningocele* do not necessarily involve lower body paralysis although people with these conditions may require crutches or leg braces to help them walk. Spina bifida is often accompanied by *hydrocephalus,* an enlargement of the head caused by pressure from cerebrospinal fluid which, if not diagnosed and treated in time, can cause brain injury. Usually, the medical response to hydrocephalus is the installation of a shunt (a short tube) in the spinal column to help this fluid drain. Hydrocephalus and the presence of a shunt, indeed spina bifida itself, usually do not preclude a student's normal progress through school. However, educational experience with children who have hydrocephalus is beginning to reveal that the condition may also produce a higher than average chance of learning disability, owing to possible anomalies in the structure of the brain. The connection, at this stage, is more suspected (through empiricism) than proven, but teachers should be sensitive to the possibility.

Spina bifida is, in a sense, fairly typical of a condition wherein the teacher's best approach is to help, but not direct, the student to manage himself or herself.

Brain Injury

Often the result of an accident or other trauma, a brain injury is almost invariably an unique condition. While the area of the brain that has suffered the injury may be responsible for a constellation of human characteristics, there is no certainty that these characteristics will be affected, or that the effects will be short or long term. Educators dealing with a student diagnosed as brain injured, perhaps more than with any other exceptional student, must truly begin their assessments and programs with no assumptions or preconceived notions.

Seizure Disorders (Epilepsy)

Epilepsy is not a disease, but rather a symptom of a brain disorder that leads to seizures. The disorder occurs in about 300,000 Canadians

---

> ### Bloorview MacMillan Centre ✍️
>
> Educators have an especially powerful ally in the many services and facilities available from the Bloorview MacMillan Centre (formerly Hugh MacMillan Centre) in Toronto. Not only can schools get useful information and advice, but very often, a student with a brain injury can be diagnosed and treated, as well as attend school for a time, at the centre. Usually, application for the services of the centre are accessed via a board's support services, or, through the Ministry of Health or Ministry of Community Services.

according to the Epilepsy Association, over half of these (55 percent) diagnosed before age ten. In the majority of cases, the cause is unknown. There are several types of seizure; the two most commonly occurring are *tonic-clonic* and *absence seizure* (formerly called 'grand-mal' and 'petit-mal'). In the first type, the tonic-clonic, an individual loses consciousness, most often convulses, and may fall. Breathing may stop temporarily. The individual may lose bowel and bladder control, or may bite the tongue. After one to five minutes or so, the person regains consciousness, but may experience confusion and headache and often goes into deep sleep. Absence seizures, on the other hand, are very brief and often go unnoticed. They may occur several times a day, usually when the person is sedentary, and are characterized by what is often called a "clouding of the consciousness", during which the individual's eyes may stare blankly, or the hands will move aimlessly. Return to normal is usually abrupt. It is not unknown for teachers to be the first to suspect absence seizures, since one-on-one learning situations are good opportunities for observation, especially if the teacher is attempting to find out why a particular student's style is marked by significant ups and downs of understanding.

Students with idiopathic epilepsy (of unknown origin) seem to function entirely normally between seizures. Those with symptomatic epilepsy (from brain injury) often have to cope with the consequences of a primary condition, of which epilepsy is one factor. Either way, epilepsy itself, is not usually the reason a student is referred to an IPRC. Very often, it is a primary condition, or the side effects of seizure-control medication, that lead to consideration for special education.

Many students who have tonic-clonic seizures seem to be extremely sensitive about the events, and teachers may find themselves more challenged by the emotional than by the physical consequences of seizure. How a teacher deals with a *post*-seizure classroom atmosphere can have a most important impact. Reassurance and emotional support for the student who had the seizure is crucial; equally vital is how the teacher educates the other students about epilepsy. (The Epilepsy Association has excellent material to assist with this issue. It also has up-to-date information on new medications for seizure control.)

Dealing with a Tonic-clonic Seizure in the Classroom

- Do not try to restrain the student; you cannot stop the seizure.
- Remove or try to protect the student from furniture and sharp objects.
- DO NOT force anything between the teeth.
- After the seizure, turn the student to one side to allow saliva to drain.
- Loosen the collar and other tight clothing.
- Put something soft under the student's head.
- Do not offer a drink until the student is fully awake.
- Let him or her rest afterward. (Often they will sleep.)
- If the seizure lasts beyond five minutes, or seems to pass from one seizure to another without the return of consciousness, it should be treated as a medical emergency.

Tourette Syndrome

Once considered extremely rare, and likely because of that, very little known or understood, Tourette syndrome (TS) is now believed to be far more common, and to have far more impact on the classroom than was originally thought. However, prevalence data still vary. The prevailing opinion has been that TS affects one in every 2000 individuals (about the same prevalence as blindness) whereas some data suggest as many as one out of every four. Interestingly, TS has become relatively well-known in our culture thanks to commercial television programs. Unfortunately, it is still not very well understood. What most people understand is that TS is a neurological disorder that usually manifests itself in childhood, and is frequently characterized by repetitive physical movements like facial tics and/or vocal sounds. In a small percentage of the cases, the sounds are obscenities or curses (called *coprolalia*). TS is a lifelong disorder, although the symptoms have been known to disappear for long periods or even disappear altogether, with and without medication.

The implications of TS for parents and teachers are significant, in part because of less well-known behaviour symptoms that are often part of the condition. Students with TS may be very hyperactive. Obsessive compulsive behaviour is common. And the condition is also marked by profound rages and aggression, provoked by what in the minds of teachers and peers and caregivers appear to be very innocuous stimuli. Common learning difficulties associated with TS are: difficulty in getting started (or finished), problems with comprehending verbal instructions, and confusion over space-time directionality. Given those difficulties, it is not hard to understand why TS can be confused with learning disability, developmental disability, schizophrenia and other conditions. Medication to control TS symptoms is improving all the time, although it may have side effects that have an impact on a student's behaviour and academic performance.

The role of the teacher, as usual, is very important in the case of a student with TS. Understanding, empathy, common sense support, and remediation strategies are obvious needs. Perhaps the most vital matter in assuring the student's security and sense of wellbeing is the way in which the teacher manages the effect of the TS on the student's peers and classmates. The Tourette Syndrome Foundation has some very helpful literature for teachers, and it is a given that this should be read by any teacher who has a student with TS in his or her classroom. In fact, teachers who encounter TS in their classroom often find that the Foundation is their most helpful ally.

Pervasive Development Disorder (Autism)

In 1980, the diagnostic term 'Pervasive Development Disorder' (PDD) first appeared in DSM-III, the Third Edition of the Diagnostic and Statistical Manual, published by the American Psychiatric Association. Even before 1980, some clinicians had been using PDD as a non-specific generic term for a group of related disorders (including autism) which share certain characteristics: impaired communication, restricted, stereotypical mannerisms, and difficulty with reciprocal social interaction. Although the DSM is the most widely used diagnostic system among mental health professionals, acceptance of its attempt to distinguish autism as one form of PDD, is far from unanimous thus far.

DSM-IV (1994) attempted to clarify the matter with a listing and description of five disorders under the umbrella term PDD.

Rare Conditions

A frequent difficulty for teachers and educational assistants is finding information on rare conditions and disorders, that have serious implications for the classroom. Mobius Syndrome, Rett's Disorder (a.k.a. Syndrome) and tuberous sclerosis are examples of conditions that are found in Ontario classrooms, but for which there is limited data. Tuberous sclerosis is marked by lesions in the brain and other organs, often the skin, and is very frequently accompanied by serious developmental delay. Students frequently have seizures, and some manifest obsessive compulsive and rage behaviours not unlike those found in students with autism or Tourettes.

Rett's has so far been found only in girls. Children with the condition, after normal development, begin to lose purposeful hand skills around age 3-5, followed by a diminution of general physical ability, decelerated head growth, and diminished cognitive function.

Mobius Syndrome (congenital facial diplegia) was first described well over a century ago (1888). In this condition, the muscles of the face gradually weaken, so much so that the individual cannot make facial expressions, even when crying or laughing. Atrophy of the tongue is common. In some cases, the forehead and eyebrows may even droop over the eyes making vision difficult. Although, there is no clear evidence of intellectual differences, Mobius is a condition that generates special needs both at home and in the classroom.

Support groups have recently been founded for Rett's, and tuberous sclerosis, but not as yet for Mobius Syndrome. Teachers can usually obtain an address for the support groups via on-line sources, or through the community support department of larger hospitals.

- Autistic Disorder
- Rett's Disorder
- Childhood Disintegrative Disorder
- Asberger's Disorder
- Pervasive Development Disorder Not Otherwise Specified (including Atypical Autism)

Needless to say, there is more than a little disagreement about these distinctions. (The last term alone is sufficient to raise doubt in even the mildest of cynics!) Nevertheless, it is probably important for teachers and educational assistants to be aware that 'levels' of what once went under the blanket term 'autism', now generally prevail. Whether or not the distinctions affect what must be done to meet special needs in the classroom is moot, for it is not likely a teacher will be helped very much by the knowledge that a student is not 'autistic', but rather, has 'childhood disintegrative disorder'. Of interest is the fact that, despite the distinctive forms of PDD, most suggestions for effective classroom instruction and behaviour management are generally similar.

Autistic Disorder: marked by very impaired development in social interaction; verbal and nonverbal communication may be very restricted or very much one-way. Students with the disorder will usually have a very restricted repertoire of activities and interests and will resist attempts to be diverted from them (and resist attempts to be introduced to new ones). If the student has quite extreme autism, he or she may engage in *echolalia* (constantly repeating words and sounds) and *pica* (ingesting non-edible objects and materials) or behaviours that to others seem very bizarre.

Childhood Disintegrative Disorder: marked by what appears to be normal development for several years, before autistic-like features become apparent. There is marked regression of verbal and social skills and development of bizarre, repetitive behaviours. (This disorder is sometimes called 'Heller's Syndrome' after author Joseph Heller's book about his child with PDD.)

Asberger's Disorder (also Syndrome): marked by less obvious and less intense autistic-like features. There is normal development (speech

For Discussion: the Case of Matt

The car crash that completely disabled Matt also caused serious injury to three of his friends and killed two others. Matt is the only crash victim with permanent spinal injury. Although his condition was at first diagnosed as 'diplegic' (the legs are more involved than the arms) after about six months of therapy, Matt had a sudden stroke and went into a coma. Doctors are sure he had another stroke while 'out', for after several weeks he suddenly came to, with extreme choreoathetosis (abrupt, involuntary, writhing movements) in all four limbs. This condition was so intense and painful that after three months it was decided to relieve it with a non-reversible surgical procedure that has made Matt a quadriplegic.

The accident happened after a weekend field party when Matt was 15 years old in grade ten. At the time, he was identified gifted and had been placed part time in a self-contained class with gifted peers, and part time in advanced grade twelve language and math classes. Matt is now 19. He returned to school about a year ago and, to everyone's delight, demonstrated immediately that although his body was largely immobilized, his intellect was entirely unimpaired.

An admirable piece of creative thinking on the part of a special education teacher solved a potentially serious obstruction to Matt's rehabilitation. Bioengineering staff at the hospital had fashioned a 'headstick' so that he can tap a computer keyboard. (Matt speaks normally; he uses the computer for writing, problem solving, and a range of activities.) But leaning over the keyboard with the headstick would exhaust him after a brief time. The teacher simply mounted the keyboard above the monitor so that Matt's neck brace supports most of his movements.

Matt has done exceptionally well since his return and will graduate with honors. Now he has asked his teachers for some career counseling. Given his exceptional abilities in language and math, given what computers can (and will) do for him, and recognizing the possible limitations imposed by his physical condition, should he seek a liberal arts degree? (He is a superb writer and editor with a highly developed sense of language.) Or should he pursue accountancy? (His math skills are very superior.) He enjoys both areas equally.

may be somewhat delayed) and usually relatively normal interactions with family members, although peer relationships may show clearer manifestations of PDD. Often have unusual or very elaborate preoccupation with certain subjects or with specific objects.

PDD Not Otherwise Specified: marked by impairments across all three areas of characteristic for autism, but does not have the number of features (as specified by DSM) to be placed in one of the above categories.*

Rett's Disorder (see sidebar, page 116)

Multiple Disabilities

Students identified as multiple-disabled or multi-handicapped have more than one exceptionality. There is limited evidence to show that certain single handicaps are more predisposed to be accompanied by others. In fact, a particularly vicious myth that continues to prevail is that all multiple-disabled students are severely intellectually retarded. Another frequently posed myth is that all multiple-disabled students have no oral language. However there does seem to be a higher prevalence associated with certain exceptionalities. Children with cerebral palsy, for example, have a very high ratio of uncorrectable visual impairments. About a third of children with significant hearing loss have additional special needs.

This particular area of special education occupies a considerable amount of professional attention. In situations, for example, where it has been decided that a multiple-disabled student will not be mainstreamed in a regular class, finding an appropriate special class can be difficult. A jurisdiction may have a total of 4 or 5 students with deafness/blindness and a special class for them, but it may have only one student diagnosed deaf/blind, physically disabled, and developmentally delayed. And it may have a total of three students who are identified as autistic (one of whom also has visual impairment). The tendency, in situations where these children are not integrated into regular classes, is to identify them as multiple-disabled and place them in a single self-contained class. The rationale for this would likely be that such

---

*In describing a syndrome, the DSM characteristically presents a list of observable symptoms and then specifies a minimum number necessary to qualify for a diagnosis.

congregation allows individualized programming and easy access to support services, that it takes cognizance of those areas where programs may overlap, and that it is economically feasible. Nevertheless, it is quite common for students with multiple, severe disabilities to be integrated into a regular class with appropriate support, very often, an educational assistant or health aide (or both).

Whatever the identification and placement of a student with several exceptionalities, three features are common in a program:

i) it is highly individualized;

ii) there is a significant amount of support available from specialized educational and health services;

iii) there is a well-above-average degree of communication and cooperation (at least attempted) with the student's home so that education and habilitation can be coordinated beyond the school day.

Chronic Health Needs

A chronic health need does not automatically predestine a student for special education. Health problems may be present in students of either regular or special education classes. Teachers will encounter students with cystic fibrosis, scoliosis, congenital malformations, muscular dystrophy, diabetes, cancer, asthma and other chronic conditions, not to mention situations like poliomyelitis or encephalitis from which a student may recover but with some disability as a result.

As well, not all needs that could come under the rubric of 'chronic health' are themselves the condition that require special education. Two examples are *allergies* and *fetal alcohol syndrome*. The latter, which can have major health implications, very often has an overriding educational need arising from developmental delay (which is why this text includes FAS in Chapter 9). Students with allergies — and teachers will readily attest that the numbers in this area are growing rapidly — may well be innocent victims of the stimuli that cause their reactions, but educators usually find themselves compelled to meet the special learning needs the allergy *symptoms* cause.

It is not the place of a text like this to present a list of handicapping and chronic health conditions. The examples above are included as typical of the more frequent situations that may be present in a classroom. It is important to repeat here, that the teacher's main responsibility is to educate, with all this implies, not to treat; and to cooperate in the health care aspects that are part of the needs of these students.

Attending school, simply being in school, is a crucial element in the normalization and growth of a student with a non-sensory physical exceptionality.

Some Issues in the Field

■ *Dealing with emergencies* may pose a serious challenge for teachers and assistants. Some are even led to resist placement of chronically ill students in their classes. Usually the resistance can be overcome simply with information and education about the particular exceptionality. However, a constant — and justified — complaint of frontline classroom personnel is that they are not kept adequately informed about students with health needs. Changes in medication, environmental triggers (e.g., of a seizure incident), crucial times of day: all these factors can be very important to the accommodation of a student with special health needs,

and teachers quite rightly argue that poor communication from health personnel, inefficient bureaucracy in a school or larger system, not to mention stringent privacy regulations, makes their jobs more difficult and even puts the student at risk. (All of which substantiates the wisdom of regular, direct communication with parents who, for obvious reasons, will likely be both helpful and informative.)

■ *Families often experience practical and emotional havoc* when they have a child with physical disabilities, or neurological condition, or chronic health need. Such a child inevitably demands a disproportionate amount of the family's resources in love, energy, money and time. Needless to say, families react in different ways, and their feelings usually have a profound effect on the way the child reacts in turn to the world at large. In whatever way the family — and the child — react, the teacher, educational assistant and a wide number of personnel in a school are inevitably drawn into this reaction, so that relative to their other students, schools almost invariably find themselves expending equally disproportionate amounts of love, energy, money, and time. How a school deals with this fact, morally and practically, can become a matter of serious debate.

For Discussion: the Case of Divora

Before Divora began attending her neighbourhood school in mid-grade one, her parents had advised the principal that their only child was "fiercely individualistic and rigorously independent". The school's primary staff soon agreed. Divora does not play with anyone in any of the 'centres', although she will spend time in them alone. Her classmates have learned to yield whatever space she wants. This apparent lack of interest in relationships extends to adults too. Divora shuts out advice, instruction, praise, even sharply worded imperatives. Although she tends to engage in repetitive behaviours (e. g., tracing the entire circumference of tabletops with each finger in specific sequence) these do not seem overtly exceptional (especially since others in the class have found them appealing enough to imitate!).

Recently, a school yard incident made Divora's teacher press the principal to refer the child to an IPRC. A kindergarten child climbed the school yard fence, cut himself seriously, then fell and was knocked out. He landed beside Divora, at that precise moment the only witness, but she appeared not even to notice, and made no attempt to raise an alarm. The principal agreed, and the IPRC, on the basis of an assessment and extensive anecdotal reports, identified the child 'autistic'. The committee decided that she would continue in her present class. Arrangements were set up to have the teacher receive regular consultative advice from the Geneva Centre, and special resource assistance is to be provided to encourage Divora to develop relationships with other people.

Divora's parents, however, disagree with the identification. They acknowledge the behaviours but do not want their daughter called 'autistic'. Unfortunately, the special consultation and resource assistance is available only to children with autism. Everyone is now looking for a creative solution.

Educational Implications

❖ Canadians live in a culture obsessed with beautiful bodies. Health and strength are not enough; we must be well formed and attractive. It is not surprising therefore that to the physically exceptional especially, there is not only a battle to overcome the limitations imposed by their own bodies, there is also a battle to be accepted by others without stigma. The same phenomenon applies to behaviour. To people with Tourette syndrome, for example, the band of acceptable or so-called normal behaviour in our culture appears very narrow, so that when their condition expresses itself, they feel very much singled out. Therefore a teacher with one or more of these students in his class often finds himself dealing as much with behaviours — the disabled students', his own, that of other students, the culture at large — as he does with curriculum and instruction. Exceptional students will have negative feelings about themselves if it is obvious that others around them do. Conversely, they may become independent and self-sufficient in response to the expectations of others. Self-acceptance and self-awareness will develop in kind with the open and honest appraisal that significant people in their lives give to them.

Classroom personnel have an enormously important role to play in this. For example, teachers will often react with caution to someone in their midst who has a surgically implanted shunt, or who has a leg brace, or who may suddenly convulse or experience an asthma attack. Such caution of course is reasonable, but it is important that the caution be just that, and not fear. Fear and ignorance are potentially as great a threat to exceptional students as the primary handicaps themselves.

❖ The treatment of conditions like epilepsy or Tourette syndrome often involves the use of medication which has sedating side effects. Teachers sometimes find they are adjusting, not to an exceptionality, but to the treatment of that exceptionality. In fact it is not uncommon for a student to be identified and placed in special education principally because of the effects of the medication which is being used to control a primary condition.

❖ The normal adjustments that every teacher makes to accommodate her students' personal needs are often intensified in cases of chronic

For Discussion: the Case of Tamhana

The fourth grade teacher had met Tamhana two years ago when she 'supplied' in a grade two class for several months. At the time, the teacher had taken note of the young girl's persistent and unusual behaviour, but followed the advice of a colleague and did not pursue the matter. Now, as the fourth grade teacher, he regrets that decision, for Tamhana's apparent oddities are much more pronounced, and more obsessive to a marked degree. She has continued a grade two habit: returning from the schoolyard according to a very specific walking pattern. But whereas she would permit intervention two years ago, Tamhana blows into a frightening rage now, if interrupted. She enters the classroom by a patterned path as well (and her peers have learned not to get in the way). Her lunch is eaten in specific sequence, and she has taken to counting aloud while chewing to ensure an identical number of 'chews' each time.

Tamhana's facial tics, very evident in grade two, have ceased, but she now makes strange sounds when sitting alone (which, regrettably, is most of the time) ranging from growls to oohs and eehs, and on one occasion, the teacher is certain, barking. Lately, Tamhana has taken to impulsively running from the room when the whole class is engaged in an activity. She allows herself to be brought back and is very remorseful for causing a disturbance. However, she cannot explain why she runs out, and often, if questioned the following day, denies any knowledge of the event.

The teacher, like many of the staff, believes Tamhana has Tourette syndrome and wants the principal to refer her to an IPRC. Unfortunately, this was attempted in grade three and then abandoned after a friend of Tamhana's family told her parents that "girls don't get Tourettes". As a result, the parents refused all requests from the IPRC for cooperation. The staff has now learned of an additional complication: that Tamhana's father does not want attention focused on a female child in any way that might bring disgrace on the family. What the teacher knows he must do is somehow convince the girl's parents that some kind of intervention is necessary, for Tamhana's strange behaviours are intensifying daily.

health need. The students often miss a great deal of instructional time through illness and absences for therapy, etc. Teachers also have to make allowances in scheduling and in monitoring so that matters of the students' personal hygiene can be addressed. As well, students with particularly serious disabilities often have attendant behavioural, even psychiatric problems that can call upon the full extent of a teacher's patience and stamina.

❖ Since a disabling condition like cerebral palsy can affect progress through the natural stages of development, teachers can safely anticipate that some students with severe conditions may not be working at the same academic level as their peers, and must therefore make adjustments in program.

✔STRATEGIES FOR THE CLASSROOM

(1) Students in both regular and self-contained classes — most especially younger children — will invariably take their cue from teachers when seeking out how to react to and behave toward people with disabilities. Accordingly, teachers need to take a very positive leadership and modeling role. Teachers also need to show other students tactfully, how to be helpful without taking over, how to react with empathy not pity, and how to treat their colleagues' exceptionalities with common sense.

(2) Where there are no secondary exceptionalities to deal with, such as learning disability or developmental delay for example, the teacher of a student with non-sensory physical limitations, or neurological impairments or chronic conditions, will likely treat the student in the same way as he or she treats everyone else, making allowance only for special needs in day-to-day functioning. These might include help in the administration of medication, help in the effective use of a prosthesis (artificial replacement for a body part) or some other adaptive device necessary for daily living.

(3) Continuing developments in computer technology accelerate far ahead of the capacity of texts like this one to describe them, and of course, teachers need to stay abreast as best as they can to utilize this progress on behalf of their students.

(4) Because many children with physical disabilities are absent from school frequently, the degree to which a teacher cooperates in out-of-school assistance can be a very important factor in academic success. Many jurisdictions appoint what are called 'itinerant' teachers, or teachers of the home and hospital-bound, whose teaching load usually involves on-site instruction at home, in hospital, or in other institutions.

(5) It is rare but not unheard of, for the classroom teacher to be the catalyst in the discovery of a condition such as absence seizures for example, which in a large and chaotic family may not be noticed if they are mild and infrequent, but in the more structured demands of school become evident. Such relatively unknown conditions like Tourette syndrome sometimes go undiagnosed even through adolescence.

(6) Effective communication among teachers, parents, and health care professionals is absolutely essential but is ignored with discouraging frequency. It is often incumbent upon the teacher to initiate this, usually by direct and regular contact with the parents.

(7) Regarding Autism: (The following advice is from an adult diagnosed autistic at age three.)

My head is like a video. The only way I learn is to see things. That's why nouns and verbs are easier to learn than other words. When you teach an autistic kid things, *show* him.

You need blocks and sticks and things like that for math.

Use art a lot.

Phonics is best for reading. So are poems. And music and songs.

Autistic kids stick with special things they like. I loved trains. Still do. My best teacher used math trains. We had train records and we read train stories. Ms. King was so cool.

When you talk, don't say so much at once. Don't talk *slow*. We're not idiots! Just don't say so much at once! I wish we had computers when I was in school. With computers you control the information coming in.

For Further Investigation

United Cerebral Palsy Associations. (1993). *Cerebral Palsy – facts and figures*. Washington, DC: United Cerebral Palsy Associations

Bauer, S. (1995). Autism and the pervasive developmental disorders. *Pediatrics in Review, 16*, 130-136.

Blum, R.W., Resnick, M.D., Nelson, R., & St.Germaine, A. (1991). Family and peer issues among adolescents with spina bifida and cerebral palsy. *Pediatrics, 88*, 280-285.

Huntinger, P.L. (1996). Computer applications in programs for young children with disabilities: recurrent themes. *Focus on Autism and Other Developmental Disabilities, 11*(2), 105-114.

Light, J. (1997). " Communication is the essence of human life": reflections on communicative competence. *Augmentative and Alternative Communication, 13*, 61-70.

Parette, H.P., Hourcade J.J., & Brimer, R.W. (1996). Degree of involvement and young children with cerebral palsy. Physical Disabilities: *Education and Related Services, 14*(2), 33-59.

For the Classroom Teacher

Batshaw, M.L., & Perret, Y.M. (1992). *Children with Disabiities: A medical primer* (3rd ed.). Baltimore, MD: Paul H. Brookes.

Bigge, J. L. (1991). *Teaching individuals with physical and multiple disabilities* (3rd ed.). New York: Macmillan.

Cohen, S. (1998). *Targeting autism: what we know, don't know, and can do to help young children with autism and related disorders*. Berkeley: University of California Press.

Fraser, B.A., & Hensinger, R.N. (1983). *Managing physical handicaps: A practical guide for parents, care providers, and educators*. Baltimore: Brookes.

Geralis, E. (Ed.). (1991). *Children with cerebral palsy*. Rockville, MD: Woodbine House.

Giangreco, M.F. (1997a). Persistent questions about curriculum for students with severe disabilities. *Physical Disabilities: Education and Related Services , 15*(2), 53-56.

Graffe, J.C., Mulligan-Ault, M., Guess, D., Taylor, M., & Thompson, B. (1990). *Health care for students with disabilities: An illustrated medical guide for the classroom*. Baltimore: Brookes.

Help From Support and Advocacy Groups ✍

Teachers often find support and advocacy groups very helpful in a variety of ways. Members of organizations like The Epilepsy Association, The Learning Disabilities Association, The Association for Bright Children, The Tourette Syndrome Foundation, The Canadian Hearing Society, The Canadian National Institute for the Blind (there are many more) are invariably well-informed and current, and usually quite aggressive in seeking out information, supporting innovative practice, or dealing with slow-moving bureaucrats, and reluctant, sometimes poorly informed health professionals. All of these are issues a teacher invariably faces, and most of the time, regular contact and help from the appropriate advocacy group can be quite helpful in addressing them. Most associations, for example, have education programs in kit form or videotape which are available to teachers who wish to enlighten their classes or their colleagues about a particular special need. Further, it is not unknown for an advocacy group to be the principal catalyst in bringing service to bear for a student for whom nothing hitherto had been available. Advocacy groups are also a remarkably effective first line of emotional support and information to a family which has just learned that a child has been diagnosed.

Students Who Are Deaf or Hard of Hearing

"If you can hear, you're at the centre of the world, right in the middle of what's going on, but if you're deaf, you're always out at the edge."
—Charley Ben, made deaf by injury at age 43

Prevailing Misconceptions About Deafness

1. Deafness diminishes intellectual ability.

The basis of this misconception lies in the fact that in school, deaf students sometimes lag academically because of their difficulties in communicating with people who hear and can use spoken language easily. Intellectual ability is distributed among the deaf in the same way as it is for the hearing.

2. Deafness leads automatically to muteness or to inability to speak.

People who are born deaf or become deaf before they have acquired the ability to speak (usually called prelingual deafness), often have difficulty developing the ability to speak with clarity, but the connection between deafness and the inability to speak is not absolute.

3. Profoundly deaf people live in a world of total silence.

Even people with profound deafness can respond to some sounds, particularly the vibrations.

4. A hearing aid restores normal hearing.

Basic hearing aids amplify sounds and do not necessarily restore normal hearing. However hearing aids have become very sophisticated, and some models now offer the user a variety of settings, individually customized to adapt to different situations. As well, other high-tech (and sometimes controversial) devices are now available. (See page 130.)

5. It is counterproductive and potentially harmful for people who are deaf to socialize almost exclusively with others who are also deaf.

Many members of the deaf community argue with conviction that the phenomenon of an exclusive "Deaf Culture" is an entirely natural outcome and should be encouraged. While others argue the opposite with equal vigor, there is as yet no conclusive evidence that the desire of some deaf people to associate primarily with one another is anything but normal.

6. Teaching sign to the deaf will retard their development of spoken language.

The teaching of sign language does not, of itself, retard the development of spoken language. However, if a deaf person chooses to learn or to use sign exclusively, the development of facility in spoken language may be affected.

7. Deaf people compensate by learning to read lips.

Many deaf persons use *speech reading* in which the receiver notes facial expression, hand gestures, and other body language in addition to simple lip movement. However this skill does not come more easily to deaf people than to anyone else. Reading of lips alone is often not helpful because of similarities in the words of spoken language, and because of the inconsistencies in the lip movements of speakers.

8. American Sign Language (ASL) is a loose style of gesturing primarily used to convey concrete ideas.

ASL is a language with its own set of grammatical rules, and it can be used to convey levels of abstraction just as oral languages do.

9. American Sign Language is a universal sign language.

While ASL has become increasingly popular, it is by no means a universal language. Of note is the fact that, just as there is no universal spoken language, there is also no universal sign language. ASL is one language among many.

Types of Hearing Loss

Most hearing losses are conductive or sensorineural (and sometimes, but not frequently, both). In the case of *conductive* hearing loss, sound is reduced or blocked before it reaches the inner ear. This may occur as the result of infection, or trauma, or wax build-up or other cause. Sometimes the blockage can be cleared, or the sound amplified to reduce the effects of conductive hearing loss.

In *sensorineural* hearing loss, the problem is in the reception of sound in the inner ear or in the transmission of electrical impulses along the auditory nerve. Sound may reach the inner ear but because of problems in the inner ear structures, it may not be transmitted

meaningfully even with amplification. There are many possible causes for sensorineural hearing loss, including such apparently simple diseases as mumps or measles, along with more complex viral infections like meningitis, and a range of congenital disorders and types of trauma. Attempts to correct sensorineural loss tend to be more radical and the results less predictable.

Some specialists in the field distinguish a third type of hearing difficulty which they call *central auditory dysfunction*. It is described as an inability to interpret correctly (i.e., in the brain) sound that comes from the auditory nerve, even though sensitivity to sound may be otherwise normal. Central auditory dysfunction is still pretty much a mystery and is not yet universally accepted as a valid explanation of hearing difficulty.

Classifications of Hearing Loss

Specialists in the field of hearing generally use a combination of four major systems to classify an individual's degree of hearing loss.

- *Site of loss:* whether the loss is conductive or sensorineural, or both.

- *Age of onset:* whether the loss is pre or post lingual.

- *Etiology:* whether the individual's loss was present at birth (congenital loss) or has arisen since birth (adventitious loss).

- *Severity:* acuity of hearing, measured by an individual's response to intensity, or loudness, measured in decibels (dB), across a range of frequencies, measured in hertz (Hz). A simple metaphor for the severity measure can be found in the controls on a radio. The volume control of a radio increases or decreases the decibel rating of sound that issues from the speaker, while the frequency or pitch is modified by how carefully the tuner is set to the signal, and also by the degree of clarity achieved by adjusting the tenor/bass setting. Most of the speech in a typical classroom will range from 400 to 2500 Hz, often depending on whether one person is speaking or whether there is classroom "buzz". The decibel rating in a typical classroom may be as low as 30 dB (a whisper) to as high as 80 or 90 dB (a shout). In most cases, comfortable human conversation has a dB rating of around 35-50, in a frequency or Hz range of about 400 to 1250. (See Figure 11B for more examples.)

The *severity* classification is the one most frequently used by teachers and teaching assistants because it can be structured into functional clusters which imply some simple guidelines for the classroom. (See Figure 11A.)

It is important to note that the characteristics described in Figure 11A are by no means all there is to know about deaf or hard of hearing persons. Just like those who hear normally, deaf and hard of hearing persons are as completely individual as anyone else, and therefore attend or tune out like anyone else. Another difficulty with classification is that, despite a certain presumed level of function in a deaf or hard of hearing person, that function will invariably be affected by the style and expressive quality of the person sending the communication.

Some Issues in the Field

■ Although there are a variety of matters that concern both educators and specialists regarding the deaf and hard of hearing, the single,

most overwhelming and consuming issue is the matter of communication method or style. On the surface, the issue appears to be a simple one of oralism versus manualism: that is, whether a deaf person should learn to develop and fully use whatever residual hearing he has available in order to communicate as normally as possible with people who hear, or, whether the emphasis and energy should be devoted to learning how to sign, in order to communicate with other signers (who, by and large, will be other deaf persons, family, and teachers).

Underlying the issue is what advocates of manualism especially, call the *deaf culture*.

Supporters of manualism argue that being deaf means being part of a culture that is distinguished by, among other things, its own language. They argue that, because experience shows most deaf persons do not become comfortable participants in the hearing culture, to deny them their own language therefore denies them their own culture and forces them into one where they are at risk, or at the very least, are not full participants. Simple observation forces the conclusion that significant numbers of deaf people support this view. The phrase *deaf community* is frequently used (especially

Loss Range	Classification*	Implications ✍
27-40 dB	Mild hearing loss	May have difficulty with faint or distant sounds, with conversations, and may have loss in groups, or settings with much ambient noise.
41-55 dB	Moderate	Frequent difficulty with normal speech, especially in conversations, groups, and class discussions.
56-70 dB	Moderate/severe	Often has difficulty with speech and with language comprehension. Conversation must be loud to be understood.
71-90 dB	Severe	Great difficulty with even loud or amplified speech. The latter may seem faint and distorted. Subject usually requires amplification and intensive speech and language training.
91 dB+	Profound hearing loss; deaf	May be aware of loud sounds and vibrations, but generally cannot deal with even amplified speech without extensive training.

A hearing loss is also often described as *bilateral* (both ears) or *unilateral* (one ear), with the severity of loss indicated according to the better ear.

(*Note that some jurisdictions choose to modify classifications such as this one for their own purposes.)

Figure 11A

by the deaf) to describe deaf persons as a cohesive group who share their own entertainments, activities — and language. This tendency toward self-exclusion does not prevail at all to the same degree among other groups with a readily apparent exceptionality.

Supporters of oralism counter that the world is dominated by, and made up mostly of, hearing persons, and that deaf persons who do not avail themselves of the opportunity to be part of the dominant culture are denying reality and relegating themselves to what is in effect not a culture, but a sub-culture with all that this implies. Some advocates on this side of the issue suggest that it may be advantageous for deaf persons to develop skill in both styles, either simultaneously or separately, in order that they can make a choice. The issue is often a particularly agonizing one for parents, for in the case of very young children, they must make the decision on their behalf since it is usually advantageous to begin either method as early in life as possible.

Educators, too, are inevitably involved in this issue, both practically and ethically. The teaching of reading, for example, is one area that can be significantly affected if a student is using ASL (American Sign Language) as her predominant means of communication. For example, a phrase that in print is written, "Yesterday I went to the store.", is typically signed in ASL as "Yesterday me store go." Because sensitivity to syntax is such a powerful component in learning to read, it follows that some deaf children using ASL may have an extra hurdle when learning to read English text.

Still another matter for teachers and teaching assistants is sensitivity to the intensity of this debate. While their primary role, naturally, is to instruct, that role can be potentially more complex if the student (or her parents) have objectives which relate strongly to one side or other of the communication and culture issue.

Common Sounds	dB Rating	Usual Effect
rustling leaves	20	pleasant
whisper	30	barely audible
2-3 people conversing	40-65	varies
hair dryer (on high)	70	interferes, disrupts
occupied cafeteria, food blender, motorcycle (at 5 m)	80-95	annoying (85 dB for 8hrs. begins hearing damage)
chain saw, snowmobile, jet flyby (at 300 m)	105-110	regular exposure without protection may cause damage
stereo (over 100 watts) boom box	120	threshold of pain sensation is 125 dB
rock concert, jet engine (takeoff at 50 m)	110-140	beyond pain threshold

Figure 11B

■ Further complicating the matter of educating deaf and hard of hearing persons is the intensity of debate within the oralism and manualism philosophies themselves. Even after a decision has been taken to emphasize one approach or the other, there is the potential for further disagreement over what is the best technique to choose. For example, among supporters of manualism, American Sign Language has become the overwhelming choice, but that choice, among deaf persons, is not unanimous. There continues to be some who argue for such manual methods as Signing Exact English (SEE) which, as the name implies, follows the syntactical and grammatical principles of English as it written and spoken.

■ In recent years, sophisticated surgical implantation technology has generated more possibilities — and difficult decisions — for dealing with significant hearing loss. One of the more vigorously debated technologies is the *cochlear implant*. In this procedure*, a receiver is implanted either within or outside the cochlea (part of the inner ear) and an external

---

* The technology is highly complex, and a full description of it is beyond the purposes of this text. More detailed information is available from the Canadian Hearing Society.

component transmits signals to this receiver. The present state of cochlear implant technology does not restore normal hearing, but there is evidence to suggest that it can dramatically improve a subject's ability to make sense of environmental sounds both natural and artificial and to interpret speech. Controversy about the procedure and the technology arises over the suitability of candidates, the type of implant to use, and the impact on the subject.

Somewhat less controversial is an at-the-ear, skullbone-anchored hearing aid system, which stimulates the inner ear by transmitting signals to the skull. This implantation technology was initially limited to subjects with conductive hearing loss, and has enjoyed a significant level of success. Research is being extended to subjects with sensorineural loss as well.

■ An issue that plagues researchers, and one that has more than a peripheral impact on educators, is determining the true prevalence of hearing loss in Canadian populations. Inconsistent definitions across jurisdictions, differences in the style of collecting and reporting data, and difficulties in assessing hearing loss among individuals with other disabilities (especially if these are multiple) leads to some confusing numbers in the field. In a study published in 1994, Schein noted that the prevalence rate in the U.S. is reported as 86 per 1000 while in Canada, it is 41 per 1000. He also showed wide variations among the reported rates in Canadian provinces (e.g., 34/1000 in NWT; 61/1000 in MB). The uncertainties implied by these differences in data affect funding, research, and even the degree of importance given to the matter by administrators.

Typical School Placements

- Special Residential schools. There are four such schools in Ontario, each of which offer day programs as well. The Whitney school in Belleville, the Robarts school in London, and

---

An experience related by Vivienne, profoundly deaf from birth

It happened in grade four. I was nine, then, I think. I was concentrating on math — I love math; the numbers follow a pattern, not like words where the rules always change. I was aware the other kids were moving. Nothing unusual about that. Class of thirty. But then the lights went out! I looked up. Everyone, including the teacher, had disappeared! I was so scared! I ran to the door and there was a class monitor — John. He was waving at me. Probably yelling too. Looked like it anyway. It was a fire drill. Mustn't run, mustn't talk. But when I caught up with the class I was shaking and sobbing.

Once again I felt ignored.

---

the Drury school in Milton are well known and highly regarded. Also held in high repute is the unique program at the Mac-Donald school in Brantford for the deaf and blind. Interestingly, over the past decade and more, the population of deaf students at these schools has declined somewhat, leading to the inference that more students with hearing loss are being educated in their neighbourhood or nearby schools.

- Special day schools, to which students commute from their homes.

- Self-contained special classes within regular elementary or secondary schools.

- Part-time integration programs. Students may attend some regular classes in a regular school. A signing interpreter, or an FM amplification system or other support might be used. This type of program may have a resource room component, especially if a trained teacher of the deaf is available to work directly with the student and to consult with the regular class teachers.

- Itinerant teacher programs. Specialist teachers offer assistance in classrooms. In this program, the student is in regular class full time.

Communication Approaches and Supports

Oral Approaches

A deaf or hard of hearing child who learns via an oral approach typically learns to take advantage of auditory, visual and tactile input. Much attention is given to auditory training, talking, speechreading, and amplification . Usually, oral programs emphasize the development of residual hearing and the exercise and development of intelligible speech. Research suggests that significant successes in this type of program tend to occur in fully integrated school programs, and in subjects with above-average IQ test scores, whose parents are fully involved and supportive, and who have above-average socioeconomic status (Geers & Moog, 1989; Paul & Quigley, 1990).

The following is a brief description of some of the methods used under the rubric of oralism. Educators and parents who wish to investigate any of these ideas further, might begin with the information available from the Canadian Hearing Society.

Speechreading

This is a process wherein a person receives a message principally by observing a speaker's face, paying special attention to the lips, and expressions and gestures in the face, body and hands. Speechreading is enhanced if the receiver is aware of and familiar with the context of the speech, but complications make this method only one avenue among others for deaf persons to receive information. Very few deaf persons rely on it exclusively.

Auditory Training

This process teaches a child to use what residual hearing she has. Also called the *auditory method* and *auditory learning,* it operates on the principle of teaching the child to learn how to listen rather than just learning how to hear. Advocates argue that only a very few children are unable to benefit from this training especially if it is begun as early as possible. Essentially, the method involves first the development of awareness of sound, then the ability to make gross discriminations among sounds in the environment, and finally the ability to discriminate among speech sounds. Supporters argue for the earliest possible use of amplification, as well as simultaneous training in speech production.

Specialized Styles

There are a number of individual and unique ideas that appear in the field from time to time, and often attract a great deal of attention because of both active support and active criticism. Two such, that have gained attention and that, while not very widespread in their use, are fiercely supported by their respective advocates, are the *cued speech method* and the *acoupedic method.* The first uses a combination of oral and manual styles. Attempts to develop the individual's residual hearing capacity and the capacity for speech are supported by eight manual configurations and four hand positions to supplement the visual manifestations of speech. The originator of cued speech, Orin Cornett, claims it can be learned in 12 to 15 hours by anyone of average intelligence.

The acoupedic method, on the other hand, excludes all visual clues in order to encourage the individual to use residual hearing to the maximum extent possible.

Manual Approaches

American Sign Language* (ASL)

In May, 1993, Ontario became the first Canadian province to authorize the use of ASL (and LSQ, Langue de Signes Québécoise) as a language of instruction for deaf students. Ontario schools for the deaf now use ASL, and written English, and allow students opportunities to use and develop their auditory and speech potential.

The predecessor of ASL is FSL, French Sign Language. It was developed as a one hand signing system by Abbé Charles Michel de l'Épée (1712-1784). The abbot also founded an institution for the deaf in Paris, in 1770.

ASL is a true language in itself, quite different from spoken language, and most emphatically not a translation of English into manually communicated words. ASL has its own vocabulary, its own grammar, its own word order, and its own history. American Sign Language is founded on combinations of symbolic gestures produced by the shape, the location, and the movement of the hands. Whereas methods like *Total Communication* (see following) very often employ iconic signs, in which the shape of the sign encodes English as much as possible, the signs of ASL are unique. Many of the ASL signs symbolize concepts rather than individual words. ASL has no signs for the grammatical markers, such as *ed* and *ing,* that express verb tense and condition. Rather, users depend on facial expression and body language to replace voice intonation and enhance meaning. ASL tends to be learned by deaf children in special settings like schools, rather than being passed on by parents in the way that language is learned by most hearing people.

Fingerspelling

This method spells out the letters of the English alphabet by using various finger positions on one hand. As a technique, it is often used as one part of the *Total Communication* method and *Rochester Method*. The alphabet in Figure 11C is the one presented by the National Association for the Deaf in the U.S. Members of the Canadian Hearing Society have varied in their endorsement of fingerspelling.

Combination Approaches

Although a deaf or hard of hearing person's communication approach is likely to emphasize one rather than several methods, she will invariably avail herself of other sources for information (like facial expressions, body language, etc.) in the same way as a hearing person. However, within the canon of communication styles advocated for the deaf, there are approaches that operate from this multi-source position both practically and philosophically. Two of these approaches are the *Rochester method* and *Total Communication*.

The Rochester method uses fingerspelling in conjunction with speech, speechreading, and amplification.

Total Communication may be defined as the use of speech, speechreading, fingerspelling and amplification, along with the simultaneous use of a school-based manual system. In a school-based total communication system, signs are usually taught in the same order as language. This teaches the child to communicate manually using English syntax. Also, unlike ASL, the signs tend to attempt to reflect English syntax.

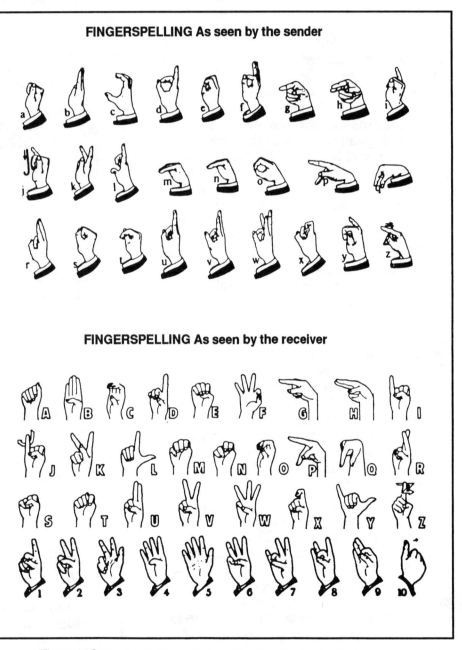

Figure 11C (Reprinted with permission of The Canadian Hearing Society.)

Worth noting is that some classrooms use ASL as part of a Total Communication approach. In any case, even those advocates who strongly support ASL to the exclusion of all else, acknowledge the potential usefulness of other support like speechreading and hearing aid technology.

Hearing Aid Technology

There was a time not long ago when fitting someone with a hearing aid meant installing a device that simply amplified incoming sound. While the basic advantage of such a system is obvious, the accompanying drawbacks were often significant. Although straight amplification is still available today and in many cases is entirely adequate for the user, the technology has become far more sophisticated and versatile. In most cases, the professionals who assess hearing (audiologists and audiometrists) can not only point to where on the range of decibels and range of hertz an individual has hearing problems, they can also point to assistive devices that can be customized to address those problems. This technological step represents somewhat of a revolution for people with a hearing loss for it means that, in many cases, they are able to acquire hearing aids (granted, at significant expense) which compensate for loss without adding new problems by amplifying other sounds unnecessarily.

In the classroom, this technology can be generalized across a very wide spectrum. One example, and there are many, is a system that uses FM radio band technology. In this system, the teacher (and/or other students) wears a transmitter and the deaf student(s) a receiver. For the deaf student, the amount of classroom ambient noise is usually less obtrusive, with sounds coming principally from whomever is wearing the transmitter. The system — between speaker and listener at least — is cordless.

However, it is important to recognize that this is only one of many systems recently developed primarily for classroom use. Thus it is important for educators involved in the acquisition of technological support for students who are deaf or who have a hearing loss, to investigate the options thoroughly, particularly in seeking out recent developments, and in seeking out the possibilities for customization of the support.

Ironically, in an age that turns readily to technology in almost every facet of life, less than a third of people who could be helped by hearing aids, actually own and use one (Schein, 1994).

Educational Implications of Hearing Loss

❖ All other factors, like quality of instruction, being equal, deaf and hard of hearing students usually do not have an easy time in school, academically, mostly because of what is in effect, a language barrier. Studies over several decades (see Allen, 1986, for example) suggest that academic achievement is affected by five elements more than any other. These are the severity of the hearing loss, the chronological age at onset, intelligence, socioeconomic status of the family,

Possible Indications of Mild to Moderate Hearing Loss in Children

In primary classrooms especially, children who experience more than the usual frequency of colds, earaches, sore throats, etc. need to be watched carefully for signs of the hearing problems that often follow. As well, the following signs merit attention, especially if a teacher or teaching assistant notices them consistently.

- Poor articulation, especially consonants, when not attributable to a factor like age, or a different first language
- Loud speech (and singing) in situations that do not require it
- Physical signs (like cocking the head)
- Trouble following directions or answering simple questions
- Unusually frequent requests for repetition
- Unusual inattentiveness

The possiblity of a hearing loss should always be considered by teaching professionals assessing a student's behaviour problems and/or failure to meet academic potential.

and hearing status of the parents; (a deaf student of deaf parents is considered to have a better chance for academic success than if the parents are hearing).

The same studies invariably point to achievement test scores for the deaf being significantly lower than the scores of hearing controls, even on specially adapted test instruments. However, it behooves educators to consider whether this lower performance is simply the result of a bad fit between the real abilities of deaf students and the way achievement is measured. Even though deaf students may lag in reading and other language skills, teachers must be on guard against interpreting a difficulty with language as an inherent lack of ability. Still, whatever the teacher's attitude toward her deaf students, the issue of language development and its effective use will be a principal, likely *the* principal, educational consideration.

❖ The difficulties deaf students have in communicating often lead to exaggerated compensatory behaviours or to frustration that is expressed in ways which cause them to be unfairly labelled as disturbed, or odd, or even mentally handicapped. In the past it was not unusual to find deaf students of normal intellectual and emotional mein, placed in segregated classes because of what was perceived to be retardation or disturbed behaviour. There has even developed over time, a so-called 'psychology of the deaf', in which the characteristics of deaf people are sometimes described in very unflattering language. One result of this perception of the deaf, no matter what its accuracy or its origins, is reinforcement of the isolation that deaf students frequently describe as the worst part of living in a hearing world. Being aware of and responding to this factor is very important for teachers and teaching assistants of integrated classrooms.

When There's a Signing Interpreter In Class

(Most frequently in this situation, the interpreter will sit with the class and face the instructor, while the deaf student will sit with the class and face the interpreter.)

- Be prepared for significant distraction at first. *It will pass.*
- Both interpreter and his or her client will benefit from a summary of the lesson about to be taught.
- Be conscious of the lag time between speech and its translation into sign.
- A visual aid (e.g., a transparency) means the deaf student has two stimuli to process with one sensory organ. (Not dissimilar, in the case of a hearing person, to being addressed by two people at once.)

❖ The classroom environment plays a major role in accommodating the needs of a student who has a hearing loss. Although matters such as locating the student's desk are always taken into immediate account by most teachers and teaching assistants, there are other issues that recent technological analyses have shown to be important. One of these is the amount of echo in the classroom, technically referred to as *reverberation* (the amount of time it takes for a sound to decrease to 60 dB [decibels] after it is turned off). Naturally, the more reverberation can be reduced, the less likely a student with hearing loss will experience interference. Interestingly, the impact of reverberation on students with normal hearing can be very significant too, a fact which makes reverberation reduction through the use of carpeting, acoustical ceiling tiles, and drapes, a matter for serious consideration.

❖ Yet another issue is signal-to-noise ratio. This is the dB level of the speaker divided by the dB level of the ambient sounds in the room. The higher the latter, the lower the ratio and, naturally, the lower the ratio, the more difficulty a deaf or hard of hearing student will experience. Signal-to-noise ratio is a powerful argument for advocates who support congregated classrooms for deaf and hard of hearing.

❖ Whether a deaf student has an interpreter, or has amplification devices, or uses total communication — whatever the approach — communicating is very hard work, both as a consequence of the concentration needed to receive information and of the effort needed to send it. Deaf students get very tired, usually more so than their hearing peers, and teachers must recognize this.

❖ Meaningful cooperation with the hearing world can be difficult to achieve. Deaf persons often describe their experiences with others in societal control (e.g., police, and other official-dom) as unsatisfactory. An important responsibility of educators because of their potential for extensive contact with deaf and hard of hearing persons is to sensitize the hearing public to their needs.

✔STRATEGIES FOR THE CLASSROOM

The following suggestions are collected from deaf and hard of hearing students who were asked to offer advice to teachers and educational assistants in regular classes.

(1) Seat her toward the front of the room and to one side with the better ear toward the teacher and class. Otherwise seat in the second seat from the front, second row from the window, or similar setting, but always with light on the teacher's face.

(2) Permit the student to move her seat if the teaching centre moves to another part of the room.

(3) A deaf student needs to see the speaker's face. Seat him two to three metres away from the place where you do most of your talking. Keep your hands away from your face.

(4) From time to time attempt to keep your mouth near the level of the student's eyes. For example, instead of always standing, sit at your desk at certain times.

(5) Be sure to have the student's visual and aural attention before giving assignments or announcements.

(6) Make a practice of asking *both* hearing and hard of hearing students to repeat directions for the benefit of the whole class. Ask the student to repeat instructions to ensure he understands.

(7) Do not turn your back while talking. Do not talk while writing on the chalkboard; a moving target is impossible to speech read. Do not walk around the room while talking about important things.

(8) Don't use loud tones or exaggerated mouth movements. Use the same tone of voice and the same inflection you use for everyone else. Avoid gestures. Excessive gestures draw attention away from the face and lips. They're embarrassing too.

(9) Many words sound the same — blue, blew; tax, tacks. This is confusing enough. But many words that do not sound the same look the same on the lips — e.g., *bat, pat, mat* look alike as do *bad, pad, mad*. Words that look alike on the lips are called homophones. Even an expert at speech reading misunderstands directions or questions. It is essential, therefore, that when dictating spelling words for example, you use them in sentences to give the student a clue.

(10) It may be helpful to explain to other students that many words look alike. Let the class try to speech read a few sentences. This procedure will help others in the class to understand. Understanding helps eliminate teasing and unfair judgements.

(11) During a discussion, ask questions to ensure that the person with hearing loss understands. If she does not understand, restate the material in a different way. Perhaps she was not familiar with the key words that you used, or some of them may have looked like other words.

N.B. (12) Names of people and places, especially new ones, are very difficult to understand. It is well to place new words or terms on the chalkboard and discuss new material from this vocabulary.

(13) Assign a 'buddy' to help explain things. A buddy can be a great fallback, but watch out for too much dependence.

(14) Try rephrasing rather than repeating. But be sure a rephrase does not add confusion.

(15) If the person with a hearing loss is completely lost, say quietly "I'm talking about . . ." This often gives her a fresh start. But be discreet!

(16) If the student seems to have trouble with certain words repeatedly, use these words often in as many ways as possible.

(17) Find out if he has a good ear and speak to that side.

(18) If your class has group discussions or cooperative learning activities, a round table is better for a deaf student than a rectangular one.

(19) If you have a good relationship with your deaf student, you can tell him when his speaking is too loud or when it's getting on other students' nerves.

(20) Encourage participation in extra-curricular activities. Deaf students are like any others. They take their lead from their teachers.

(21) *If a visit is being planned,* or a visitor is coming, prepare for it. Write new and unusual words on the chalkboard; help the deaf student become familiar with the names of persons or objects she will be seeing. Explain any special rules ahead of time when you can be sure that she understands them. The brief discussion will help her associate lip movements with new words and promote her understanding of their meaning. By telling the student in advance what unit of activity will be studied, she has an opportunity to find material on the subject and will be able to follow along much better because she will be more familiar with the vocabulary.

Always, in history, or science, and geography lessons where there will be new vocabulary or new concepts, try to give the student a brief written statement, e.g., "Today's topic is the Introduction of The War of 1812. Key words are Niagara Frontier, Sir Isaac Brock, York, James Madison", etc.

(22) *Deaf students tire more easily* than others. You can help by planning the day's work so the periods when they must pay attention are interspersed with other activities.

(23) *Encourage the student* to keep trying. Please be patient. Repeat instructions as often as necessary.

(24) *If possible, try to help* the student learn to use a dictionary pronunciation key.

For Discussion: the Case of Nils

Nils' thirteenth birthday was more dramatic, if not traumatic, than most such days for a young adolescent. To begin with, on that day he boarded a plane in Stockholm, with his mother, to come to Canada. She had accepted a three-year diplomatic posting, with an option of a three-year extension.

On the day of their arrival, Nils and his mother learned their first lesson in Canadian geography: the school for deaf students that had agreed to accept him was too far away from his new home for him to be a day student. Even more distressing, they learned that the school used a communication style quite different from that which Nils used. From age six, Nils had attended a private, residential school for the deaf that uses sign exclusively. Moreover, the style of signing is one the school has developed, and it is quite significantly different from any form of sign used in any general way in North America. This difference might not have been an issue for Nils in his home country, for the school provides personal interpreters for students who leave to enrol in neighbourhood schools. However, with Nils' move to Canada, the matter has become far more complicated.

Over a series of meetings during the first month of his life in Canada, (which fortuitously, was during the summer vacation) Nils and his mother have decided, and the local (Ontario) board has agreed, that he will enrol in the neighbourhood school. At this point, however, the boy and his mother have a further decision to make, choosing from among these options:

1. The Swedish diplomatic service will provide and pay for a personal, in-class, signing interpreter trained in the signing style used by Nils' former school.

2. Given that Nils has some residual hearing (his loss is severe to profound but he wears two powerful and sophisticated hearing aids) one consultant has recommended that a style of Total Communication be used.

3. Inasmuch as Nils is already familiar with sign, that style can be continued, but using ASL.

4. Some combination of the above.

One piece of good news for Nils is that the teacher of the class where he will attend is both qualified and interested in special education. She acknowledges that she has preferences in the matter of communication, but has pointed out in meetings with Nils and his mother, that she will happily accommodate whatever decision is made.

Nils' school career has demonstrated that he is both very bright and very resourceful, and although his language skills are typically lagging behind those of his hearing peers, his superiority in subject areas like mathematics suggest that he would likely respond to any or all of the above. The question to be solved: what is best for him?

(25) Note that many students hear better on some days than others.

(26) Talk with the deaf students every day. Talk often, rather than for a long time. Ask questions about movies seen, T.V. programs, hobbies, travel, work, etc.

(27) A hearing aid makes speech louder. It does not make speech clearer. It also amplifies all the other noise. See if some of the other noise can be reduced.

(28) If it has not already been investigated, look into the possibility of using an FM system. This system can be more effective in a classroom than a hearing aid.

(29) There is a lot of computer software that is really helpful. The computer is patient too and doesn't get tired of repeating something. If the student is in control of the keyboard, the number of repeats then is just what is needed. Not too many. Not too few. While you are at it, most computers with sound capacity will take earphones. Earphones are always better for people with a hearing loss. It concentrates the sound and blocks out all the background. Half the time it's the background that's the problem anyway.

N.B. (30) *(Author's note:* The following is verbatim (orally) from a very bright twelve-year-old student with a severe hearing loss.) *"Our teaching assistant this year was the best help I ever had. And she wasn't a hearing specialist. Couldn't sign or nothing. But she was helpful. You don't really need a specialist very often. Just a good T.A."*

READINGS & RESOURCES

For Further Investigation

Allen, T. (1986) Patterns of academic achievement among hearing impaired students, in Schildroth, A., & Karchmer (Eds.), *Deaf children in America*, San Diego: Little Brown.

Counterpoint. (1992). Deaf Students invited to eye their futures. *Counterpoint*, p.17.

Davis, J. (Ed.). (1990). *Our forgotten children: Hard of hearing pupils in the schools* (2nd edition.). Bethesda, MD: Self Help for Hard of Hearing People.

Feher-Prout, T. (1996). Stress and coping in families with deaf children. *Journal of Deaf Studies and Deaf Education. 1*, 155-166.

Geers, A. & Moog, J. (1989). Factors productive of the development of literacy in profoundly hearing impaired adolescents. *The Volta Review*, 91, 69-86.

Greer, A.E., & Tobey, E. (1992). Effects of cochlear implants and tactile aids on the development of speech production skills in children with profound hearing impairment. *The Volta Review, 94*, 135-163.

Jacobs, L.M. (1989). *A deaf adult speaks out* (3rd ed.) Washington, DC: Gallaudet Press.

Jaussi, K. R. (1991). Drawing the outsiders in: deaf students in the mainstream. *Perspectives for teachers of the hearing impaired*, 9, 12-15.

Karchmer, M.A., Petersen, L.M., Allen, T.E., & Osborn, T.I. (1981). *Highlights of the Canadian survey of hearing impaired children and youth*. Washington, D.C.: Gallaudet College, Office of demographic studies.

Moores, D.F. & Meadow-Orlans, K.P. (Eds.) (1990). *Educational and Developmental Aspects of Deafness* (Gaulladet Univ. Press).

Padden, C., & Humphries, T. (1988). *Deaf in America: Voices from a Culture*. Harvard University Press.

Paul, P.U., & Quigley, S.P. (1987). Some effects of hearing impairment on early language development, in *Hearing Disorders in Children: Pediatric Audiology*. Austin, TX: Pro-Ed.

Quigley, S.P., & Paul, P.V. (1992). *Language and deafness*. San Diego: Singular Publishing.

Schein, J. (1994). "Deafness in Canada and the United States", *Deaf American Monographs*, 93-99.

Schildroth, A.N., & Hontto, S.A. (1994). Inclusion or exclusion? Deaf students and the inclusion movement. *American Annals of the Deaf, 139*, 239-243.

Schirmer, B.R. (1994). *Language and literacy development in children who are deaf*. Needham Heights, MA: Allyn & Bacon.

Stokoe, W.C., Casterline, D.C. & Croneberg, C.G. (1976). *A Dictionary of American Sign Language on Linguistic Principles* (2nd ed.), Linstock Press.

Stone, P. & Adam, A. (1986). Is your child wearing the right hearing aid?: Principles for selecting and maintaining amplification, *Volta Review*, 88, 45-54.

Vernon, M. & Andrews, J. (1990). *The Psychology of Deafness: Understanding Deaf and Hard of Hearing People*. New York: Longman.

Vygotsky, L.S. (1962). *Thought and Language*. New York: Wiley.

For the Classroom Teacher

Bergman, T. (1989). *Finding a common language: Children living with deafness*. Milwaukee, WI: Gareth Stevens.

Flatley, J.K. & Gittinger, D.J. (1990). Teaching abstract concepts: keys to the world of ideas, *Perspectives for Teachers of the Hearing Impaired*, 8, 7-9.

Gaty, J.C. (1992). Teaching speech to hearing impaired children. *The Volta Review*, 94, 49-61.

Gdowski, B.S., Sanger, D.D. & Decker, T. N. (1986). Otitis-media: effect on a child's learning, *Academic Therapy*, 21, 283-291.

Greenburg, J. E. (1985). *What is the sign for friend?* New York: Franklin Watts.

Hearing and Communication - All Division resource guide (1992). MET - Pub# 104169

Holt, J., & Marshall, W. (1994). *Classroom attributes and achievement scores for deaf and hard of hearing students*. Silver Speng MD: Registry of interpreters of the deaf.

Kluwia, T., Moores, D. & Gaustad, M. (Eds.) (1992). *Toward Effective Public School Programs for Deaf Students: Context, Process, and Outcomes*. New York: Teachers College Press.

Luetke-Stahlman, B. & Luckner, J. (1991). *Effectively Educating Students With Hearing Impairments*, (Longmans).

Sanders, D.M. (1988). *Teaching deaf children: techniques and methods*. Boston: College-Hill.

Schirmer, B.R. (1995). Mental Imagery and the Reading Comprehension of Deaf Children. *Reading Research and Instruction*, 34, 177-188.

Very valuable material on curriculum development and teaching methods for the deaf, along with specialized information in the form of videos, films, books for children and adolescents, are available from a variety of sources including:

The Canadian Association of the Deaf/Association des sourds du Canada #205, 2435 Holly Lane, Ottawa ON, K1V 7P2 (613)526-4785.

Canadian Hard of Hearing Association/Association des malentendants canadiens (same address as above) (613)526-1584.

Canadian Hearing Society, 271 Spadina Road, Toronto, ON, M5R 2V3 (416)964-9595; TTY 526-9292.

The Gaulladet Bookstore (of Gaulladet College) Box 103, Kendall Green P.O., Washington, D.C., 20002 (202)651-5380.

12

Students Who Are Blind
or Partially Sighted

" TRY THIS. Close your eyes for a full hour — if you can! And just listen to the noise. That's my biggest challenge. Noise. I need to get information. But picking the <u>right</u> sounds . . . Not easy."
—Sarah-Lynne Neb, student, aged 16

Misconceptions About Blindness and Partial Sight

1. Blind people have no sight at all.

Only a small percentage of legally blind people have absolutely no vision. The majority have a useful amount of functional vision.

2. Legally blind people use braille as their primary method of reading.

The majority use print — often large type — as a primary source of reading. An increasing trend among blind people who cannot see print is to use audio technology — recordings and other conversions of print — rather than braille.

3. An extra sense enables blind people to detect obstacles.

Blind people do not possess an extra sense, but often develop a strong sensitivity to nearby objects especially if they have the ability to hear.

4. The blind automatically develop better acuity in their other senses.

Through concentration and attention, blind persons often learn to make very fine discriminations in the sensations they obtain. This is not automatic, but rather, represents a better use of received sensations.

5. If partially sighted students use their eyes too much, their sight will deteriorate.

Only in rare conditions is this true; visual discrimination ability can actually improve through training and use. Strong lenses, holding books close to the eyes, and using the eyes does not harm vision.

6. Blind children automatically become good listeners.

Good listening is primarily a learned skill. Although many blind people develop good listening skills, it is the result of effort because they depend on these skills for so much of their information.

7. Instructing children in mobility techniques should wait until elementary or even secondary school age.

The adage of "earlier the better" applies to blind children as easily as to their sighted peers. Even the use of a cane at an early age has been shown to have advantages.

8. Seeing-eye dogs take blind people where they want to go.

The proper term is *guide dog* (or *dog guide*). It does not "take" the blind person anywhere; the person must first know where he or she is going. The dog is primarily a safeguard against dangerous areas or obstacles.

9. Using the long cane is simple and natural.

The task is not simple. There are specifications not just for using the cane but for its manufacture as well.

Definitions of Blindness

Legal blindness in Canada is defined as a distance acuity of 6/60 m or 20/200 ft. or less in the better eye after the best available correction. That means the person must stand at six meters or less to see an object which would normally be seen at sixty meters. Persons whose visual field is reduced to an angle of twenty degrees or less at its widest diameter are also legally blind. (Normally sighted people have a visual field of 180 degrees.) A partially sighted person is one whose distance acuity is 6/13 or less in the better eye. It is important to recognize that someone with visual acuity of 6/60 can probably read, or at least *see*, print. Total blindness, i.e., inability to see anything at all, is actually uncommon.

Classifications are usually presented as follows:

Near normal vision. These individuals are able to function without special training, but will use corrective lenses.

Moderate functional impairment. People in this group require specialized aids and lighting.

Reduction in central vision. A moderate field loss. People with this disability may qualify for special services as legally blind.

Low vision. Even after correction, vision is lower than normal, although correction is usually very helpful.

Poor functional vision and possible poor central vision with marked field loss. For this condition, standard correction is of little or no benefit. Usually strong reading aids and other technologies are needed instead.

Blind. Total field loss as well as total detail loss. May, in some cases, distinguish between lightness and darkness.

Some Typical Causes of Blindness

Retinal detachment: The retina can become separated through injury or disease, making it incapable of receiving images.

Retinoblastoma: a known genetic disease that presents with malignant tumors. Treatment usually involves chemotherapy and local eye-saving measures. According to the Ontario Cancer Institute, the majority of eyes are salvaged. The Institute advises genetic counseling for the families involved.

Retinopathy of Prematurity (formerly known as *Retrolental fibroplasia):* a condition occurring in babies who are exposed to a greater than normal concentration of oxygen post-natally.

Rubella: a syndrome occurring as a result of maternal rubella infection during the first months of pregnancy.

Sympathetic ophthalmia: When there is a penetrating wound to one eye, the other eye may reflect the same characteristics as the injured eye.

Some Typical Causes of Partial Sight

Albinism: A known genetic disease in which the eyes are light sensitive. Minimum illumination is needed, and tinted glasses are usually prescribed.

Astigmatism: This defect causes an error in refraction. Images are blurred and there is generally poor visual discrimination. Glasses are prescribed, usually with positive results. Good illumination usually helps too.

Cataracts: Any lens opacity is a cataract. Such an opacity causes blank areas in what is seen. Depending upon the nature of the opacity, adjustments in lighting are usually necessary.

Colour deficiency (a.k.a. *colour blindness*): unable to distinguish colours. More boys than girls are affected.

Glaucoma: a problem caused by increased intraocular pressure. Glaucoma patients require constant medical attention and sometimes suffer headaches. Quite often peripheral vision is poor. Good illumination is recommended.

Hyperopia: The hyperopic eye is far-sighted. A student with this condition usually functions well in gross motor activity but finds reading and other near work difficult and tiring until correction is provided.

Macular degeneration: The centre of the field of vision blurs causing most detail to be lost. Some peripheral vision usually remains but with limited strength.

Monocular vision: Through disease, accident, or defect, a person is left with only one seeing eye.

Myopia: The myopic eye is near-sighted. Distance vision is blurred so that gross activities can be difficult. A student with this condition is more comfortable with reading and other close work.

Nystagmus: The involuntary movement of the eyeball caused by this problem makes focusing and fixation difficult.

Optic atrophy: The optic nerve sustains permanent loss of its ability to carry clear images to the brain. A person may have restricted fields of vision. Visual behaviour may be inconsistent.

Peripheral vision: This is the ability to see only those activities and objects outside of the direct line of vision. Because of defective central vision, the student may have to tilt the head or raise or lower the eyes in order to read.

Retinitis pigmentosa: Pigment deposits in the retina cause loss of peripheral fields resulting in tunnel vision. Major difficulties occur in dim light. Good illumination is needed.

On Being Blind: Words by Ginny de V.

"... what took me till adulthood to realize, was how much sighted people talk to each other with their bodies — I mean — I still don't actually see it, but I'm more sensitive to it now that I know. You see I always talk a lot — can't you tell? — and most of the time I just keep on going until someone stops me — well, wouldn't you?

Anyway I didn't understand that sighted people have all these ways of saying 'shut up' without actually saying it — you know? Like — they turn away, or they stand up suddenly. Stuff like that. I never interpreted that as 'shut up' even when I knew it was happening, until someone told me about it. I'm glad I was told though. It helps to know. That's one of the things about being blind. Everybody treats you with kid gloves. We don't need that. We're people too. We've got to be told to shut up too just like everybody else. I mean ..."

Strabismus: An imbalance of the eye muscles causes failure of the two eyes to focus on the same object. The eyes can cross or eyes deviate upward or downward. Early treatment is vital, or a "lazy eye" (amblyopia) can result.

Tunnel vision: The field of vision is so reduced that a child sees only what is directly in front. It creates the same visual image that others see when looking through a tube or a straw. This severely affects a person's mobility and the collection of information from the environment.

Some Issues in the Field

■ Perhaps the most significant issue for blind and partially sighted people is successful adjustment to the world at large. This adjustment calls for mobility and a sensitivity to the environment that is natural in sighted persons but not so in those whose vision is limited. Much of a blind person's energy, life force, education, and time, are devoted to this matter, especially when they are young. At the same time, because they are normal human beings in every other respect, blind people naturally wish to live the lives that the rest of the world does. A great deal of the initial social exchange between visually disabled people and the sighted people in their lives is devoted to finding a mutually comfortable, appropriate and effective means of associating.

■ The failure of individuals and families to have regular eyesight examinations continues to be a nagging concern of health care professionals and educators. Infants as young as three months can now be tested with considerable accuracy. Optometrists urge that all children be examined by three years of age and again at school entrance. This is because many vision problems are more correctable if a response is made early. It is also important to begin teaching visual *efficiency* early, if visual *acuity* is poor or weakening. Testing is especially important if there is a familial pattern of such problems as strabismus, cataracts, etc. Despite the logical and impassioned arguments of both educators and health professionals, the response of families and even educational jurisdictions to the need for early and regular eye examinations is, surprisingly, less intense than one might expect, given the ease and limited expense with which these examinations can be conducted.

■ Treating learning disability as a vision problem was not uncommon in the early to mid-1970's and still has some residual currency today, even though evidence of the connection is hard to find. A student presumed to have learning disabilities should always have his vision checked, but only to determine whether his academic difficulties are being caused by poor vision, not to find a visual/learning disability connection.

Some Educational Implications of Special Visual Needs

❖ Empirical evidence suggests that in the classroom, especially among younger students, cognitive abilities in the blind and partially sighted

Classroom Checklist of Possible Vision Problems

Although the ultimate diagnosis of a student's visual problem — or even its existence — would naturally be determined by an optometrist or ophthalmologist, teachers and educational assistants can play an important role in early detection. While this is a more common occurrence in the very early grades, teachers of older students should not exclude themselves since eye disease and poor vision can begin at any stage in life and grow serious rapidly. Any of the characteristics in the Classroom Checklist, especially if observed over time, might indicate real or potential visual impairment.

1. Appearance of eyes
- One eye turns in or out at any time?
- Reddened eyes or lids?
- Encrusted eyelids?
- Frequent styes on lids?
- Eyes tear excessively?

2. Complaints by student
- Headaches in forehead or temples?
- Burning or itching of eyes after reading or deskwork?
- Nausea or dizziness?
- Print blurs or moves after reading a short time?

3. Behavioural signs of visual problems
- Head turns while reading across the page?
- Loses place often during reading?
- Needs finger or marker to keep place?
- Tilts head extremely while working at desk?

- Rereads or skips lines unknowingly?
- Too frequently omits or substitutes words?
- Complains of seeing double (diplopia)?
- Misaligns number columns regularly?
- Squints, closes or covers one eye?
- Consistently shows gross postural deviations?
- Orients a worksheet unusually?
- Must feel things to understand?
- Disorderly placement of words or drawings on page?
- Blinks excessively at desk tasks?
- Blinks to clear chalkboard after near task?
- Holds book too closely?
- Avoids all possible near-centred tasks?
- Closes or covers one eye when reading?
- Squints to see chalkboard?
- Rubs eyes a great deal?

tend to develop more slowly than the norm. There is a good deal of support for the view, however, that this apparent lag is owing more to differentiated early learning experiences rather than to any inherent intellectual difference. Blind children simply have not had the opportunity to experience some of the things that sighted children have.

❖ It is difficult for students with serious vision problems to develop a spatial map of their environment. However, it is possible to develop the concept of space with other senses, such as noting the time it takes to walk various distances, or feeling the dimensions between objects. Because the amount of information that can be taken in at one time is limited, the process is understandably slower. This fact makes the time to acquire learning an important factor — as it is with almost all students with exceptionalities.

❖ For students who cannot see, or who see poorly, it is often difficult to understand abstract concepts without the aid of concrete materials. Such students then, will benefit from three-dimensional models, exaggerated bas-relief maps and globes, manipulative games and materials.

❖ Blind and partially sighted students are often overprotected by the adults in their lives and treated over-delicately by fellow students. Although this is not an unnatural response, it is important that independence be a prominent and continuing objective in the education of students with vision problems. Fostering this independence calls for frequent and delicate judgments by the teacher.

❖ Blind students must be taught social and communicative skills that many sighted persons acquire naturally (at least some of the time). Most cultures, for example, attach great importance to whether or not a speaker looks at her listener, and many advocates for the blind urge that this habit be taught. However, some so-called natural skills are much more difficult to teach. For example, sighted people make constant use — albeit subconsciously much of the time — of a system of communication that has come to be called 'body language': important markers that indicate responses like reinforcement, enthusiasm, reluctance, disagreement, uneasiness, etc. Body language thus enables an alert speaker to detect the need to modify a particular communication. Sometimes even

more important, it is body language that indicates whether or not a communication is finished — or should be! For obvious reasons, the very notion of body language, and the means of dealing with it is something that blind and partially sighted students cannot be expected to acquire naturally.

❖ The less a person is able to know the world through sight, the more important it becomes that she be a good listener. Although it was assumed in the past that good listening skills automatically develop as a consequence of sight deprivation, it is now known that such skills must be taught.

❖ Professionals dealing with the very young must be particularly conscious of the fact that many children are not aware of a visual problem if they have one. Or if they are aware, they often do not understand its extent or its implications. This is important for the teacher, not just in discovering the presence of the problem, but in helping the child to deal with it.

❖ For educators, a point of importance is recognizing that academic success is more closely related to social, cultural, and familial factors than to degree of visual impairment.

Education and Communication Technology

Braille

This well-known writing system is named for Louis Braille, who was responsible for the system currently in use, but Braille was not, in effect, the inventor: more a modifier. The system originated in the hands of Charles Barbier, an officer in the army of Napoleon Bonaparte. Barbier devised a system of raised dot writing that could be read by touch in the dark. He called it *écriture nocturne*. It was enthusiastically received by the Academy of Sciences in France in 1808, but proved somewhat impractical for the blind. Braille published his modified system in 1834. Within twenty years it was adopted by the Paris School for the Blind, but took another half century to penetrate North America.

Braille is a tactile communication method. Cells of from one to six raised dots on paper represent the letters of the alphabet (and numbers). Although it is a direct transliteration of

English (or other language) braille resorts to contractions regularly to save time and space. (For example, in English braille, the letter 'r' by itself means 'rather'.) Although it has been established that braille is easier to read than raised letters of the alphabet, it is still a much slower process than reading print is for the average sighted reader.

Students can begin learning braille in the first grade, and have a number of technologies available to them, beginning with braille books. A brailler is a six key device not unlike a typewriter. (Integrated classrooms where a brailler is used must become accustomed to its noise.) There is also the *Optacon** which converts print into braille electronically.

Computer-Assisted Technology

Computer technology continues to develop at a rate that almost outpaces the capacity of special education to use it effectively. Some examples of recent technology — to which modifications are continually being added — are the *Versabraille II+** a laptop computer that combines brailler and word processor technology, the *Kurzweil Reading Machine** which converts print to audio output, the *DragonDictate** a speech-activated word processor, and the *Braille Blazer** which prints braille at 10-15 characters per second.

As this text is being written, the World Wide Web offers tools like an Internet browser called *ZoomText Xtra* and *Windowbridge* which translates *Windows* icons and graphics into the spoken word.**

Optical Aids

Teachers and their blind and partially sighted students are assisted by still other devices which, although they may appear simple in comparison to computer technology, are remarkable examples of technical common sense. These include items like embossed rulers and tape measures, braille watches, three

---

* Brand names are used in these descriptions. Further information about these and other technologies is available from provincial and territorial ministries of health.

** Industry Canada has a community access program to help with access to the Internet. The program has been particularly helpful in cases of the blind. Educators may wish to try their site at http:// cap.unb.ca

dimensional maps, hand-held and stand mounted magnifiers, special lighting, etc.

Mobility Assists

The *long cane* is one of the most effective and simplest devices yet devised for safe, efficient mobility. It's important to note that although the use of one seems simple to sighted people, learning to use it effectively requires some training and practice. For very young children the *Connecticut Pre-cane* has been developed but is still in the early stages of proving itself. (For more information, see Foy, C.J., et al, (1992) *Journal of Visual Impairment and Blindness*, 86 (4), pp. 178-81.)

Guide dogs are reported by their users as extremely helpful in alerting them to changes in the immediate environment, to potential dangers, and in guiding them through complex situations. The dogs are also excellent companions and many users describe them as important in connecting them socially to their communities. It is important to recognize that not every blind person will benefit from a guide dog. There are several complex and expensive hurdles to overcome, not the least of which is the training of the dog, along with training the person and then bringing the two together in what is, hopefully, a compatible relationship.

Electronic devices like laser canes and sonic guides (worn on the head) are still experimental and very expensive.

Educational Placement

Increasingly, and with marked success, blind and partially sighted students are being educated in the regular classroom. Special assistance may be delivered by an itinerant specialist teacher who provides advice on strategy, materials, and possibly on curricular modification. Such modification may be intense instruction on how to listen, how to make "mental mobility maps", etc. The assistance may also take the form of one of the educational aids listed above, or it may be a combination of aid from several sources. As with all other areas of special education, teaching assistants in the classroom have proven to be invaluable for blind and partially sighted students.

For some students, a resource room is their primary placement. This arrangement may offer a more certain guarantee of the specialized instruction they may need, but still permits a high degree of integration with the rest of the school.

A more specialized placement, used particularly for students whose vision problems are quite seriously disabling, is an entirely self-contained classroom, or even a residential school devoted to blind students (and students who are blind and have other special needs as well). In these environments, where there are usually very low pupil-teacher ratios, students receive regular school curriculum adapted to their needs, along with very specialized instruction related to their blindness.

For Discussion: the Case of Lori

When she was three years old, Lori fell off the dock at the family cottage in Muskoka. No one saw it happen because a very noisy barbecue was occupying the attention of the adults and most of the other children. As a result, Lori was in the water for what was later estimated to be about three minutes. She was unconscious when rescued but responded immediately to resuscitation. Nevertheless, both her parents and her nursery school teacher were especially watchful that fall, because Lori seemed to bump into things and fall over her playmates far more frequently than seemed normal for her age. Both teacher and parents suspected that the near-drowning incident might have caused some as yet unspecified brain injury

That suspicion was given altered focus two years later by a very observant kindergarten teacher and an equally perceptive educational assistant. After the first week of school, both instructors began to keep an "events journal" on Lori, noting specifically those behaviours that suggested Lori had impaired vision. Within ten days they were both convinced that their young student was using peripheral vision to accomplish what other students did by focusing face on. A conference with Lori's parents led to a visit with an opthalmologist and then, confirmation of what the two suspected: that Lori had macular degeneration.

The quick and careful thinking by Lori's kindergarten teacher and educational assistant, made a huge difference in her life. Macular degeneration usually means that the individual has blurred or completely obscured centre-of-field vision, while retaining some vision at the edges of the field. Very often it is progressive and intensifies over time. The early intervention in Lori's case meant that she was able to receive special training at a crucial time in her development. Lori's average to above-average ability, and what every adult in her life calls "high-profile spunk", along with this training, meant that she was able to progress quite smoothly through the next eight years of her school career. She was in a regular class in her neighbourhood school for this time.

Now, in the seventh grade, a problem has arisen. Lori's condition has worsened over time so that essentially, she has lost all her vision. For funding purposes, she has been identified as legally blind for several years now. None of this has denied her full participation in all class activities, something she and her parents insist on, even though her "accidents" have increased in number and seriousness — most recently a broken arm in gym when she missed a parallel bar during a routine performed against her gym teacher's wishes. Other difficulties have arisen as well. Lori is in the school band, but she does not have a natural ear, cannot see the notes, and plays her trombone badly — and loud. The dropout rate from the band has now reached a crisis level. Because of an incident during a natural science field trip last year (Lori fell over an embankment and pulled two other students down with her; no one was hurt) this year's cross-country skiing trip (an overnighter) can't attract enough volunteer parent supervisors and may be cancelled.

A meeting of Lori's teachers, assistants and parents has been called for next week by school officials. The agenda specifically sets aside the legal issues involved. What the administration wishes to discuss is what is best for Lori and her schoolmates in terms of their education and social development. Should her program be restricted?

✓STRATEGIES FOR THE CLASSROOM

(1) It is usually very beneficial for a teacher of a regular class with a blind or partially sighted student to establish the practice of holding regular, informal, and private discussions with that student to work out special means of communication,* or to clarify misunderstandings, to develop routines, and otherwise plan for the — usually simple — special accommodations to the student's needs. It is an ideal time for both student and teacher to learn and discover.

(2) It may be necessary for a teacher to set up the classroom with the expectation that physical arrangements will not be altered, at least for a significant period of time. While this may contradict the style a teacher likes to follow, it may be a necessity for simple reasons of safety.

(3) At the same time there is the student's normal need to be physically mobile, to explore, to expand her capacity, as well as the need to perceive the self as both part of and separate from the environment. A great deal of professional skill is demanded of teachers in marrying this need with the obvious requirements of safety and efficient function described above. The key phrase is *responsible independence*. Students need supervision of course, but the ultimate goal of it must be, as with all special education, to become unnecessary.

(4) Another vital phrase is *common sense*. A student with partial sight for example, should always be permitted to sit near the chalkboard, to borrow notes, to have another student take carbon-paper notes. (Yet the exceptionality need not be emphasized. If other students are blindfolded in an activity, the blind student should be too.) An overhead transparency can be photocopied for someone who cannot see the screen. Partially sighted students almost always respond to better lighting. Additional time may be necessary for tests or a variety of other activities. Doors should always be fully open or fully closed. *Name students being addressed*; if an instruction is given to another child, a blind child may automatically follow it with perhaps disastrous results. By the same

---

*A quite loquacious blind student in one of my classes did not sense that her extensive contributions to class discussions often wore out her classmates' receptivity. We worked out a simple and very subtle pencil tap so that she would know when to quit.
— K.W.

token, be explicit in giving instructions, particularly those involving movement from one place to another. A blind student cannot be expected to compensate for obstacles. If told to "come here", he may well come in a straight line regardless of hazards, because of his trust in the teacher.

(5) Teachers, assistants, and sighted fellow students often have to make allowances for communication style. Blind and partially blind students usually do not reinforce others with eye contact or facial expression — a phenomenon that takes some getting used to. In the same vein, the students often place great interpretive value on the expression and tone of their teacher's voice. This can be very important in some situations. Also, when a blind person responds to a communication with total silence, it may be because he is taking in and interpreting available cues. This too, requires adjustment from the teacher.

(6) "Blindisms" are characteristic mannerisms such as rocking, head shaking, hand shaking and eye poking. Most advocates suggest that teachers and educational assistants adroitly discourage these behaviours for they may isolate the student as irremediably different in a way that goes beyond merely being blind.

(7) Many blind people have grown to associate physical contact with being guided. Gestures such as patting and hugging may have negative connotations for some students, or may be misinterpreted. (Another reason for having regular, informal meetings.) When a blind person is being guided, let her be the one who maintains and controls the physical contact. Don't grab her arm and steer; let her hold your arm.

(8) A blind person who is lost or disoriented, needs *position* in order to work out *direction*. If a sighted person has occasion to help a blind person in this situation, it is important to make the blind person understand where she *is* first. Once she is oriented as best as possible, *then* explanation about direction can follow. A subset of this issue is the matter of snow-covered surfaces. Blind people often describe snow as their "fog" because the snow covers the surface references they use to orient their position. It follows then that they will often need more assistance in winter.

(9) A tactful classroom buddy or advocate is always helpful, but this should never be an unnaturally long-term arrangement.

(10) Perhaps the single most important role a teacher plays is being the classroom leader in developing a positive attitude (a crucial role in any case). Sighted students will take their cue from their teacher in determining how to react to and inter-relate with a blind student in their midst. An accepting atmosphere for this student, with realistic expectations, will build his self-esteem, his sense of success, and his willingness to deal with the world. It will also contribute in a major way to the maturing of all students in the class.

READINGS & RESOURCES

For further Investigation

Attmore, M. (1990). *Career perspectives: interviews with blind and visually impaired professionals.* New York American Foundation for the Blind.

Bailey, I.L., & Hall, A. (1990). *Visual impairment: An Overview.* New York: American Foundation for the Blind.

Bishop, V.E. (1996). *Teaching visually impaired children.* (2nd ed.). Springfield, IL: Charles C. Thomas.

Curry, S.A. (1993). A model assessment program. *Journal of Visual Impairment and Blindness, 87*(6), 190-193.

Canadian National Institute for the Blind (*CNIB*). (1993). *History of the CNIB.*

Erin, J. (1996). Children with multiple and visual disabilities. In *Children with visual impairments: A parents guide* (pp. 287-316). Bethesda, MD: Woodbine House.

MacCuspie, P.A. (1992). The social acceptance and interaction of visually impaired children in integrated settings. In S.Z. Sacks, L.S. Kekelelis, & R.J. Gaylord-Ross (Eds.). *The development of social skills by blind and visually impaired students* (pp. 83-102). New York: American Foundation for the Blind.

Warren, D. (1984). *Blindness and early childhood development.* New York: American Foundation for the Blind.

For the Classroom Teacher

American Foundation for the Blind (1991). *A picture is worth a thousand words for the blind and visually impaired person too: An introduction to audio description.* New York.

Blind and visually impaired children....Can do! Visually Impaired Preschool Services, 1215 South Third Street, Louisville, KY 40203.

Harrell, L. (1992). *Children's vision concerns: Look beyond the eyes!* Placerville, CA: L. Harrell Productions.

Heydt, K., Clark, M.J. Cushman, C., Edwards, S., & Allon, M. (1992). *Perkins activity and resource guide* (vols. 1 & 2). Waterdown, MA: Perkins School for the Blind.

Hill, E.W., & Snook-Hill, M. (1996). Orientation and Mobility. In M.C. Holdbrook (Ed.). *Children with visual impairments: A parents guide* (pp. 259-286). Bethesda, MD: Woodbine House.

Olmstead, J.E. (1991). *Itinerant teaching: Tricks of the trade for teachers of blind and visually impaired students.* New York: American Foundation for the Blind.

Sacks, S.Z. & Kekelis, L.S. (1992b). Guidelines for mainstreaming blind and visually impaired children. In S.Z. Sacks, L.S. Kekelelis, & R.J. Gaylord-Ross (Eds.). *The development of social skills by blind and visually impaired students* (pp. 83-102). New York: American Foundation for the Blind.

Scholl, G. (Ed.). (1986*). Foundations for education for blind and visually handicapped children and youth.* New York: American Foundation for the Blind.

Smith, E.S. (1987). *A guide dog goes to school: The story of a dog trained to lead the blind.* New York: Wiliam Morow.

Valuable information for teachers on matters of curriculum, resource support, technology etc. is available from:

Canadian National Institute for the Blind/ L'Institut national canadien pour les aveugles 1929 Bayview Avenue, Toronto ON, M4G 3E8 (416) 480-7580

Students With Speech and Language Disorders*

" Try this. Just for a day, or even an hour. Stop in the middle of each sentence. But leave your mouth open and make it clear you're trying to talk but can't. Then watch how others look at you. Like you've got two heads. Now think of living your life like that. "
— Ronnie Kargill.

Misconceptions About Speech and Language Disorders

1. Stuttering affects all ages and both genders equally.

Stuttering affects more boys than girls and more children than adults. The child over adult ratio is usually ascribed to the fact that, by adulthood, many people with a stutter have been helped by speech and language specialists.

2. Speech and language disorders are not related to intelligence.

Prevalence data show that although the disorders may occur among very intelligent individuals, they are found more frequently among persons with lower intellectual ability.

3. Articulation disorders, in very young children especially, are not serious, and correction is rarely worth the effort or the risk of trauma.

Although many small children have unique speech patterns, articulation disorders should never be dismissed as insignificant. "He'll grow out of it." is often an inappropriate substitute for remedial action.

4. If an individual has a speech or language disorder, she also has a learning disability.

The connection is not an absolute one, although difficulties with language affect both areas. Speech and language disorders also overlap other areas of special need, such as deafness.

*Speech and language disorders have traditionally been the responsibility of specialists in the speech and language field, and generally in Ontario, this continues to be the case. In part because speech and language therapy and remediation was solidly established in schools well before special education became more or less universal, this particular area of support tends to continue to be somewhat of a separate unit in most jurisdictions, even though, administratively, it is often grouped with special education or with psycho-educational services. Speech and language specialists work cooperatively with special educators and regular classroom teachers, but because the principal responsibility lies largely outside the domain of special education, at least in practice, what follows here is only a brief overview, offered for information purposes.

5. Speech disorders and language disorders are really the same thing.

Most people with language disorders, especially children, also have articulation problems. But it is quite common for a person to speak (i.e., articulate) clearly without making sense.

Defining Speech and Language Disorders

The development of speech and language is a complex process. How children acquire both can have a dramatic effect on their ability to understand and function in both the social and academic worlds. Communication, or the exchange of ideas, can take many forms, a word, an expression, a movement of the body. The ability to tell a joke, carry on a conversation with peers and authority figures, or whisper after lights out, are all important parts of communication. Nor does it all come from the vocal chords. Language is often spoken, but it is also gestured and certainly enhanced by tone, facial movement, and body positions and movements.

It is important to distinguish between speech and language disorders. In the field of communication, speech disorders are characterised by impairments of voice, articulation of sounds, or fluency. Language disorders encompass both receptive and expressive language and manifest in a student's inability to use and comprehend semantic and grammatical conventions.

Types of Speech Disorders

Speech disorders, while more common in particular types of populations, are not exclusive to those populations and can be found across a wide diversity of students. Diagnosis and treatment of the disorders are generally done by professionals in the field, in particular, speech and language pathologists, although it can often be a teacher or educational assistant who first notices that something may be amiss.

There is a wide range of terminology in this area of special need, so that different terms often refer to the same or very similar types of conditions.

The following are presented here because of their familiarity and frequency within the field.

Articulation disorders: Atypical production of speech sounds in a language; e.g., *rabbit — wabbit.*

Voice disorders: Atypical production of vocal quality, pitch (high/low), loudness and resonance; e.g., a harsh or whispery vocal quality.

Fluency disorder (stuttering): Abnormal flow of speech characterised by impairment of rate and rhythm; e.g., repetitions of a particular syllable of a word — *ca ca cat.*

Types of Language Disorders

As with disorders of speech, language disorders are found across a wide spectrum of the population. Students with language disorders can be at risk in the development of literacy. In the very early stages of infancy, children begin to acquire language skills. Small infants respond to voice by turning their heads and smiling. At two to three months, they start to coo, and by the age of four have approximately 1,000 to 1,500 words. By the time a child starts grade one, more complex parts of language, such as the use of irregular verbs, are being mastered.

Not all children reach these milestones for a variety of reasons. They may have difficulty hearing; some do not have the mental ability; others are not sufficiently exposed to language.

Articulation Expectations

Children typically learn to express sounds in speech very early in life. By the age of 8, most children have in their repertoire all the sounds that they will use for adult speech. The acquisition of these sounds in speech follow a similar pattern for most children.

In a normal population distribution, 90% of all children will have mastered these sounds:

By the end of age 3 — m/, n/, ng/,p/, f/, h/, w.

By the end of age 3½ — y.

By the end of age 4 — b/, d/, g/, k/, r.

By the end of age 4½ — s/, sh/, ch.

By the end of age 6 — t/, l/, v/, th (as in then).

By the end of age 7 — z/, zh (as in treasure)/, j/, th (as in three).

Some children may experience difficulty with expressive language, as in the use of incorrect tenses: *"I go to the store yesterday."* Other children may have difficulty with receptive language. A set of directions like, *"Get your red jacket from the closet and make sure to put on your scarf and mittens"*, may present a great deal of difficulty. (In the latter situation, it is not hard to understand why the complication intensifies in a school setting where this kind of instruction abounds. *"Discuss the impact of agricultural versus urban society as a root cause for the revolution."*)

Language is comprised of a variety of components, including morphology, phonology, syntax, semantics and pragmatics. These components, when impaired or not developed in any way, result in language disorders. The following are some simple examples.

Morphology: understanding and using sections of words that have meaning. (The dog *bark* when the car went by.)

Phonology: combining sounds to form words and manipulating sound sequences to form coherent speech. (brush – *bwush*)

Syntax: the rules that govern the combining of words to form coherent sentences. (What he is doing?)

Semantics: combining words and sentences to convey meaning. This may include difficulty with words that express concepts related to time and space, cause and effect, synonyms, and in general, abstract terms. (I'll go to bat for you – in reference to defending a person.)

Pragmatics: using language socially: to greet others, to request needs or information, to protest, pretend, and respond. (A child with a pragmatic language disorder may be unresponsive to normal social greetings.)

Central Auditory Processing Disorders

Some students seem not to be listening, although their hearing may be perfectly intact. More and more professionals in the speech and language field believe this is owing to a 'central auditory processing' (CAP) disorder: an inability to recognise as meaningful, acoustic signals sent to auditory areas of the brain. Normally, people generally use both ears to fuse information and to "tune out" auditory distractions (selective attention). People who demonstrate CAP difficulties may lose both messages, mix them up, or cannot integrate the information coming in via both ears.

According to specialists in speech and language disorders, students with CAP disorders generally exhibit the following types of behaviours. (However, it should be noted that the behaviours may also be associated with many students who have other types of difficulties. This is likely a reason why the notion of central auditory processing disorder has not yet been fully accepted across the broad area of special education.)

- Inconsistent response to oral speech.
- Better response to oral speech in quiet environments than in noisy environments.
- Poor response to speech in environments that distort speech, such as a gym.
- Better response to speech when the speaker is close.
- Frequent communication checks such as "what?" or "huh?"

Brent, in senior kindergarten, was the eldest of five children. For the first two months of school his only form of communication was a slight nodding of his head. Brent seemed unwilling to follow class routines, did not socialise with the other children, and refused to comply with direct requests by the teacher. While Brent eventually did begin to speak, his utterances were mumbled and scant. At times, it seemed as though his answers were designed to cause difficulty or mock the teacher.

Following kindergarten, Brent was placed in a self-contained behaviour class with an emphasis on behaviour modification. His disruptive and non-compliant behaviour persisted in the new low enrolment setting. Brent's special class teacher suggested to the in-school team that Brent have an assessment by the board's speech and language pathologist. The principal followed up on this suggestion and obtained permission from the parents to conduct the assessment. Test results showed that, in both expressive and receptive language, Brent was functioning at the age level of a two and a half-year-old, results which had profound implications for the boy.

An IPRC is to be held next week to discuss Brent's situation. Neither the teacher nor the educational assistant in the behaviour class has any training in areas of speech and language. However, they are willing to undertake any program to help Brent, as long as they are given professional advice and supervision. The school board has one full time speech and language pathologist with a very busy schedule. She visits the school twice weekly where she works with two children in a regular grade one class. If Brent were placed here, she would include him in her twice weekly sessions.

The grade one class, though, is a very busy and somewhat noisy setting, in a pod-style room with three other primary classes. The pathologist feels that given the intensity of Brent's language needs, this may not be as good a setting as the behaviour class, where things are much quieter and more controlled. The principal is now seeking opinions from other teachers on staff.

Getting Help

Many, if not all, school boards in the province employ speech and language pathologists to provide support and expertise to teachers who may suspect that a student is in need of help. What varies from board to board is the availability of these specialists to provide direct intervention on an ongoing basis. Often, there are just too many students that require support. Given that this is the case, the special education teacher or classroom teacher, with specific direction from a speech and language pathologist, may be enlisted to work directly with students to improve language skills. The intervention may involve working on a particular sound, such as 'r', or playing a word game designed to develop expressive language skills, and other relatively straightforward activities.

Where more extensive assistance is required but unavailable at the school board level, a speech and language pathologist may refer cases to government support services outside the jurisdiction of the board. Some parents may also choose to get support privately.

Clues to a Speech or Language Disorder

- Does the student follow simple directions?
- Does the student understand the meanings of words that others understand?
- Does he or she have a limited vocabulary compared with age peers?
- Does he or she understand longer, more complex sentences?
- Does the student follow the general rules of grammar?
- Does the student often have difficulty finding the correct word to express himself?

General Suggestions For Teachers

- Repeat student's comments in a more grammatically correct way.
- Structure the environment to allow for increased opportunities for interaction.
- Check for comprehension by asking the child to repeat what has been said.
- Gain the student's attention initially before speaking (eye contact, tap on the shoulder).

- Don't turn away when you are speaking. Monitor that the student is listening.

- Speak in a clear voice.

- Be aware of the level of language of the student with whom you are working.

- Paraphrase your own ideas after speaking to ensure comprehension on a variety of levels.

The Teacher's Responsibility

As indicated previously, the teacher's role is usually governed by a specialist in speech and language and will be particular to the needs of the child. The more severe the case, the more likely the teacher will be part of a team and will be fulfilling responsibilities for part of a program developed by someone else. However, since nothing in practice is as straightforward as it appears in theory, it will still be incumbent upon regular classroom teachers and special education teachers to provide leadership in several ways. These would include providing many extended opportunities for the student to talk, making the classroom an enjoyable place for him or her to work on speech and language, and modeling an appropriate response to abnormal, difficult to understand language for the student's age-peers to follow.

In short, the teacher's role with speech and language disorders is similar to that which he or she fills with all students: to be a compassionate professional who takes responsibility for developing the whole individual. An essential difference in the speech and language area lies in the tradition that considerable expert help is usually available.

Suggestions for Teachers' Voices

- Designate a signal for silence in the classroom.

- Try to address students when there is no other talking and students are attentive.

- Go to the person you wish to talk to instead of shouting across the room.

- Encourage quiet periods during the day when no talking is allowed (silent reading time).

- In the gym or on the playground, use a non-vocal way (e.g., whistle) to get attention.

- Try to humidify the environment. A closed door and plants may help.

- Curtains and carpet muffle noise.

- Keep water handy.

READINGS & RESOURCES

For Further Investigation

Beukelman, D.R., & Mirenda, P. (1992). *Augentative and alternative communication: Management of severe communication disorders in children and adults.* Baltimore: Brookes.

Bobrick, B. (1995). *Knotted tongues: Stuttering in history and the quest for a cure.* New York: Simon & Schuster.

Byrne, B., & Feildling-Barnsley, R. (1990).*Acquiring the alphabetic principle: A case for teaching recognition of phonemic identify. Journal of Educational Psychology*, 82, 805-812.

Fey, M.E. (1986). *Language intervention with young children.* Austin TX: Pro-Ed.

Gallagher, T.M. (1991). *Pragmatics of language: Clinical practical issues.* San Diego: Singular Publishing.

Hedge, M.L., & Kaiser, A.P. (1994). *Introduction to communicative disorders.* Austin, TX: Pro-Ed.

Hulit, L.M. & Howard, M.R. (1993).*Born to talk.* New York: Macmillan.

Morrison, J. & Shriberg, L. (1992). Articulation testing versus conversational speech sampling. *Journal of Speech and Hearing Research, 35*(2), 259-273.

Niedecker, E.A. (1987). *School programs in speech-language: Organization and management* (2nd ed.) Englewood Cliffs, NJ: Prentice Hall.

Nippold, M.A. (1988). *Later language development: Ages nine through nineteen*. Austin, TX: Pro-Ed.

Ownes, R. (1996). *Language development: An introduction* (4th ed.). Boston: Allyn & Bacon.

Palmer, J.M. & Yantis, P.A. (1990). *Survey of communication disorders*. Baltimore: Williams & Wilkins.

Shames, G., Wiig, E., & Secord, W. (1993). *Human communication disorders* (4th ed.). New York: Macmillan.

Stark, R.E., Bernstein, L.E. & Demorest, M.E. (1993). Vocal communication in the first 18 months of life. *Journal of Speech and Hearing Research, 36*, 548-558.

Thomas, P.J., & Carmack, F.F. (1990). *Speech and language: Detecting and correcting special needs*. Allyn & Bacon.

Wang, P.P., & Baron, M.A. (1997). Language and communication: Development and disorders. In M.L. Bathshaw (Ed.), *Children with disabilities* (4th ed.) Baltimore: Brookes.

For the Classroom Teacher

Bush, C. (1980). *Language remediation and expansion: School and home program. Communication Skill builders.* Can. Dis: Moyer Visco Corp.

Dan, J., & Hicks, K. (1987). *Games make alpha-betics fun.* Newport Beach, CA: Better Teaching Games Publication

Good Talking to you – 5 tape series on Language Simulation. Education Production Inc. 7412 SW Beaverton Hillsdale Highway, Suite 210, Portland Oregon, 97225.

Hatnes, W.O., Moran, M.J., & Pindzola, R.H. (1994*). Communication disorders in the classroom* (2nd ed.). Dubuque IA: Kendall/Hunt.

Ostrosky, M.M., & Kaiser, A.P. (1991). Pre-school environments that promote communication. *Teaching Exceptional Children, 23*, 6-10.

Ownes, R.E. (1991). *Language disorders: a functional approach to assessment and intervention* (2nd. ed.). Boston: Allyn & Bacon.

Plourde, L. (1985). *Classroom listening and speaking (CLAS)*. Tucson: communication Skill Builders.

Ward-Leeper, G. (1991*). Disorders of speech and language.* London ON: The Department of Communicative Disorders.

14

Assessment
Identifying Strengths and Needs

" The thing that surprised me most when I made the switch from private clinical practice to working for a school board, was the faith so many teachers have in tests. Faith isn't surprising in clinical practice because you're dealing with the general public mostly. But teachers are professionals. I rather expected them to be a bit more — how shall I say it — agnostic? I mean, a test can help, but it's really only as good as the person who gives it."

— Ed Seip

The Role of Assessment

If a cornerstone of special education is the Individual Education Plan (IEP), then a first step in establishing that important foundation is an educational assessment. When students are assessed, relevant information is gathered and interpreted from a variety of sources, such as curriculum-based assessments by the teacher, formal tests of the student's behaviour and abilities, observations by the teacher, assistant and parent, to name just a few. What is uncovered, at least theoretically, is some insight into an exceptional student's abilities, intelligence, strengths, needs, behaviours and so on. The discoveries help in making more informed decisions. Matters of placement, and certainly the structure and content of a student's program,

can all be refined through a competent assessment. Follow-up evaluations of a program's success or failure, or of the need for modifications in it, almost always refer to the initial assessment for comparisons.

Once regarded as the exclusive realm of specialists, assessment has moved toward a more team-oriented approach with participation, responsibility and accountability being shared by a number of key people, especially the classroom teacher who is most likely to deliver the program. Others involved include the student's parents (and occasionally, in the case of some adolescents, the student himself) the assistant, the school's special education teacher (who may be responsible for some of the more formal investigations), and, if need demands and the personnel are available and accessible, various individuals with special expertise.

The Reality of 'Loose Probability'

No matter how much teachers may desire specialized information about their students, and no matter how acculturated we may be to the belief that such truth can be revealed, the simple fact is that the very best that an educational assessment can produce is a kind of loose probability. Still, however loose, it is nonetheless an important probability. Education itself is not an exact science, and effective teaching is often much closer to art than to the mere mechanics of instruction. An assessment provides information gathered in an organized way that, at the very least, confirms in a presumably unbiased way, the view of the people working with the student. At the very best, it may reveal factors that no one had known or possibly even suspected.

Granted, there are reasons to harbour doubts about some of the procedures and components in an assessment and, quite possibly, reasons to be wary of the results, but to ignore the possible contribution of an effective assessment to an exceptional student's case would be a disservice indeed. Assessment has an important role to play. What shapes the quality of that role is the quality of the assessment procedures, and the way results are interpreted and applied.

When Are Assessments Completed?

There are those who argue that assessment happens every moment in a school. Whether they are monitoring a student's behaviour in the halls, observing while he shoots baskets in the gym or evaluating while he writes a spelling test, teachers are always provided with opportunity to collect data that will improve programming and identify needs or strengths. Assessment is an integral part of teaching. Choosing when to assess, what to observe, which piece of work to add to a portfolio, or to whom to listen in reading — these are all part of the daily challenges for classroom teachers.

However, for students who may be exceptional, the process may well go beyond the typical day to day assessment decisions that teachers make. In a situation, for example, that might be resolved with just a bit of help, a teacher may feel the need to bring the case of a student before a School Team. If so, she will usually prepare for this referral by making an initial assessment based on observation, classroom performance, portfolio, samples of the student's work and, possibly, a rating scale/checklist (especially in potential 'behaviour' cases). It is not unusual for the teacher to have engaged in curriculum-based assessment: gathering information over a period of time, of the student's performance in a particular curriculum area (like reading, or mathematics).

When a student's situation is more complicated or demanding, then in addition to the assessment described above, more intensive, formal, and specialized procedures (perhaps an IQ test or standardized achievement test, or even in some cases, a diagnostic test) will be carried out. One point when a fairly extensive assessment is sure to be carried out is prior to the development of an IEP.

In cases where a student is being identified as exceptional by an IPRC, assessment tends to be very thorough. Usually, information is collected through a number of sources, and a variety of assessment strategies are used. The IPRC will then use this data to aid in the identification of the student as exceptional, and to help decide on appropriate placement. The data collected is then utilized in the development of the student's IEP. At the review stage, this assessment data will be utilized again with more current and perhaps additional or different information being added.

Yet another common procedure is 'screening'. This is a fairly formal but broad procedure used to determine if more intrusive testing is needed. Groups of students are screened via an achievement test or test of cognitive abilities or other instrument. (Some boards have their own systems of screening to be used along with, or in place of, commercially published tests) The purpose is to discover, in a general way, whether there are any students at risk or potentially gifted. Those students are usually assessed then, in a more formal and extensive way, to confirm (or dismiss) their suspected risk or giftedness. Screening may take place at the preschool level where children entering school are screened for vision, hearing and general readiness. Later in a student's career, screening helps to identify those students who fall outside what is judged to be normal performance criteria. These students are then tested further to assess the nature of the discrepancy.

Who Does Assessments?

Given that the regular teacher spends a majority of the day with the student, the process, quite naturally, begins in the classroom. It is the teacher who can best observe a student's response to text, her reaction to the physical environment, and relationship to peers and adults. Teachers collect samples of student's work: journal entries, tests, and portfolios. These are the materials which, along with the teacher's own professional opinions and views, establish the initial, basic, and often, most important information. Further testing (and observation) may then be done by the school's special education teacher. The combination has distinct advantages in that the two (or more) teachers can then cooperate in the next step: designing the program the assessment implies.

In larger jurisdictions, there is often a separate unit responsible for assessment, known by descriptors such as psychological services, or psych-support, etc. This unit does almost all the assessing for special education outside the classroom setting. Psychologists, or personnel working under their guidance and direct supervision, conduct much of this assessment. Smaller jurisdictions make alternative arrangements where classroom and special education teachers may be given more responsibility for formal types of assessment. However most boards, even the smaller ones, have these types of assessments done by a person for whom this is a primary role.

For Discussion: the Case of Larry

Each of Larry's eight years in the same elementary school has contributed to his reputation as a complete enigma. In fact, he is secretly (and kindly) known by the staff as "What Next Larry" because tales about him invariably attract that phrase.

In kindergarten and grade one, Larry did not seem to learn to read or write or even print his name. When he returned for grade two the next September, he immediately showed language skills well above grade level, and by Christmas was leading the class. However, by the end of the year he had begun to manifest odd behaviours, the most serious of which was eating chalk. That too, disappeared over the next summer, but when Larry returned in the fall, it appeared he had become an elective mute. Nothing his teacher or assistant did, could penetrate the mutism. His parents (who were, then and now, as baffled as his teachers) reported the same behaviour at home, *and* that Larry was being emulated by his immediately younger brother! Like the previous mysteries, this too passed, and in grade four Larry took up music. The school has a grade 7-8 band, and Larry showed he could play the clarinet well enough to join this older group and even become a soloist. Again, his parents had no explanation. Larry never had lessons, they reported, and although they kept a clarinet in the attic, no one (except Larry, now) could play it.

Grade five saw sports enter the picture. Rather, sports*casting*. This class devoted a part of each morning to current events and media study, and two or three times a week, Larry, would report — pleasantly, but obsessively and in total detail without notes — all the scoring from the previous night's NHL games. In grade six, Larry began writing his novel. He abandoned that venture before completion, but the writing took up almost all his time until winter break. A standardized achievement test that year showed Larry at grade in language but well behind in math. However, he had been completely absorbed in his novel, especially when math was being taught. In grade seven, Larry became officially eligible for the school band but then dropped out. Instead, he got permission to form a school chess club. By the end of the year, this club had a higher membership than the band.

It is now the first month of Larry's grade eight year. The principal (who is both fond of and protective of Larry — the affection is returned, fully) has held a meeting of all staff who have taught or otherwise dealt with Larry. What he has proposed, with the strong support of the boy's parents, is that, since Larry will go to a secondary school next year, it would be to his benefit if his arrival there were preceded by a confidential assessment. The principal wants the teachers to suggest to him, just what kind of information such an assessment should seek out, and how it should be obtained.

Some larger school boards may employ speech and language pathologists to assess children with language difficulties. Physical screening for vision and hearing is generally under the jurisdiction of the public health nurse. Assessments done by physiotherapists and occupational therapists are also outside the jurisdiction of the school boards, though schools may, with the cooperation of the parents, request such assessments.

Parents sometimes obtain an assessment privately, even though, by law, they have access to any data the school has. They may offer these data to the school (or to an IPRC) or, if they choose to, may keep it to themselves.

Components of an Assessment

A majority of the assessment information collected about a student, if not all, revolves around what the student is seen to be doing (observation), a systematic collection of student work products, discussions and information sharing by stakeholders in the child's education (including, of course, parents) and, finally, testing. Historically, in special education, emphasis has been placed on the latter element. The mystique of testing has often overshadowed, and even delayed, action on behalf of an exceptional student. The phrase "We are getting him tested" was — and still is! — an oft-heard one, and it's not unusual for a teacher to be caught in the frustrating position of waiting on results before modifying a program. The benefits of more formalized types of testing can indeed inform the process of program planning. But for some time now, the experience of special education teaches that formal tests are only one component in a much more complex process; one that starts with teachers in the classroom suspecting something, acting on that suspicion, and ultimately trying out possible strategies to ameliorate the difficulty.

The 'Battery'

Curiously, the pieces that make up a formal assessment are often described collectively by an artillery term: assessment 'battery'. What follows here is a description of components that *may* be used in a battery, although certain of them will almost always be included. (It is difficult, for example, to conceive of an assessment being useful and valid without the observations of the teacher and assistant.) The decision

regarding what components to use is typically governed in part by school and board policy. For example, many boards have complex and stringent requirements for identifying students as gifted, and specify that certain test instruments be used as part of the identification procedures. Some boards discourage or even forbid the use of certain components. However, once the school and board policies are met — and on the matter of components these matters are flexible for the most part — how an assessment is actually conducted, and what is used, will typically be the choice of the professional personnel involved. That choice will vary according to their knowledge, competence and personal preference.

Informal (Teacher Made) Tests

A growing awareness of the benefits when assessments are conducted by the person working directly with the student on an ongoing basis, means there has been an increase in the use and acceptance of informal measures designed by classroom teachers. A disadvantage to these measures is that there are no norms for them, and thus they usually do not have acceptance beyond the immediate situation. But then, that is not their purpose. Their advantage is that they can often be tailored to meet specific needs. For example, an informal test can be designed to reveal the presence or absence of a very specific skill, and thus may provide a picture of *why and when* a student fails to grasp a skill (like subtraction) instead of simply confirming that he has not grasped it (which the teacher already knows in any case).

Other informal measures may include a teacher using parts of rating scales and checklists so that she can be more certain to have covered all the points. Informal inventories are used here as well. Still another practice (albeit of questionable legality and efficacy) is to use parts of different published tests to put together the desired information about a student.

Curriculum-Based Assessment

This concept involves measuring a student's performance according to curricular expectations the school has established. Many observers suggest that curriculum-based assessment, despite the extensive explication and argument that surround it, does not differ very much from the way evaluation in schools was conducted well before special education became commonplace. In the case of an exceptional student, detractors say, curriculum-based measurement is not really a true alternative, since all it really does is confirm that the student is not responding appropriately to the curriculum, a fact that was already evident.

Supporters argue, however, that curriculum-based assessment emphasizes the identification of a student's personal, unique and complex characteristics as they relate directly to the curriculum, and that this uniqueness is superior to the type of assessment which merely establishes the presence of some disability.

To be effective, curriculum-based assessment must be carried out frequently; it should be specific (i.e., directed exactly at what has been taught); the results should be considered as a reason for possibly adjusting the instruction, in addition to just determining how the student is doing; and, testing should consider small, subskill gains in addition to the acquisition of more global matters.

Formal Tests

Intelligence tests

Traditional intelligence testing continues to be popular in Ontario in spite of the grave concerns of many educators about the value of the procedure. Generally, IQ tests give a relatively accurate assessment of what an individual has been taught (and what he remembers) and of what he has been exposed to thus far in his life. In this sense, an IQ test is a measure of current performance. What continues to be hotly debated is whether the test measures intellectual potential and can thereby be legitimately regarded as a *predictor* of future school performance. Despite these concerns, IQ instruments continue to be used for that purpose. Among the several commercially available IQ tests, the most widely used test by far in the province of

---

Keys to an Effective Assessment

For reasons of economy, availability of personnel and appropriate instruments, and because of politics and the chronic problem of special education, lack of time, not all educational assessments will meet every one of the criteria listed here, every time. Yet when these criteria are not met as a basic standard, the results of any assessment should be weighed accordingly.

❶ Has the assessment used a broad spectrum of sources (e.g., teacher, parent, other professionals if appropriate, test instruments if appropriate)?

❷ If test instruments have been used, are they known to be *valid* and *reliable*? Is the examiner adequately trained in the administration of the tests and interpretation of the results?

❸ Was the assessment individually tailored? (i.e., Did it take into account matters like the the subject's dominant culture, his language, age, school experience, physical abilities?)

❹ Was the assessment 'ecological' in the sense that it examined the whole student in relation to her total environment: (e.g., program, classroom situation, home situation)?

❺ Does the assessment imply or recommend responses: avenues of remediation or enrichment (as opposed to presenting only an enumeration of deficiencies)?

❻ Do key persons in the life of the subject (teacher, educational assistant, parent) acknowledge that the assessment has sampled genuinely representative factors?

Ontario, has been the *Wechsler Intelligence Scale for Children III*, known colloquially as the 'WISC III'.

Projective Tests

Gestalt psychology and psycho-analytic method propose that an individual will project her inner life, especially her inner feelings, when presented with an ambiguous stimulus like a picture of an inkblot. When asked to draw pictures of a situation or an object (e.g., her family or a tree) or when asked to describe "What is going on here?", while being shown a picture, an individual will, according to this theory, expose more of her deeper self than she would if asked directly. Projective tests have been fiercely criticized for lack of norms, insufficient standard-ization, entirely subjective interpretation, and even for revealing more about the examiner than the subject! Although their use has declined significantly in Ontario schools, they still appear in some assessments. Some examples are the *Rorschach Inkblot Test* (1932) and the *Human Figure Drawing Test* (1968).

Tests of Academic achievement

These are the most widely used formal test instruments of all — and possibly the most abused. There are achievement tests for large groups (e.g., the *Canadian Achievement Tests*, 1983) and there are individual tests as well (e.g., the *Peabody Individual Achievement Test, Revised*, 1988). Administrators of achievement tests can be any-one from a classroom teacher to a professional psychometrist. Publishers provide detailed administration manuals and

Some Important Terms in Assessment*

Band of Confidence: a relatively new means of reporting test scores. Because of the Standard Error of Measurement factor (See below) a test score can never be considered absolutely correct. Thus some test manuals now offer a range *around* the given score about which there can be some confidence.

Criterion Referenced Test: a number of specific behaviours or performances are stated (e.g., Subject knows the alphabet? Can count from 1-20?). These are the criteria. The subject's ability in this particular area is then assessed. (See Norm Referenced Test.)

Grade Equivalent: a subject's raw score on a test is applied statistically to produce the school grade he would be in if he were in the sample group of students used to determine the norms for the test. (A subject's grade equivalent of 6.2 means that if he were in the group sampled to produce the norms, he would stand at the second month of sixth grade.)

Norm Referenced Test: a test which rates a subject's performance relative to the results obtained in a known comparison group (or *norm* group).

Norms: the results obtained by a supposedly representative sample of students as a particular test was being developed. After it is then published, students who write the test have their results compared to these norms to produce scores like Percentile, Stanine, Grade Equivalent, etc.

Percentile Rank: a subject's percentile rank of 82 means that she scored higher than about 82 per cent of the norm group.

Reliability: the level of consistency and dependability of a test. (Will it produce similar results over variable conditions?)

Split-half Procedure: this involves administering the same subject(s) half of a test instrument (e.g., the odd-numbered questions) at a different time from the other half (e.g., the even-numbered questions).

Stanine: a reporting scheme for test results based on an equal interval scale of 1 to 9. (5 is average; 6 slightly above, etc.).

Standard Error of Measurement: the extent to which a subject's score is "out". These data are reported (or should be!) in the technical manual available with published tests.

Validity: the degree to which a test measures what it purports to measure.

* See also glossary in Appendix.

recommend that examiners attend training seminars

Very often in special education, achievement tests are used as screening tests. Other uses include general comparison, since the test results are calculated in terms of the results — called *norms* — developed across a wide, randomly selected population. In other words, the test takers reveal where they stand *in terms of the test*, relative to a general population.

Diagnostic Tests

The term is misleading. These tests do not diagnose in any absolute sense but rather, present specific information about a student's performance in a specific area. The true purpose of these tests is to suggest areas for remediation. Subtests of the *Woodcock Reading Mastery tests — Revised* (1987), for example, deal with specific areas like 'Word Attack' 'Word Identification', and 'Word Comprehension', presumably giving indication about the extent to which a student is competent in these areas. Critics of this and other similar tests question the value and even the validity of this kind of subskill breakdown in an area like reading. However, they acknowledge it may have value in areas like mathematics, where steps in the process of subtraction, for example, can be broken down and illuminated more clearly.

Tests of Cognitive Ability

The jury is still very much out on the issue of whether or not testing for cognitive abilities is any different from testing for intelligence with the IQ instruments already in use. Cognition is about thinking. Whether testing for thinking is any different from testing for IQ is moot. In Ontario, supporters of the distinction generally opt for the *Canadian Cognitive Abilities Test* (1983).

Developmental and Readiness Tests

These are primarily administered by classroom teachers — especially teachers of early grades — to determine the level of ability of students. For exceptional students, their purpose is generally for screening. Very often these instruments are used in conjunction with checklists and skill inventories. Two of these, popular in Ontario, are the *Boehm Test of Basic Concepts — Revised* (1986) and the *Brigance Inventories, (various)*.

Rating Scales, Inventories and Checklists

These instruments usually offer descriptive statements about areas like behaviour, attitude, self-esteem, self-care, etc., in lists. Each item in a list is followed by a frequency ranking (like 'almost all the time, frequently, sometimes, occasionally, rarely') or sometimes just by 'yes' or 'no'. Responses are entered by the student's teacher, educational assistant, parent, social worker, or child care worker (sometimes all of these for comparison and time/place/situation diagnosis). A reasonably popular example of this type is the *Child Behavior Checklist* (1983).

Some rating scales are designed to be completed by the student. The *Coopersmith Self-Esteem Inventory* (1983) for example, presents statements to the student like "I often wish I were someone else" followed by "like me___' and "unlike me___'.

Most often, the results of these scales are used to determine a developmental profile from which educational or social or self-care objectives are developed. Occasionally, the information may be used to indicate a developmental level, and sometimes decisions about placement for example, will be influenced by the level indicated. The *AAMD Adaptive Behavior Scale: School Edition (1981)* often called an adaptive behaviour 'test' is frequently used this way.

The rating scale type of instrument invites, quite obviously, considerable subjectivity and, interestingly, is both praised and criticized for this factor.

Interviews and Informal Commentary: Teachers and Parents

Any effective assessment procedure will seek out the opinions of the responsible adults who associate with, and have responsibility for, the student most directly. In Ontario, most boards invite the classroom teacher, and sometimes the educational assistant, to meet with an IPRC to present information. Very often this face-to-face discussion is preceded by written information that may vary from a simple referral form, to anecdotal information, to a fully developed case study. Parents can offer certain vital information to an assessment or evaluation team. Their information is invariably current and intimate (if biased sometimes); they also have the advantage of knowing the student's full history. Ontario Regulation 181 requires that parents be an integral part of the process when a child is being considered for special education.

Medical Information

This is included only when it is germane. Information may range from data about hearing, sight, and physical ability, to the general health and neurological conditions that may be relevant to a student's situation. These data, if available, will come from the appropriate health professionals; they are almost never prepared by a school board. Experience has demonstrated that without cooperation and impetus from parents, the data, along with accompanying useful advice, are often hard to come by. Health professionals are understandably wary of privacy regulations but at the same time, often show a curious reluctance to share more than sketchy information with schools.

Reports and Analyses: Other Professionals

For reasons that do not require elaboration here, it is obvious that members of the behavioural science professions can offer very helpful insights into the situations of certain students. What educators must weigh, however, when receiving information from these sources, is the proportionate amount of time any one of the assessors has been able to spend with a student and, of that time, the amount in an actual classroom situation. Because of this factor, together with what seems to be somewhat of a weak track record for predicting behaviour on the part of these professionals, educators often find it more helpful to use assessment information from these sources for general understanding of a syndrome rather than for specific programming.

Alternative Assessment Procedures

Alternatives to traditional assessment procedures are continually being suggested to school systems. Five of these are described briefly here.

Authentic Assessment

Based on the premise that traditional types of assessment instruments fail to measure a

---

Involve the Parents

What parents have to offer an assessment about a student's abilities is essential for obvious reasons. Answers to the following questions are useful.

- What are your concerns regarding your child's learning/behaviour at school?

- How does what we do at school affect him at home (reaction to homework, frustration level, general attitude to coming to school)?

- Has she had particular success in the past, with a strategy or program?

- What other reports do you have that we may need to be aware of?

- What goals do you have for your child?

- Do you have a preference in method of communication from home to school?

- What questions do you have of us?

---

student's performance in an authentic way, this type of assessment focuses on forming a complete and 'realistic' picture of what a child can or cannot do. Authentic assessment allows for a collection of data based on 'real' situations in which the students can be engaged in an interactive way, and during which they can access help from teachers and peers alike. The focus is on allowing students to translate information that is taught in a classroom situation, and apply this knowledge in a problem solving way. This type of assessment is designed to produce the learner's best performance based on interaction and practice.

Portfolio Assessment

Portfolios are a collection of a student's work that represents growth and development over a specified period of time. Rather than being a haphazard collection of work samples periodically collected, a portfolio is a representative sampling. The goal of portfolio development is twofold: first, to provide a vehicle for the teacher to measure progress, and secondly (and perhaps more importantly), to allow for the student himself to monitor and evaluate his academic growth, and thereby help to make informed decisions on how to proceed.

Salend (1998) suggests the following guidelines for effective use of portfolio assessment in the classroom.

- Identify the goals of the portfolio.
- Determine the type of portfolio to be used (showcase, reflective, cumulative, goal based).
- Establish procedures for organizing it.
- Choose a range of authentic classroom products that relate to the objectives of the portfolio.
- Record the significance of items included in a student's portfolio.
- Review and evaluate portfolios periodically.

Ecological Assessment

This concept includes an amalgam of formal and informal methods, along with careful evaluation of the teaching-learning variables in the student's case. The idea is to examine the context in which the student learns, as well as the student himself. Thus, matters like the teacher's management style, the curriculum, teaching strategies, and instructional materials are examined; work samples produced by the student are evaluated, as well as his success and error patterns inside and outside of school, etc. All this is in addition to the use of the usual formal test instruments. While ecological assessment is most attractive in principle, management and economic factors make it very difficult to carry out.

Learning Style Assessment

An initially well-received proposal in the 1980's offered the idea that by examining how a student learns, and discovering under what conditions or through what style of presentation he learns most naturally and effectively, remediation then becomes a relatively straightforward case of making appropriate adjustments when he does not learn. While the idea was successful in promoting attention to individualization programming as an assessment method, it has proven exceedingly complex for the rewards it might generate. Another problem is that in the development stages of their growth, students' styles are not necessarily stable and therefore accessible to reliable measurement.

Dynamic Assessment

Feuerstein (1979) and his colleagues propose an alternative that is most exciting, conceptually, for special education. Generally critical of traditional assessment procedure for its habit of assessing a student *statically*, i.e., at a single

For Discussion: the Case of Kyeesha

Kyeesha's parents call her their "divine gift". She was born to them when they were in their mid-forties, after they had experienced several unsuccessful pregnancies over a period of years. Both have successful careers (in art history and microbiology) and their home is intellectually and culturally stimulating.

When Kyeesha was four years old, the parents had her assessed for intelligence and general ability in a private clinic. The clinic's test results placed Kyeesha in the Very Superior range intellectually, and for the next two years her parents enrolled her in a private pre-school. Prior to enrolling her in Grade one of their neighbourhood elementary school, the parents requested an IPRC. The committee, having little information available to it except the clinic's test results as provided by the parents, along with anecdotal accounts from them, quite readily accepted their opinion that Kyeesha should be identified gifted and placed in a primary gifted program.

After considerable success initially, Kyeesha began to lag behind her colleagues in achievement seriously enough that by the end of grade two, the school requested, and was granted by the parents, permission to conduct another assessment. The school board's chief psychologist somewhat reluctantly reported his conclusion that, intellectually, Kyeesha is in the Average to High Average range. Not unexpectedly, her parents find this difficult to believe. However, because they are naturally disposed to cooperate, and no matter what, wish to make decisions that are in their little girl's best interests, they have asked for a meeting with the school. What they want to have explained to them is: how can results of two assessments of the same child differ so greatly? And, is there other information the school can provide that would help make clear to them what Kyeesha's real status might be?

point in time, with all the attendant drawbacks, Feuerstein argues for *dynamic* assessment. In essence, this is a test-teach-test model that stipulates the subject first be assessed to reveal needs; then it directs the examiner to interact constantly with the subject, teaching him the content and concepts that were first assessed in an attempt to address the needs; and third to re-assess to see if the subject has learned and to identify what strategies were the most successful in the process. Feuerstein's thesis is that it is more valuable to discover whether and what and how a student can be taught (his word is 'modified') and what strategies work best in the teaching, than it is to simply learn or have confirmed what he cannot do. Although dynamic assessment has a minority of firm converts in Ontario, it has not gained the attention it perhaps deserves.

Some Issues in the Use of Formal Tests

■ More than in any other area of special education, the issues and concerns — the problems — of assessment are very much interwoven and interrelated. One issue spills over into another in a way that makes both more serious than they might be individually. A good case in point is the issue of test mystique and the issue of just how accurate is the picture of a student that a test produces?

The mystique factor is powerful. Educators, including those who should know better, seem to willingly ascribe to tests a kind of mystical capacity to open a window into a student's inner being and the workings of her mind. The result is that some educators will often defer to test results or interpretations of test results — the supposed picture of a student — even if the results contradict their own observations and conclusions, arrived at over months of intimate observations and analyses. Ironically, the professionals who administer and interpret the tests rarely push for this; in fact they are usually the ones who point out that a formal test instrument is just one of several looks at the subject. Yet so strong is the effect of a test result that almost everyone involved in a student's case will, however tacitly, acknowledge its superiority, with the effect that the importance of a test in the general assessment of a student can be shockingly disproportionate.

Professional Expertise? ✎

Faust & Ziskin (1988), in a major review that traced expert psychiatric and psychological testimony in the U.S. court system during the twentieth century, shocked both the legal and behavioural science professions by showing that the predictions of behaviour by these experts in testimony, proved later to be wrong more than half the time! The fact that this excellent study has had almost no impact on practices in the judicial system or on behavioural science practices suggests how firmly entrenched is our cultural urge to believe in supposed expertise.

■ Other nagging problems are the aging of test content and the matter of cultural bias and tacit discrimination against lower SES groups. Producers of commercial tests claim to have addressed this matter in their revisions, but estimates of their success, as published in professional reviews, are conservative at best.

■ In tests administered to groups, the questions are typically phrased so that the answers can be machine-scored, with multiple-choice format being the most popular. Almost every question therefore, must be responded to with a single, confined answer. Such a structure invites a great many dull and simplistic questions and devotes an excessive amount of space, time, and effort to minutiae. Needless to say, it also leaves little room, if any, for the reflective or creative student.

■ It is not uncommon, in tests of language and reading, to find lists of single words, out of context, to be read aloud. (See, for example, the *Wide Range Achievement Test-Revised,* 1984.) These lists are often separated in subtests under titles like 'Word Recognition', with the results interpreted as a measure of general reading ability, rather than word recognition alone.

The practice also assumes that testing an isolated skill like word recognition is possible, and worth doing in the first place.

■ In tests of achievement especially, each item tends to be scored with the same value (usually 1 or 0). Since the tasks typically increase in difficulty, Student A, who correctly answers only questions sixteen to twenty, earns the same score as Student B, who correctly answers questions one to five. Granted, a careful item by item analysis would reveal that Students A and B attained a raw score of five by different routes, but in practice, consumers of test information rarely see, or have time to see, an item analysis.

■ Tests are usually rigorously timed, with all the difficulties that causes for slow thinkers (not to mention deep thinkers).

■ Over time, commercially produced formal tests have come to be called 'standardized' (distinguishing them from teacher tests which by implication therefore, are *un*standardized). Many test consumers have come to accept 'standardized' as though these tests are based on a standard against which students are judged. This is not at all the case. Test results are indeed compared to a scale of values or 'norms', but these norms are not an absolute standard; they are the scores obtained from the population samples used by the test publishers to establish a basis for comparison. Publishers usually contend that their norms represent the range of results (in a perfect bell curve) that could be expected in a normal or typical population. That claim notwithstanding, the comparison is still relative; it is not standard. What *is* standard in formal tests are the procedures of administration and scoring. A 'standardized' test is one which is administered and scored the same way every time, in order to reduce examiner interference.

■ Another well established practice is to generalize test results. If student C takes test X in reading comprehension and scores a grade equivalent of say 4.2, *those results are for that particular test.* Yet it is regular practice by educators to make the assumption that the student's absolute reading level is 4.2

■ Easily one of the most misunderstood and ignored elements of formal tests is the standard error of measurement (SEM). Because no test is absolutely accurate, a subject's true score is never known. The score that a subject gets — his 'obtained' score — is actually only an estimate of his true score. What the SEM does then, is give a statistical reflection of how close to a true score the subject's obtained score actually is. If, for example, he scores 110 on a test with an SEM of 3.8 then approximately two-thirds of the time, statistically, his true score would fall between 106.2 and 113.8. The impact of the SEM can be very powerful (not the least because it is so often ignored). If students are identified for a program on the basis of test scores, it is easy to see how the spread, the looseness implied by the SEM, can be significant.

■ Taken together, the problem with formal tests (not all of which by any means are the fault of the tests or the examiners) have led to a decrease in their use in Ontario in assessing exceptional students. Although the testing tradition is still quite solidly established, alternative sources are more frequently being used, and tend to have greater credibility than they did. What still remains for special education, at least in some jurisdictions, is to narrow — hopefully eliminate — the gulf between the conducting of an assessment of an exceptional student and the developing of their program.

The Case Study

A case study is an efficient executive summary that collates information from a number of sources into one document. In situations where an exceptional student's case has become complicated over time —and many do — and when it has involved a variety of personnel, some of whom may not know one another, or have never worked together, a case study brings together history, current status, and needs. If written with some care, it can be the most effective means by far, of bringing a group of professionals with diverse interests up to speed on a situation for which they share responsibility.

Usually, an educational case study is prepared by the teacher nominally responsible for the student in question. Ideally, it is written according to two principal criteria:

✓ The best case studies are succinct. Effective writers always aim at a maximum of two pages if at all possible.

✓ A case study does not make judgemental or evaluative statements but *reports fact.*

CONFIDENTIAL

I. <u>Carter F-R.</u>   Date: <u> 12 Dec. </u>

Address: <u>123 Street, City, ON</u>   DOB: <u>12 Oct. 19xx</u>   Age: <u>9.2</u>

School: <u>ABC Elem. , City, ON</u>   Placement: <u>Gr. 3-4</u>

Lives with: Mother ✓ (Judith)   Father ✓ (Stanford)

Writer: <u>D. APPLEYARD</u>   Distribution: PRINC. ✓ SPEC. ED. RES. ✓ PARENTS ✓

II. Educational Issue: Carter appears to be extremely bright. Teacher nomination, peer nomination and IQ test results all match the school's 'gifted' indicators. His parents have declined to offer an opinion. Carter himself insists he is not very intelligent.

By the end of kindergarten, Carter could read fluently and do arithmetic at about the grade three level. He continues to excel in both areas. Carter has an impressive vocabulary and speaks in a very mature, very adult fashion, although he participates during class only when the topic is serious (e.g., world issues, etc.). He has never been seen playing, or smiling, or appearing to be enjoying himself. Several observers have commented that "he is a miniature 40-year old" and that "he's almost not a kid at all". Carter belongs to a chess club and has qualified for inter-provincial competition in an age group one above his own.

In his split grade 3-4 class, Carter leads somewhat of an isolated existence. It is difficult to tell whether this is his decision or not, although any invitations by peers to become involved are invariably declined. As a result, the boy has no friends in the class, and except for a fellow chess player in grade eight, none in the school.

A decision must be taken whether or not to transfer Carter to the self-contained gifted program at XYZ school. In discussions with his teacher, Carter has revealed that he does not see himself as very bright, that he feels deeply insecure, and that he feels no one likes or cares for him. This nine-year-old recently said to his teacher: "I am the saddest person I know."

III. Family History: Carter is the youngest child in an intact family of five. His father is president of a large import-export firm, and travels internationally about half the year. Mother is an opthalmologist with a well-established practice. His two siblings (age 22 and 24) are cum laude university graduates. One is studying for a doctorate; the other has started her own investment service. Carter's principal care-givers have been nannies, none of whom has stayed with the family for more than nine months.

IV. Physical and Health Status: No significant matters; Carter is very healthy.

V. Social and Behaviour Matters: Except for the social behaviour described in II, there are no exceptional matters in Carter's school behaviour. In class he is quiet but not withdrawn, and cooperative but not submissive.

VI. Supplementary Reports: A letter from XXX Academy, a private residential school where Carter was enrolled for two months in grade one, states that he was withdrawn by his parents "by mutual consent". There are no other reports on file.

VII. Assessment Data: In a board wide achievement test (C.A.T.) administered to the third grade during the week of 21 September, all of Carter's sub-test scores were above the 98th percentile. (See OSR.) Carter was given the WISC-III with the permission of his parents; his full scale score was in the Very Superior range; the verbal score was higher than performance by 2 points. Following the board administered test, Carter's parents had him assessed privately but have declined to share the results.

VIII. Present Program: Carter is in a split grade three-four class. (Officially, he is in grade three.) The program here is very organized and very much individualized, with emphasis on academic achievement. There is plenty of opportunity for enrichment and extra study. The other students in the class are, by and large, bright achievers.

IX. Recommendations: Carter will be presented to IPRC on Jan. 7. Recommendations to follow. (See OSR.)

The Case Study (continued)

It is important to keep in mind that a case study is a beginning point. It is at the meeting(s) for which the study has been prepared, in advance, where judgements, evaluations, speculations, opinion, interpretations and so on, are aired.

For a case study *in education* the following components are most often preferred:

I.   Demographic data

II. Description of the educational issue

III. Family history

IV. Physical and health status

V.   Social and behavioural matters

VI. Supplementary reports

VII. Assessment data

VIII. Current program and placement

IX. Recommendations. (This section is usually not completed until after discussions have been held and decisions have been made for a next step.)

I. For reasons of privacy, the amount of demographic data is usually limited to bare essentials, including the obvious elements like name and address, age, birth date, school and placement, and parents' names.

II. The educational issue is the heart of the study and should give the reader the essence of the situation. Details that expand or explain are usually entered in different sections.

III. Appropriate, useful information about the family is often very helpful but for reasons of privacy, the writer of a case study should err on the side of less rather than more — unless the family situation is, in the writer's opinion, a major factor.

IV. Information about physical development is included only if germane. Where it is not an issue, the case study should state only that.

V. In some case studies, the section on behaviour and social matters will require some detail. The writer of a study, however, must be careful to avoid drama and to stick to relevant facts.

VI. Supplementary reports usually include medical data, reports from other schools or agencies, etc. In some case studies, it suffices to state only that these reports have been made, and then if possible, indicate where the originals may be available.

VII. Assessment data are usually the product of tests. It is important to include them, but often, because of privacy regulations, they may not be available to the writer of a case study. If possible, the writer should try to determine what tests were administered, under whose authority and when. At the very least, the writer should be able to state whether or not tests were administered.

VIII. A description of program need not be elaborate. Usually an overview is sufficient.

IX. Recommendations are not usually made if the case study is going forward to a school team or to a committee. (On the other hand, if the study is not going forward, then this section becomes the whole purpose of the activity.)

READINGS & RESOURCES

For Further Investigation

Algozzine, B., & Ysseldyke, J. (1992). *Strategies and tactics for effective instruction.* Longmont, CO: Sopris West.

Bagnato, S.J., Neisworth, J.T., & Munson, S.M. (1997). *Linking authentic assessment and early intervention: Advances in curriculum based assessment* (3rd ed.). Baltimore: Paul H. Brooks.

Benner, S.M. (1992). *Assessing your children with special needs: An ecological perspective.* New York: Longman.

Bufkin, L.J., & Bryde, S.M. (1996). Young children at their best: Linking play to assessment and intervention. *Teaching Exceptional Children, 29.* 50-53.

Feuerstein, R. (1979). *The dynamic assessment of retarded performers: The learning potential assessment device, theory, instrument and techniques.* Baltimore: University Press Park.

Gajris, M., Salend, S.J. & Hemrick, M.A. (1994) Teacher acceptability of testing modifications for mainstreamed students. *Learning disabilities Research and Practice, 9,* 236-243.

Hammill, D.D., Brown, L., & Bryant, B.R. (1989). *A consumer's guide to tests in print.* Austin TX: Pro-Ed.

McGloghlin, J.A. & Lewis, R.B. (1984). *Assessing special students* (4th ed.). Upper Saddle River, NJ: Merrill/Prentice Hall.

Meltzer, L., & Reid, D.K. (1994). New Directions in the assessment of Students with special needs. *Journal of Special Education, 28,* 338-355.

Neisworth, J.T., & Bagnato, S.J. (1996). Assessment for early intervention: Emerging themes and practices. In S.L. Odom & M.E. McLean (Eds.) *Early intervention / early childhood special education: recommended practices.* Austin TX: Pro-Ed.

Overton, T. (1992). *Assessment In Special Education.* New York: Merrill.

Salvia, J., & Ysseldyke, J.E. (1995). *Assessment* (6th ed.). Boston: Houghton Mifflin.

Taylor, R.L. (1989). *Assessment of Exceptional Students,* (2nd Ed.). Englewood Cliffs, NJ: Prentice Hall.

Thurlow, M.L., Ysseldyke, J.E., & Silverstein, B. (1995). Testing accommodations for students with disabilities. *Remedial and Special Education, 16*(5), 260-270.

For the Classroom Teacher

Arter, J.A., & Spanel, V. (1991). *Using portfoios of students work in instruction and assessment.* Portland OR: Northwest Regional Educational Laboratories.

Bufkin, L.J., & Bryde, S.M. (1996). Young children at their best: Linking play to assessment and intervention. *Teaching Exceptional Children, 29.* 50-53.

Gajris, M., Salend, S.J. & Hemrick, M.A. (1994). Teacher acceptability of testing modifications for mainstreamed students. *Learning Disabilities Research and Practice, 9,* 236-243.

Howell, K. W., Fox, S. L., & Morehead, M.K. (1993). *Curriculum based evaluation: Teaching and decision making* (2nd ed.). Pacific Grove CA: Brooks/Cole.

Kubiszyn, T. & Borich, G. (1996). *Educational testing and measurement: classroom application and practice* (5th ed.). New York: Harper Collins.

Meisils, S.J. (1993). Remaking classroom assessment with the work sampling system. *Young Children, 48,* 34-40.

Paulson, F.L., Paulson, P.R., & Meyer, C.A. (1991). What makes a portfolio a portfolio? *Educational Leadership, 48*(5), 60-63.

Reed, Lorrie C. (November 1993). Achieving the aims and purposes of schooling through authentic assessments. *Middle School Journal, 25*(2), 11-13.

Salend, S. (1998). Using portfolios to assess student performance. *Teaching Exceptional Children,* 31 (2), 36-43.

Salend, S.J., Whittaker, C.R., & Reeder, E. (1992). Group Evaluation: A collaborative peer mediated behavior management system. *Journal of School Psychology, 29,* 319-329.

Sarouphim, K. (1999). Discovering multiple intelligences through a performance based assessment: Conistency with independent ratings. *Exceptional Children 65*(2) 151-163.

Valenca, S. (1990). A portfolio approach to classroom reading assignments: The whys, whats and hows. *The Reading Teacher, 43*(4). Pp. 38-40.

15

The Individual Educational Plan (IEP)
A Team Approach

❝ Special education cannot be defined in a single statement. It is a process, a journey that takes different routes for different students at different times in their educational careers. An IEP provides the roadmap for the completion of that journey. ❞

— Andrea Jack, School Principal

Practice Becomes Policy

Special education as a journey is a popular metaphor for the experiences of those in the field. The Individual Education Plan (IEP) is a roadmap for that journey, for everyone involved with an exceptional student needs to know where they are going, how to get there, and how to recognize when they have arrived. The IEP roadmap is neither new nor revolutionary. Documentation, after all, has always been an integral part of education. Teachers plan lessons, and assess learning, and use that assessment to shape what follows: in essence, educational planning. With exceptional students, however, the planning necessarily becomes more complex because their needs, learning characteristics, and abilities are more diverse and challenging.

Until the late 1990s in Ontario, official requirement of an individual education plan for every exceptional student was implied (in a Ministry document called *Schools General*), but really not enforced. Yet for most Ontario teachers, as with their colleagues in other jurisdictions, using IEPs in various forms and designs was pretty much standard practice anyway. Therefore, in 1998, when the province revised* and reissued its regulation governing the identification and placement of students with special needs (Reg. 181), and this time made IEPs a clear and official requirement, most educators in the province already had considerable experience with the concept.

---

* Subsequent to this revision, the Ministry of Education issued provinve-wide standards for school boards to follow in developing, implementing, and monitoring IEPs.

What an IEP Is...

It is a written plan of action for a student whose needs require modification of a regular school program.

Important components of an IEP are a summary of the student's strengths and needs, a statement of goals and expectations, and essential information regarding resources, program, teaching strategies, personnel, etc.

The plan is an ongoing, flexible document, developed by a school staff, usually under the leadership of one or two persons, supported by a team.

An IEP is a document in common, available to teachers, assistants, resource personnel, administrators, parents, and the student, so that all concerned can direct their energies to the same purposes.

What an IEP is *Not*...

An IEP does not cover every moment and every activity of a student's day. An overly detailed and minutely controlled plan would be impossible, if not detrimental, to implement in a classroom. What the IEP does provide is consistency, continuity and clarity of purpose. It allows teachers to act within the requirements of their job, while permitting the flexibility to adjust curriculum activities and assessments in a planned and systematic way to support the exceptional student. While an IEP provides specific guidelines for the direction of a student's program, it should also allow for the day to day flexibility required for any student in a classroom setting.

What Regulation 181 Requires

Regulation 181/98 requires Ontario principals to ensure an individual education plan be developed for every student identified 'exceptional' by an Identification, Placement and Review Committee (IPRC)*, and that the plan include:

- specific educational expectations,
- an outline of the special education program and services to be provided to the student,

---

*An alternative employed by some boards across the province is the development of an IEP for a student without a prior IPRC. In some cases, this route may provide services for students with special needs, without using the potentially complex and bureaucratic IPRC process.

- a description of the methods that will be used to review the student's progress.

Principals must ensure that the plan is developed no longer than 30 days after the student is placed in a special education program, *and that it is completed in consultation with the parent* (and the student if he or she is 16 years or older). The plan must take into account any recommendations by the IPRC that identified the student. A copy of the completed plan must be forwarded to parents (and to the 16-plus students) within the 30-day time frame, and a copy of the plan must also be included in the student's Ontario Student Record (OSR).

Preparing IEPs: Steps in the Process

While the designation 'Individual Education Plan' would suggest a finished product, an IEP is really more a process than an end result, principally because an IEP is a working document, one that is modified as needs and purposes require. The process by which an IEP is put together is pretty much standard in special education, no matter where it is offered. The sequence presented here represents the pattern suggested by the Ministry of Education and Training for use in Ontario. For the most part, although individual boards in the province frequently add their own variations, all of them generally follow these steps.

I.   Assigning Primary Responsibility

II. Gathering of information

III. Setting a direction

IV. Developing the IEP

V.   Implementing the IEP

VI. Reviewing and updating

I. Assigning Primary Responsibility

In most schools, IEPs are developed collaboratively, ideally by an 'In-school Team' under the direction of the principal. The Ministry of Education and Training recommends this approach (and the authors of this text support it, strongly). However, because of the inevitable time constraints in a typical school, and for reasons of efficiency, the primary responsibility for preparation of an IEP is usually given to one person, or sometimes two. Very often, that

When Ms. Kumar found out she would be having a grade two class in September (her first job since graduating) she immediately began to develop and collect materials for the new school year. She came into the school early to decorate her room and make it feel welcoming. Ms. Kumar learned from her principal that she would be having 25 grade two's, all of whom had had little difficulty in the grade one program.

During the first two weeks of school, despite a few minor adjustments and the establishing of classroom practices Ms. Kumar's class seemed to settle into an active and productive routine. At the beginning of the third week of school, a new child moved into the neighborhood. Joey was of grade two age but had not yet attended regular school. He had spent senior kindergarten and grade one in a day treatment program for children with social/emotional difficulties. His mother had not informed the school of Joey's history and he began school on the Monday as number 26 in Ms. Kumar's room.

Within the first hour it became obvious that something was wrong. Joey had become very frustrated at journal writing time and got out of his desk frequently. At one point Joey decided that another child was bothering him, got out of his seat and spit on the child's desk. When Ms. Kumar reprimanded him, he responded by swearing at her and running from the room.

When Joey's mom came to get him at the end of the day, she confessed that she was extremely worried about her son. She had been afraid to tell the school too much about Joey's background in the hope that perhaps a new school meant a fresh start. The principal explained that Joey was now a member of their school and that in this school, teachers were willing to do everything in their power to plan and implement a program that would meet Joey's needs.

While Ms. Kumar agrees philosophically with the ideal espoused by the principal, she feels ill equipped to deal with a child with such complex problems. What she feels would be helpful is a "roadmap", some form of written guide with specific directions and ideas.

primary person is the classroom teacher of the student under consideration, or one of the school's special education teachers. (A fairly common practice is for the classroom teacher and a special education teacher to work in concert.) This individual will gather the basic information, and then after consultation with the in-school team, will take responsibility for writing the plan, for seeing to its implementation, and will also likely oversee or perhaps actually do, the monitoring of progress. In a well-run system, the team is regularly available for consultation, assistance, and an insertion of fresh ideas.

II. Gathering Information

The OSR: For all students in the province of Ontario, an Ontario Student Record (OSR) is maintained and continually updated. Information such as previous report cards and reports by teachers and other professional staff, medical information, and school history are customarily available in this file. One especially useful document often found in the OSR is a previous IEP. The OSR then, is a logical place to start gathering details.

Insights from key persons: Information from people who have different insights and perspectives on a student is valuable in the development of the IEP. The classroom teacher has the most contact with a particular student and the information that she provides within this process is essential. Yet she does not work alone; nor will she have all the answers. Parents, principals, special education teachers, previous teachers, other professionals, and indeed students themselves, where appropriate, can and should be participants in the IEP process. Parents, most of the time, have an in-depth understanding of 'how their child works'. Having seen their child's progress (or lack of it) from year to year, they provide a picture no one else has. Their picture may have important features too, like updated medical information, likes and dislikes, other community involvement, relevant family information, etc.

Formal tests: Where appropriate professional personnel are available to administer standardized assessments (e.g., an IQ test, a test of motor skills, etc.) and if the results from such tests would be useful in a student's case, the results may help inform the process. In most cases, however, test results will not be as important, at least initially, as the careful, daily, in-the-classroom observations of teachers and educational assistants. Formal tests tend to be more important in situations that are at the relatively complex or intractable end of the scale.

Classroom observations: For many years, special education was thought to be a special and distinct type of knowledge, and nowhere was this mystique more prevalent than in the area of assessment. Surprisingly, the perception persists. Special education teachers, just like teacher-librarians or computer specialists, do indeed possess some expert knowledge and training. But this expertise does not replace the essential role that regular classroom teachers or educational assistants play in gathering crucial information. Front-line personnel can assess things like the students' interaction with text, how they respond to new tasks, whether they work best in groups, or individually, their response to authority and routines, and their response to environmental conditions such as lighting and noise level. Information like this may be recorded in a variety of formats: anecdotal records, checklists, interviews of students and others, even audio/visual recordings. No matter where or in what form this information is recorded, it is most valuable.

Student's work: Samples of a student's previous and current work reveals strengths, needs and rates of progress. Portfolios of student work, test papers, journal entries, assignments and artwork all contribute insights.

In most cases, the types of information above will offer enough substance to develop an IEP. Naturally, there are situations where it is necessary to return to the sources and dig deeper or wider. In some cases, additional personnel and resources may be needed to conduct other types of assessments (e.g., diagnostic tests). As well, especially in the case of students with special physical or health needs, a school may seek information from medical professionals (although this is almost always done with the help, and certainly the permission, of parents).

After all the information is consolidated and checked for accuracy, and after any gaps are filled, and possible discrepancies resolved, the material is then summarized on the IEP form that the board or school uses.

III: Setting the Direction

It is after the basic information has been gathered (usually by the one or two persons primarily responsible for the task) that the strength of collaboration comes into play, for the simple reason that involving more than one person in the process usually produces a more thorough and relevant — and creative — plan. Most schools in Ontario turn to a more or less formal team approach for this, because the majority already have in place some form of active In-School Team* that meets on a regular basis to share information about students with special needs. Accordingly, these teams, with members added on an ad hoc basis (i.e., people with a stake in the case, like the classroom teacher, assistant, parent, etc.) are commonly used to shape and give direction to IEPs.

A school team generally includes the principal (or designate), certain classroom teachers appointed by the principal, and the school's special education teacher(s), along with ad hoc members. The principal (or designate) is primarily responsible for the establishment and maintenance of the team approach to IEP development, but all members of the team play an important role. Each one has a perspective in terms of the information they can offer, and the support or services they may be able to provide. This is where the collaboration factor finds strength. Once the different perspectives are aired and consolidated, with both the professional and the personal insights that each has to offer, the results will generate a more complete picture of the student's strengths and needs, along with a more informed and more creative set of strategies, and actions for implementation.

Notwithstanding the potential collaborative and creative power of a school team for developing IEPs, there are schools in the province where this style is not used. Although Ontario provincial policy specifically requires an IEP be prepared for all students identified exceptional, it does not stipulate that a team be used anywhere in the process (even though it is clear, in its support and explanations materials, that the Ministry of Education strongly supports the

---

*Also known by other titles like School Support Team, Special Support Team, or just School Team. *For a more detailed explanation of the In-School Team, and it's value and purpose in the collaborative development of IEPs, see page 175.*

team principle). Therefore, in some schools, the entire process is begun, developed, written, implemented and monitored by one or two persons. Most frequently, where this approach is taken, the responsibility rests with the school's special education teacher(s). However, because this teacher will be running a number of IEPs, what happens in practice is that he or she works very closely with the classroom teacher (and assistant) of the student concerned. And since the parent is involved too, in many cases, and possibly one or two supporting professionals (e.g., speech and language) even this "single-responsibility" style must be, in effect, a collaborative one.

> "An IEP is not a pristine piece of paper that is filed in the OSR and referred to only on occasion. Rather it is a working document to be filled with crossed out expectations and remedial attempts, scribbled revisions and 'post-it' reminders. It resides on the teacher's desk providing easy access to all concerned during the instructional day."
>
> — *Ruth Daigle, Special Ed. Consultant*

IV: Developing the IEP:

List strengths and needs: Much of this information will likely come from the observations of classroom teachers, assistants, and parents, gathered in the first phase. (The primary person or the team may choose to refer to the statement of strengths and needs included in the IPRC decision.) Including the student's strengths and needs is a prelude to understanding the program modifications that will be set up. A strength might be expressed as "...follows directions willingly and cooperates well in group activities." A need might be expressed as "...must develop independent self-care skills, like toiletting, etc."

Establish goals and expectations: Goals and expectations are based directly on the strengths and needs of the student, and should reflect the expected level of performance academically, behaviourally, and physically. Goals are considered more global targets for students (e.g., "The student will develop basic computational skills in mathematics."). Expectations, on the other hand, are more specific about what the student will be *doing* (e.g., "The student will be able to recite subtraction facts between 1 and 10.").

For Discussion: the Case of Mr. Pickett

Mr. Pickett has taught English to grades 9, 10, and 11 for some years now, and has always felt he is doing good job. His peers would agree, and note that Mr. Pickett always seems well prepared for his classes, has innovative ideas, and students seem to enjoy being in his class. In the past, under the direction of the previous principal, any students receiving special education support were withdrawn from Mr. Pickett's class and programmed for solely by the special education resource teacher. While Mr. Pickett has never objected to implementing some of the special education resource teacher's suggestions in his class, he has always been comfortable in the knowledge that the primary responsibility for an exceptional student's program rested elsewhere. This year, under a new principal, the focus of special education service delivery has shifted, with the primary responsibility of the programming for exceptional students now placed squarely on the shoulders of regular classroom teachers, assisted by the special education resource teacher.

Mr. Pickett has two students this year, identified learning disabled. Both read far below grade level and require a great deal of assistance in completing any written work. Mr. Pickett has been reluctant to take ownership for their program, and is very resistant to altering his teaching practices in any significant way to accommodate their needs. Although he does not share this with the rest of the staff, Mr. Pickett has grave doubts about his ability to program for the two, fearing he lacks the necessary expertise. He is willing to help them, but does not feel he has the skills.

An in-school team meeting has been called this week to discuss the students. Mr. Pickett, while not a regular member of the in-school team has been asked to provide in advance, some information about these students, and then attend the meeting to discuss it. He is unsure of what kind of information he should provide. Nor is he sure about how much he can or should tell the team about modifications and accommodations he has already tried with the students. Mr. Pickett is feeling very hesitant and would like some guidance.

Both goals and expectations, especially the latter, should be reviewed and updated frequently.

Specify strategies and resources: Once goals and expectations are outlined, the task then becomes one of choosing strategies and identifying resources that will help the student and teachers meet them. This section of an IEP stipulates what materials will be used, what programs and teaching methods will be employed, and who will work with the student, how often, and where.

Monitor the results: Once the team or person(s) has prepared the IEP, an essential question becomes how to know if the goals and expectations are being achieved. Thus a crucial step in the development of an IEP is establishing the features of a monitoring cycle: Who will track the student's progress? How will the record keeping be handled? Who will be responsible for communicating to whom, and what is the time frame for accomplishing the goals?

Special Case: The Transition Plan

For students 14 and older, with the exception of students identified as gifted, regulations require schools to include a *transition plan* in his or her IEP. The plan is designed to allow for a smooth transition from school to school and/or school to workplace or training center. It must include specific transition goals, and actions required to achieve those goals (e.g., in the case of a deaf student who plans on post secondary education, a plan would identify those institutions especially geared to meeting that special need; in the case of a developmentally disabled student, the plan might identify work and community living options.) Under the regulation, the principal is responsible for consulting with appropriate community agencies and/or post-secondary institutions for purposes of completing a meaningful transition plan.

V: Implementing the IEP:

Implementation of an IEP centres around communication, and around practical application of the decisions made by the team. Teachers who will be delivering service to the exceptional student need to be informed and prepared for the upcoming changes (although, if a collaborative process has been used, it is very likely that key personnel will have been involved in the plan from the beginning). Parents are also informed of what changes or adjustments will take place.

The plan itself is translated into the day to day operation of the classroom with all practical considerations being taken into account. At the same time, the monitoring plan is established, because even though an IEP will usually be updated at least once every reporting period, it must always be viewed as a working document that will evolve and develop as new information arises. There are very few IEPs that do not require some modifications early on.

Once again, it is important to point out that the IEP does not cover every minute of every day in the exceptional student's school life. It is a general document that records how a modified-from-regular program will be conducted and monitored.

Individual Education Plan for Eddy Y.

(See below and next two pages.)

(The following is part of a report submitted to an IPRC by Eddy's grade two teacher. The IPRC, on the basis of this and other assessment material, including input from his parents, identified him 'Exceptional-Behaviour'.)

"When Eddy is frustrated (frequently) he will either have a temper tantrum or impulsively run from one learning centre to another in the classroom. It is not unusual for him to run out of the room. Also, Eddy has difficulty staying on task during periods of "quiet time" and "seat work". Waiting for his turn is difficult. He will aggressively insinuate himself into group or pair activities in class, and is often very confrontational in the schoolyard. Immediately post-recess and post-lunch are Eddy's most difficult times, as well as opening exercises — if he has come to school on the bus. Two negative outcomes of Eddy's behaviour are that he does not have friends, and that he is achieving at a below-average level in language arts and math. Despite his parents' willingness to cooperate, supervised homework and re-mediation-at-home activities have caused difficulty in the home.

It is important to note that Eddy completes tasks under adult supervision, or with the help of members of the grade seven/eight 'buddy program'. He works at the arts and crafts centre for long periods without supervision. One of his singular skills seems to be with animals. His work in a month-long theme study on herpetology was outstanding, and he was one of only two students willing to care for the snakes on loan. Eddy's parents report he is taking lessons at a riding stable and is said to be a "natural" around horses. I agree with the opinions of the pediatrician and the psychologist that Eddy is not AD/HD, although he manifests a number of the symptoms."

Transition Plan for Lisette B.

(See below and page 174.)

Lisette was identified learning disabled in grade four. Since the sixth grade, she has been in special resource classes full time. Although she achieves below grade level academically, Lisette can read reasonably well. She does not read for pleasure. In math, she has mastered the basic ASMD functions, but her teachers long since decided that it is more productive to emphasize the use of a calculator. Although Lisette does not appear to have close friends, years of effort on the part of her teachers, in close cooperation with her parents, have resulted in her developing some social skills, but she continues to have difficulty in situations requiring tact.

An IPRC review recently reconfirmed the LD identification, and Lisette's IEP is designed to address her needs. With the strong support of her parents, her Transition Plan is oriented toward preparation for full time employment, and it has been much influenced by her cooperative education work experience assignment at the local public library. Incidents like the following, apparently, were typical and frequent. On one occasion, Lisette walked three short blocks to get coffees for the staff (part of her duties). Despite having a written list, she telephoned from the coffee shop to ask how many coffees to get. The number, customarily written on top of the list, was at the bottom this one time. A day later she was sent to another room to get a printer (another regular duty). When she returned empty-handed, her superior went to get it. The printer, normally on a table, had been put on the floor beside the table. On her last day, Lisette was asked to put bar code stickers on newly purchased paperbacks, and she pasted the codes over the book titles. The In-School Team feels these are indications of the principal issues that the Transition Plan must address.

Individual Education Plan

Student		D.O.B	IEP Start Date
Eddie Y.		July 10, 1991	Sept. 15, 2000

School /Year	Grade	Teacher(s)
Ontario School, 2000/01	Three	J. Forrester

IPRC Date	Identification	Placement
May 1, 2000	Exc: Behaviour	Reg. Class, Dir/Ind Support

IEP Developed By
Jane Forrester with Cecile King (Sp. Ed.) assist - IST, parents

Special Education Services Involved
Psych - Serv (assessment)
Special Ed. Resource

Personalized Special Instructional Equipment
n/a

Related Health Issues
seizure (one) at c. age 4
Ritalin (20 mg/day) Jan.-June '98, discontinued
very small physical stature (issue??)

Areas of Strength	Areas of Need
- unusually good with animals - natural athlete (small size limits achievents) - responds well to adult/older student supervision - will stay on task when supervised - artistic, esp. in crafts	- very distractible - impulsive, erratic, impetuous - social skills, esp. with peers - language arts, esp. written - basic math operations

Program Description — level of support required (frequency and duration)

- Regular class/program, Gr. 3
- EA daily: 9-10 (a.m.) 2-3:30 (p.m.)
- JF to have resource/consult 2x-week
- Parent to oversee daily short ass't (use communication book)

Assessment Data

WISC-III : VS-Low Av PS-Average
PIAFR : 1-2 grades below age norm
Connors Bel. Checklist
- acting out-impulsive
Teacher/ Spec.Ed. Res / Psych observations:
- impulsive/aggressive, off-task

General Classroom Accommodations

- Eddy to have personal "office" (carrel). May be withdrawn to Sp. Ed. with C. King when urgently required.
- E.A. works 1-1 (a.m.); EA assists whole class (p.m.)/attention to Eddy
- 9 a.m. daily, review of routines and schedule; review expectations
- 3:15 daily, review of day; progress chart with E.A./teacher

Note: Parent will transport. No bus riding until situation reviewed (Dec.)

Program Area
- Behaviour
- Social Skills
- Language Arts / Math

Goal(s) Eddy will stay on task and complete work without direct supervision
- will manifest age-appropriate social skills (esp. peer interaction)
- will achieve at grade in Lang Arts and Math

Current Achievement Level	Methods of Progress Review
- on task only if directly supervised	- observation
- social skills with peers are as yet undeveloped	- monthly discussion review with parents, principal, 1ST
- Lang Arts 1-1.5 grades below norm	- assessment Dec 15 with
- Math 1 grade below norm	split half of PIAT-R

Education Expectations (show dates)	Accommodations, Strategies, Resources	Evaluation of Progress (show dates)
By Dec 15: increase time on task. reduce impulsive behaviour to age-appropriate level	- "proximity" support by teacher and EA - "start meetings" at 9 a.m. post recess, post-lunch - all adults and Eddy focus on one routine until firm	Oct. 15: enter/leave behaviour much improved. On-task better but still below age-level. Recommend: JF continue program to next review, Nov. 15
Immediate: eliminate peer confrontations and interference	- review expectations before lunch/recess - use of progress chart - To Sept. 30: yard supervision of Eddy by EA	Oct. 15 Noticeable progress. Classroom disputes much reduced. Recommend: Phase out reviews by Nov. 15 JF
by Dec 15 - increase written production; raise achievement level	- daily writing (p.m. with EA) of "Eddy's Animal Care Manual"	Oct. 15 High task commitment Recommend Continue JF

Parent/Guardian (or Student 16+)

☑ I was consulted in the development of this IEP

☑ I have received a copy of this IEP

☐ I have made comments (see over)

_____   10/12/99
Signature   Date

Transition Plan

Date Sept. 19, 2000

Name Lisette B.
(See page 1 for other demographic details)

D.O.B. August 12, 1984

Goal(s) See also I. EP (in O S R)

Lisette will work independently under general (not direct) supervision. Lisette will recognize that repeated assignments may vary. Lisette will review all facets of situation before seeking help.

Action	Responsibility	Date
To Date: enrolled in co-op ed. co-op experience and resource program co-ordinated one session work exp.	L. Farmer (co-op. ed) and H. Leprich (Sp. Ed)	Since Nov. '99
Current: (to Dec.) continue coop/sp. ed co-ordination	as above	To Dec. Review Oct. 15 Nov. 15 Dec. 15
Lisette to be ass't mgr. for girl's field hockey team (30 Sept. – 8 Nov.)	C. Leech (phys. ed)	
begin daily instruction in cognitive style using, (SRA) Thinklab	H. Leprich	
Next Term (Jan/01 →) public library work exp. Review (with IEP)	Farmer/Leprich with M. Fleetwood (Lib.)	N. B. Review meeting on Jan. 15, 2001

	Parent/Guardian	**Student**		
I was consulted in the development of this Plan	✓	✓	_(signature)_ Signature	9 June '00 Date
I have received a copy of this Plan	✓	✓	Lisette Bremer Signature	June 9, 2000 Date

VI: Reviewing and Updating the IEP:

A student's IEP needs to be reviewed on a regular basis. Considerations in such a review would include:

- Does the plan still reflect the student's needs?
- Are the strategies and resources still effective?
- Is the student progressing at the rate that was expected?
- Should changes be made to the assignment of responsibility?
- Has any new information emerged that means the plan should change?
- Is the student displaying responsibility and commitment to the learning process?
- Are family/student commitments in the plan being carried out?

Dangers and Trouble Spots

Despite the appeal of IEPs and even though experience has proven their value, there are some potential difficulties to be aware of, both in preparation and implementation. Many teachers feel they are ill equipped to develop what they consider a radical departure from their normal planning. Even teachers with training in special education may have little experience in coordinating a team and developing plans. There can often be confusion, if not tension, over who has responsibility for the various components of the process. And, even though a multidisciplinary approach is useful, a lack of systematic training for school personnel and sporadic attendance at meetings can make the approach difficult to maintain.

Some educators are concerned that the relatively formal nature of the IEP creates yet another level of bureaucracy, and thereby moves education even further away from its intended recipient, the student. The use of computer programs to develop IEPs, and programs that spin out computer generated strategies to complete a plan, have raised legitimate concerns over "paper compliance" to the very important IEP process. Yet paper compliance is a natural response for teachers faced with increased workload, heavy demands from administration and parents, excessive paperwork, insufficient support and lack of training. One very legitimate criticism of most IEP forms is that, notwithstanding their theoretical excellence, they are too demanding a document for the typically overwhelmed teacher to maintain well.

Ultimately, an IEP is only a tool. A proven one, but a tool nevertheless. To put it to effective use requires the same skills, resources, and above all, *willingness*, that any other educational tool requires. One way to circumvent the possible problems with an IEP and to ensure a more beneficial outcome is to manage its preparation and implementation through the power of a school team. Experience proves that a team approach to the IEP not only enhances the quality of an IEP, it also offers greater likelihood that its contents — and its ideals — will take effect.

The In-School Team

The Role a Team Plays

The role and the style of an in-school team varies from school to school and board to board. Some schools have teams that meet on a regular, scheduled basis; others meet only when a certain number of students have been referred for discussion. Some teams meet to help a teacher with ideas for students who are having only mild difficulty, while other teams meet only if a child is already identified as exceptional or at risk of being so. Team style and function depends on a variety of other factors too, like the expertise, experience and beliefs of the staff, the nature of the student population, and the needs of the school. There are some schools, for example, that organize the team role quite bureaucratically, making it policy that any student being considered for presentation to an Identification, Placement and Review Committee, must first be presented to the team. Other schools involve the team only after an IPRC

> "A team is everybody and that is why we have such a diversity of people: so that they will come from different backgrounds in their teaching. I know that I don't know everything and I don't think there is any one person who knows everything, but if we have a group, we can pool our knowledge and come up with the best for the student."
>
> —Audrey Walsh, Spec. Ed. Resource Teacher

has identified a student exceptional and therefore in need of an IEP. Still others use a combination of these two approaches. Still, although there is wide variation in the types of in-school teams at work in Ontario, and an equally wide variation in the way their strengths are put to use, one very important, widespread, and effective role for this group is the collaborative development of individual educational plans.

Who Joins the In-School team?

Usually, a team has a relatively permanent core of people, e.g., the principal (or designate), classroom teachers, and special education teacher. Other teachers, professionals, parents and advocates may be added to suit the needs of an individual case. The group works as a team, but each member usually has a particular role in the team process, a role defined by a variety of factors: their knowledge base, their experience with the student under consideration or, in general, their capacity to provide information or support at a particular level.

❖ *The principal* (or designate) is nominally the head of the team. From a purely practical perspective, administrative power is needed for scheduling, and for making personnel and resources available. Usually, it is the principal who assigns one team member to carry primary responsibility for a particular IEP. The principal is also officially responsible for meeting provincial requirements (timelines for developing a plan, notifying participants, storing information, etc.)

❖ *The special education teacher* in a school is often the person assigned the responsibility for scheduling, chairing and maintaining the records for team meetings. Usually, she is the teacher on the team with skills and training in assessment, as well as the person with readiest access to a multitude of program modification ideas and additional resources. In most cases, the special education teacher plays a direct role in the implementation of strategies, or else arranges for implementation. It may be the special education teacher who describes and models a new technique for a classroom teacher, arranges for support personnel, works with the student directly, etc.

The special education teacher is also a gatekeeper of sorts. He communicates regularly with other professionals (e.g., speech and language pathologists, counselors, assessment services) and is usually the one who can access these resources, depending on the decisions of the team.

❖ Many teams have *classroom teachers* as regular members who attend every meeting whether or not the student being discussed is in their class. Their role is to help generate solutions for students in difficulty, and to provide support for implementing these solutions. Regular classroom teachers provide information about curriculum expectations in particular grades; they are aware of combinations of students who may be appropriate for social interventions with students having difficulty; classroom teachers have the best line into school sports and clubs and other activities. They are also a creative source of ideas.

Representation from each school division on an elementary team, or from subject areas in the case of secondary schools, provides a better rounded pool from which to draw information and solutions.

❖ A *classroom teacher who is an ad hoc team member* because the student under consideration is in her class, will have similar, but slightly more onerous responsibilities. Usually, this teacher will collect much of the assessment data, often in collaboration with the special education teacher. She will bring in observations of the student's behaviour and work habits across a variety of settings and subject areas, samples of work, results of teacher-made tests, and information gathered through discussions with family members or other involved persons. Perhaps most important, the regular classroom teacher will likely be the person to carry out instructional plans generated by the team, and she must therefore make sure the rest of the team understands clearly what can be accommodated reasonably in the real world of her classroom. One real world factor is that she will probably do most of the communicating with the parents.

❖ An educational assistant is usually an ad hoc member with particular insights about a student he may know better than most, so the EA can play a crucial part in the formation of an IEP. In the implementation of the developed plan, the educational assistant, under the direction of the teacher, may be responsible for particular types of instruction or assistance within the classroom setting. Along with the classroom teacher, the educational assistant often takes on responsibility for monitoring.

❖ Other important team members are the *parents* of the student being discussed, for they have a wealth of information to be considered. The reasonableness of interventions, such as a behaviour plan, for example, that would require home support, is far easier to discuss productively if a parent is present. Perhaps most important, parent participation helps foster the bonds of trust and communication so essential for the success of many students.

Naturally, parents are almost always ad hoc members. Experience has shown that parents often find it difficult to get to meetings, but the

For Discussion: the Case of Ms. Wall

The grade 4/5 split that Ms. Wall was assigned this year presented quite a few challenges in classroom management. Like many experienced teachers, she has a repertoire of strategies to maintain class attention and, while they are effective for many of the students, the behaviour of one student, Audrey, has led her to seek extra support and ideas from the in-school team.

Audrey first came to the school at the beginning of grade three. She had been identified as developmentally disabled, but had always been in a regular class. During the grade three year, many discussions were held with concerned individuals, including the parents, as to how to best meet Audrey's academic needs. A suggestion that she move to a segregated class was considered and rejected but now, with the increasing academic demands in the grade four setting, Ms. Wall is seeing what she considers a dramatic change in Audrey's behavior. Audrey has become extraordinarily quiet and withdrawn. She does not participate in class discussions and spends much of her time staring out the window. In music class, which used to be her favorite subject, Audrey keeps her head down and does not seem to have learned any of the songs.

At the first team meeting, attended by the principal, special education teacher, two regular classroom teachers and Ms. Wall, it was decided that Audrey's curriculum expectations be decreased with a focus on basic instruction. This instruction would be delivered in part by the special education teacher in a resource room, but for a majority of the program Audrey would stay in the regular class, with Ms. Wall getting planning help from the special education teacher. It was also decided that Audrey would join the grade one class for music as an assistant to the teacher, and to help the students learn and sing the songs. The immediate result was that Audrey seemed to regain her interest in music. She relishes being "assistant teacher". And in her grade four class, Audrey has begun to participate, not just in music class, but in her other subjects as well.

As the team meets to review her case there are several concerns. Ms. Wall is making every effort to incorporate the curriculum changes, but sees a broadening gap between Audrey's achievements and what is expected of the rest of the class. Audrey's parents are encouraged by the progress, but are also concerned about Audrey's ability to fit in academically and socially. They have accepted the school's invitation to attend the meeting called to come up with what everyone feels would be the best plan to meet Audrey's academic and emotional needs.

provincial regulations, not to mention effective teaching practice, means they are still kept informed.

❖ By regulation, *students who are 16 years and older* may participate in a team meeting in which an IEP is being developed. If the student is a participant in the actual meeting, he may play a very special role in describing needs and perspectives, at the very least, offering some insights into what is possible and realistic.

❖ *Support personnel* may be involved in a team meeting, but usually are not permanent members. These individuals, physiotherapists or attendance counselors, for example, attend meetings where their information, expertise, and intervention may be needed. Their role, as with all members of an in-school team, is to act as an information resource. Especially with secondary school students, who have considerably more independence, and a wider circle of activity that is not necessarily known to their parents or classroom teachers, support personnel may be vital to the implementation and monitoring elements in a plan.

> "It's not so much that I shell out advice, because if that were the case we would not hear the expertise of others. I more or less stimulate the discussion, try to encourage suggestions from other members of the team, bounce ideas off them. They bounce ideas off each other, so, in a way, I am a facilitator."
> — *Joan Christopher, Spec. Ed. Resource Teacher*

When Teachers Collaborate

Teachers collaborate naturally. Before and after and in-between classes, in the hall, over lunch, they share strategies they have found useful, seek opinions about their concerns for a student at risk, borrow materials, plan mutual projects for their classes, the exchanges are part of their day (and beyond). But a team situation is more formalized, and the process, as a consequence, requires a somewhat more formal structure. To put together an IEP, most teams follow a variation of this problem-solving technique.

• identify/clarify the problem,

• formulate a plan,

• initiate the plan,

• assess the success of the plan,

• revise as necessary.

Yet even these steps can be more effectively and efficiently realized if members of a team consult and collaborate with some appreciation of team dynamics.

What Makes A Team Succeed?

For collaboration to be successful, all members of the team must, at the very least, share a common focus, a sense that they are each trying to achieve the same goal. But by itself, a mutually understood purpose is still not enough. Realistically, members of a team must be voluntary participants, with a sense of voluntarily shared responsibility and accountability. Above all, to function truly without impediment, team members should have parity. The latter issue can be awkward, particularly given the fact that teachers exist in a hierarchical structure in which parity, even on a philosophical level, can be difficult to establish. On the plus side, however, teachers are members of a profession, and as a team, they are professionals united to achieve a goal for which they are better equipped than any others.

There is a practical side too. No matter how professionally a team may approach its tasks, there are some simple but fundamental requirements if it is to apply its collective strength effectively. Schools that have been benefitting from the team concept in special education for some time now, unanimously attest that to succeed, a team must

• have administrative support,

• meet at regularly scheduled intervals,

• keep group size manageable,

• receive pertinent information *prior* to meetings,

• set time limits,

• follow an agenda,

• set review dates,

• keep records,

• share accountability and responsibility.

Some Issues in Team Practice

Collaboration with colleagues in a school setting is sometimes a complex dance, and ensuring that everyone is in step can prove difficult. Here are a few of the issues that must be kept in mind.

Personal beliefs: In any group of individuals, there is bound to be a variety of perspectives and beliefs. This indeed is one of the strengths of a team: the multiplicity of perspectives. But perspectives and absolute commitment to an idea or ideal, if held to the exclusion of all else, can interfere with the problem-solving goal of an IEP. It is important to be aware and respectful of the beliefs of team members, and to remember that it is the needs of a student, not the power of a principle, that ultimately must rule.

Administrative support: Administrators, whether they be at the school level or at the school board level, hold the keys to a variety of resources and decision making powers that are not generally available to other members of the team. Within a school, the principal sets the tone for discipline and the delivery of curriculum. In team meetings, a principal's active participation as a member of the team lends a status and aura of responsibility to that team that it would otherwise not attain. Without administrative support from within the school and at the board level, in-school teams may continue to function, but do so with their hands tied.

Time: As any teacher will attest, there is never enough time – for anything! Thus team meetings can often be viewed as an unwelcome extra in a teacher's schedule. This is even more strongly the case when a team is run inefficiently, decisions are not made or followed up, communication is poor, procedures are not well established and there is no support. Given that time is a precious commodity, it is essential that team time be seen as worthwhile and, in the end, a time *saving* activity. When teams are run well and teachers are given the opportunity to work with their colleagues in an effective way, the benefits to the school far outweigh the time spent at the meeting.

Dealing with resistance: It is a reality that, at times, there will be clashes in team meetings. For a variety of reasons, team members may disagree over anything from the identification of a student's exceptionality, to the solutions proposed, to the amount and nature of resource being brought to bear. At times, the disagreement may be subtle, as in a case where a participant remains silent or strays from the topic, trying to change the subject. Other forms of resistance — like anger — are anything but subtle. Whatever the type of resistance, it can create an impediment to effective communication. Often, just recognizing that it exists, can help to move the meeting to a more productive level.

READINGS & RESOURCES

For Further Investigation

Adams, L., & Cessna, K. (1991). Designing systems to facilitate collaboration: Collective wisdom from Colorado. *Preventing School Failure, 35*(4), 37-42.

Cole, E. & Brown. R. (1996). Multidisciplinary school teams: A five-year follow-up study. *Canadian Journal of School Psychology, 12,* 155-168.

Cook, L., & Friend, M. (1993). Educational leadership for teacher collaboration. In B. Billingsley (Ed.), *Program leadership for serving students with disabilities* (pp. 421-444) Richmond, VA: Virginia Department of Education.

Dettmer, P.A., Dyck, N.T. and Thurston, L.P. (1996). *Consultation, Collaboration and TeamWork for Students with Special Needs.* Allyn and Bacon. Toronto.

Evans, S.B. (1991). A realistic look at the research base for collaboration in special education. *Preventing School Failure, 35*(4), 10-14.

Friend, M. & Cook, L. (1992). *Interactions: Collaboration Skills for School Professionals.* Toronto: Copp Clark Pitman.

Fuchs, D. & Fuchs, L.S. (1996). Consultation as a technology and the politics of school reform. *Remedial and Special Education, 17*(6), 386-392.

Heron, T.E., & Harris, K.C. (1993). *The educational consultant: Helping professionals, parents, and mainstreamed students* (3rd ed.). Austin, TX: Pto-Ed.

Idol, L., Nevin, A., & Paolucci-Whitcomb, P. (1994). *Collaborative consultation* (2nd ed.). Austin, TX: Pto-Ed.

Johnson, L.J., Pugach, M.C. & Hammitte, D.J. (1988). Barriers to effective special education consultation. *Remedial and Special Education, 9*(6), 41-47.

Jordan, A. (1994). *Skills in Collaborative Classroom Consultation*. New York: TJ Press (Padstow) Ltd.

Lamont, I.L., & Hill, J.L. (1991). Roles and responsibilities of paraprofessionals in the regular elmentary classroom. *B.C. Journal of Special Education, 15*(1), 1-24.

Lynch, E.C. & Beare, P.L. (1990). The quality of IEP objectives and their relevance for instruction for students with mental retardation and behavior disorders. *Remedial and Special Education, 11*, 48-55.

Mills, M. (1994). The consultative role of school based resource teachers. *B.C. Journal of Special Education, 18*(2), 181-189.

Napier, E. (1995). *Integrating students with special needs: Effective stategies to provide the most enabling education for all students.* Vancouver: EduServ.

Ontario Ministry of Education and Training (1998). *Individual Education Plan (IEP) Resource Guide.* Queens Printer for Toronto.

O'Shea, D. & O'Shea, L. (1997). Collaboration and school reform: A 21st century perspective. *Journal of Learning Disabilities, 30*(4), 449-462.

Phillips, V., & McCullough, L. (1990). Consultation-based programming: Instituting the collaborative ethic in schools. *Exceptional Children, 56*, 291-304.

Pugach, M.C. & Johnson, L.J. (1995). A new framework for thinking about collaboration. In *Collaborative practitioners collaborative schools* (pp. 27- 44). Denver, CO: Love.

Putnam, J.W., Rynders, J.E., Johnson, R.T., & Johnson, D.W. (1998). Collaborative skill instruction for promoting interactions between mentally handicapped and non-handicapped children. *Exceptional Children, 55*, 550-557.

Safran, S.P., & Safran, J.S. (1996). Intervention assistance programs and prereferral teams. *Remedial and Special Education,17*(6), 363-369.

Shea, T.M., & Bauer, A.M. (1991). *Parents and teachers of children with exceptionalities: A handbook for collaboration.* (2nd ed.). Boston: Allyn and Bacon.

Sheridan, S.M., Welch, M., & Orme, S.F. (1996). Is consultation effective? A review of outcome research. *Remedial and Special Education,17*(6), 341-354.

Stanovich, P. (1996). Collaboration - The key to successful inclusion in today's schools. *Intervention in School and Clinic, 32*(1), 39-42.

Westby, C.E., & Ford, V. (1993). The role of team culture in assessment and intervention. *Journal of Educational and Psychological Consultation, 4*, 319-341.

Whitten, E., & Dieker, L. (1993). Intervention assistance teams: A collaborative process to meet the needs of students at risk. *B.C. Journal of Special Education,17*(3), 275-283.

Wiener, J. & Davidson, I. (1990). The in-school team: A prevention model of delivery in special education. *Canadian Journal of Education, 15*(4), 427-445

Appendix

Assessment Instruments • Definitions •Teacher Qualifications

Some Assessment Instruments Popular in Ontario

- Titles appear in alphabetical order, and include the 'familiar' or 'nick' name in each case.
- Many instruments are used for more than one purpose, e.g., to produce both an IQ score and some ability level information. For ready access and reference, the chart immediately below organizes the instruments under purpose headings. (Note that in the interest of simplicity, the chart uses the familiar name of each instrument.)

Achievement / Academic Skills	Developmental / Readiness	Intelligence / Adaptive behaviour	
Boehm	ABS	ABS	WRAT-R
Brigance	Boehm	Binet	Gates-MacGinitie
CAT.	Brigance	C-CAT	K-ABC
CTBS	PPVT-R	Detroit	PIAT-R
Gates-MacGinitie		K-ABC	PPVT-R
K-ABC	*Diagnostic*	Leiter	Slingerland
Keymath	Brigance	McCarthy Scales	Spache
PIAT-R	Keymath	Ravens	TORC
PPVT-R	McCarthy Scales	Woodcock	Woodcock Reading
Spache	Slingerland		
TORC	Spache	*Language (& Reading)*	*Non-Verbal Instruments*
WRAT-R		Brigance	
Woodcock	*Emotional / Behaviour*	CAT	Leiter
Woodcock Reading	ABS	CTBS	Ravens
	BES		
	CBCL		

The AAMD Adaptive Behavior Scale, School Edition ("The ABS") (1981): The American Association On Mental Deficiency.

This is an individually completed scale used principally to aid in classification, placement, and general programming decisions for mentally handicapped individuals. It has two parts, yields percentile ranks; age range is 3-69. The sub-sections deal with areas like social adjustment, community self-sufficiency, etc. The rater (test completer) can be the parent, teacher, social worker, etc.

<u>Strengths and Weaknesses:</u>

The ABS enjoys popularity with educators and health professionals who emphasize adaptive behaviour in assessing mental handicap. It is used most frequently to assess an individual's ability to thrive in a particular placement (independent, group home, etc.). Validity and reliability are criticized. Generally it is not used for severely handicapped persons.

The Behavior Evaluation Scale ("The BES") (1984): Pro-Ed.

The BES is a scale for evaluating behavior in students K-12. It is filled out by the teacher or other adult, and covers areas like learning problems, interpersonal difficulties, unhappiness/depression, etc. It takes about 15 minutes to complete, and produces a number that can be used to judge a student's behaviour comparatively.

Strengths and Weaknesses:

The instrument is useful for comparison purposes if it is completed by several of the significant adults in the subject's life. However, this or any evaluation scale should never be used as a sole determiner for identification or placement.

Boehm Test of Basic Concepts ("The Boehm") (1967; Form A, 1969; Form B, 1971): The Psychological Corporation.

This test is a standardized, individual (or group, for screening) test of comprehension, quantity and time concepts designed to assess knowledge basic to early academic success. The grade range is K-2; it takes 30-40 minutes to administer; and produces a percentile score.

Strengths and Weaknesses:

Most young people find *The Boehm* interesting. Illustrations are clear. The test is well organized with an excellent manual, and is easy to administer. Unfortunately, no documentation is offered to support the concepts in this test as crucial to the early years of school.

Brigance Diagnostic Inventories ("The Brigance") (1981): Curriculum Associates.

This is an individual, non-standardized (but field-tested in Canada and the U.S.) instrument, designed to assess pre-academic, academic, and vocational skills so that teachers can more easily define objectives and plan individual programs. The grade range is pre-school to 12; it takes 15-90 minutes to administer, and only in some subtests produces a grade or age level score. (There are several other similar instruments by Brigance.)

Strengths and Weaknesses:

There is an excellent, well-organized record-keeping system which will be of real assistance in planning student programs. This test can be administered easily by paraprofessionals under supervision. The somewhat informal procedures tend to encourage carelessness, but properly used, this test can be a useful planning aid.

The Canadian Achievement Tests ("The C.A.T.")(1983): McGraw-Hill-Ryerson.

This is a standardized, norm-referenced and criterion-referenced, group test, designed to assess achievement. The grade range is 1-12; it takes a flexible time period to administer (depending on the number and combination of subtests); and produces percentile, stanine, scaled, and grade equivalent scores.

Strengths and Weaknesses:

The major content areas of this test are reading, spelling, language, mathematics, reference skill. Given the many pieces to it, the test is reasonably easy to administer. It produces a detailed Student Diagnostic Profile (SDP) that can be very useful if all personnel are prepared to take the time to interpret it. Potentially a very valuable addition to the canon of available tests, it has been quite sharply criticized for being too unwieldy and threatening to both subjects and examiners.

Canadian Cognitive Abilities Test ("The C-Cat") (1982): Nelson Canada.

This is a standardized, norm-referenced group test designed to measure cognitive abilities in the verbal, quantitative, and non-verbal areas. The grade range is 3-12; it takes 1½-2 hours to administer; and produces standard, percentile, and stanine scores for age groups, and percentile and stanine scores for grade groups.

Strengths and Weaknesses:

The C-Cat has high validity and reliability estimates, and reviewers compliment it for careful norming and standardization. Supporters state that this test has better predictive value than I.Q. tests, although critics argue that cognitive ability by itself is not a simple or straightforward entity to assss.

The Canadian Test of Basic Skills ("The CTBS") (1988): Nelson Canada.

This is a Canadianization of the Iowa Test of Basic Skills and is very popular in Ontario. It is a standardized, norm-referenced, group-administered achievement test for K-12. *The CTBS* produces mounds of data. It can be hand scored, although a computerized scoring system is preferred. Scores range from percentile to scale to grade equivalent. Intra-class data as well as other, extensive comparative data can be made available.

Stengths and Weaknesses:

Although the The CTBS can be extremely time-consuming to administer, there are many educators who argue it is worth the effort. Validity and reliability data are generally good and the test generally is well-received by reviewers. The most severe criticisms are not directed at the test itself but at the general abuse to which achievement tests especially, are subject.

Child Behaviour Checklist (The "CBCL") (1983): Queen City Printers, Burlington, VT.

Focuses on social relationships and general behaviour, using three forms. There is a teacher report form with 168 items that allow rating of behaviour problems, plus an item on academic performance and one on adaptive functioning. A second form is 'direct observation' which requires an evaluator to observe the subject in ten minute time samples and then complete 96 items that provide a behaviour and an on-task score. The third is a 'youth report form', 112 items that the subject completes. Data produce a series of profiles that differ for boys and girls and for three different age levels (4-6, 6-11, 12-16).

<u>Strengths and Weaknesses:</u>

The test is carefully developed and has good reliability scores. Reviewers consider the CBCL one of the better rating scales available. It is *not* simple to administer, nor is the raw data conversion easy. Proponents of the instrument, however, insist the results are worth the effort.

Detroit Tests of Learning Aptitude - 2 ("The Detroit") (1985): Pro-Ed.

This is a revision of a once popular standardized, individual test designed to measure general intelligence functions, such as verbal ability, reasoning, time and space relationships. The age range is 6-18; it takes 1-2 hours to administer; and it produces percentile scores, and a General Intelligence or Overall Aptitude Score.

<u>Strengths and Weaknesses:</u>

The revised Detroit is sharply criticized for lack of validity and reliability. Reviewers suggest that results should be interpreted cautiously, which is a more than mild dismissal.

Gates-MacGinitie Silent Reading Tests ("The Gates-MacGinitie"), Second ed., (1978): Riverside Publishing Co.

This is a standardized, norm-referenced, group test designed to measure silent reading skills. The grade range is 1-12; it takes 50-60 minutes to administer; and it produces grade level, standard, and percentile scores.

The Gates-MacGinitie is offered at eight levels, and gives two basic measures: vocabulary, comprehension. (The older, first edition also had a measure of speed and accuracy.) They are pen and paper tests completed by the subject(s) usually in groups.

<u>Strengths and Weaknesses:</u>

These tests are a useful screening device and are often used for test-retest procedures because alternate forms are available. However in their usefulness rests the inherent weakness: a silent reading score does not give any diagnostic information. The comprehension sub-tests are criticized as being not very well done. The questions often rely on factors not present in the passages to be read. They measure a very low level of comprehension. A most serious criticism is that the *Gates-MacGinitie* tests do not offer a teacher more than he or she already knows about a student, except a number with which to satisfy a bureaucracy.

Kaufman Assessment Battery for Children ("The K-ABC") (1983): American Guidance Service.

This is a standardized, individual, norm-referenced test of intelligence and achievement. The age range is 2½-12½ years; it takes 30-90 minutes to administer; and produces age level, standard, percentile, scaled, and grade level scores. Three dimensions — sequential processing (serial or temporal order problem-solving), simultaneous processing (a gestalt approach), and achievement — are assessed in 16 sub-tests, which in turn report four global scales: the three above plus a global estimate of intellectual functioning.

<u>Strengths and Weaknesses:</u>

It is a complex and involved instrument that requires expertise, time, and patience in the examiner. The authors urge examiners to take training courses.

An important feature of the test is its purpose of assessing disabled and minority students, and pre-schoolers, but as with the Woodcock-Johnson Psycho-Educational Battery (see page 160) *The K-ABC* does not yet have widespread acceptance. It draws heavily on neuropsychology and cerebral specialization theory, and whether or not a test based on these elements can be educationally useful is still uncertain.

Keymath Diagnostic Arithmetic Test ("Keymath") (1971): American Guidance Service.

This is a standardized, individual, criterion-referenced test designed to assess mathematics skills. The grade range is pre-school-6; it takes

30-45 minutes to administer; it produces grade level and percentile scores.

Strengths and Weaknesses:

Keymath is easy to administer, diverse, colourful, and widely applicable. It has some unique sub-tests (such as missing Elements) and is generally very motivating. On balance, *Keymath* is an excellent screening instrument, but is criticized for some elements of construction which leave gaps in the continuum of difficulty. Another criticism is that grade level scores tend to be inflated.

Leiter International Performance Scale ("The Leiter") (1948): C.H. Stoelting Co.

This is a non-verbal test producing mental age and I.Q. scores. Usually it is used for individuals with hearing and language difficulties, for severely disabled and for non-English speakers. The directions are pantomimed and gestured. Age range is 2-18. It measures areas like specific relationships, quantitative discrimination, immediate recall, etc.

Strengths and Weaknesses:

There are no time constraints and the scoring is very objective. Subjects usually enjoy the test process. However there is no leeway for partial scoring, which seems contradictory when there is no guarantee the subjects have fully understood the tasks, or are fully capable of responding. *The Leiter* is heavy and awkward to use and store. However it is a popular and potentially useful instrument for certain subjects. (There is an adaptation known as the Arthur (1950) Adaptation.)

McCarthy Scales of Children's Abilities ("The McCarthy Scales") (1972): The Psychological Corporation.

This is a standardized, individual, norm-referenced test of general intellectual ability which is frequently offered as an instrument to identify children with possible learning disabilities. The age range is 2½-8½ years; it takes an hour to administer; and produces mental age, standard, and percentile scores.

Strengths and Weaknesses:

The McCarthy Scales include several verbal tasks that are appropriate for children with suspected learning disabilities, and has good reliability support. Ironically, no exceptional children classified as exceptional were included in the norming sample, part of a criticism that

suggests more validity studies are needed. This test also has a very small age range, which makes re-testing comparisons difficult as the child grows. It is not an easy test to interpret.

Peabody Individual Achievement Test — Revised ("The PIAT-R") (1988): American Guidance Service.

This is an individual, norm-referenced, standardized test, designed to give a wide measure of general achievement, with particular emphasis on reading, spelling, and arithmetic achievement. The grade range is K-12; it takes 30-40 minutes to administer; and produces age level, grade level, standard, and percentile scores.

Strengths and Weaknesses:

The PIAT-R uses a multiple choice answer format. It requires recognition of correct spelling (not written spelling) and tests sentence comprehension as well as mathematical problem-solving skills. It can provide a quick, overall, preliminary view, but should not be regarded as the last word. Nor should sub-test scores be regarded as truly and finally indicative of a student's ability in a particular area (like reading).

Peabody Picture Vocabulary Test—Revised ("The PPVT-R") (1959; rev. 1965, 1981): American Guidance Service.

This is a standardized, individual test of single word receptive vocabulary of standard (American) English. The age range is 2½-40 years; it takes 10-20 minutes to administer; and produces age level, standard, percentile, and stanine scores.

Strengths and Weaknesses:

Because The PPVT-R has a format of presenting pictures to elicit a response to a word, it is non-threatening. It is a good first test in a battery, and is well-designed and normed. But because it is simply a test of single word vocabulary, not too much should be made of the results. The fact that the subject must understand a word and a picture (or drawing) means more than vocabulary is being assessed.

Progressive Matrices ("The Ravens") (1956): H.K. Lewis & Co.

The test requires a subject to complete progressively complicated visual analogies. It is entirely non-verbal, and is available in Standard and Advanced levels. There is a coloured version for younger children.

Strengths and Weaknesses:

Reliability and validity data are acceptable, but norms are poor for school use. (It was standardized on patients in a veteran's hospital.) *The Ravens* can be used very effectively for a test-teach-test approach (See Chapter 13) and because it is non-verbal, may reveal some enlightening cognitive strengths in poor readers.

Slingerland Screening Tests for Identifying Children With Specific Learning Disability ("The Slingerland") (1962; rev. 1970, Form D, 1974): Educators' Publishing Service.

This is a non-standardized, informal group test of visual, auditory, and kinesthetic skills related to reading and spelling, designed to identify students with a specific language disability. The age range is 6-12; it takes 60-90 minutes to administer; and it produces no scores but has guidelines for evaluating test performance.

Strengths and Weaknesses:

The tests in this instrument are strictly informal measures and permit a great deal of subjectivity. Some students become very frustrated during administration because extensive writing is required. Administration procedures are complex and difficult. Because it lacks validity and reliability data, and because of severe criticism of its value, use of *The Slingerland* has declined significantly.

Spache Diagnostic Reading Scales ("The Spache") (1963; rev. 1972, 1981): McGraw-Hill.

This is an individual, standardized, criterion-referenced test, designed to measure oral and silent reading, and listening comprehension. The grade range is 1 to 7; it takes 30-45 minutes to administer; and the test produces grade level scores.

Strengths and Weaknesses:

Because the battery includes 3 graded word recognition lists, 2 reading selections at each of 11 levels (from grades 1.6 to 7.5) and 12 supplementary word analysis and phonics tests, it purports to give fairly good information about students' reading skills. What must be considered however, is to what extent a knowledge of phonics can be equated with reading ability, and to what degree of accuracy, one can establish grade levels of a passage to 1.6 or 7.5. Many of the questions are yes-no type which gives a 50 per cent probability in guessing. The test offers a silent reading rate score which, given individual differences, is not very meaningful.

Generally, The Spache is not highly regarded because of its very serious flaws; however the author has written an excellent manual in which he shares his extensive knowledge of reading, and this one element is quite worth while.

Stanford-Binet Intelligence Scale, Fourth Edition ("The Binet") (1986): Riverside Publishing.

The fourth edition retains many features of previous editions. Its authors claim that this edition is designed to help differentiate between mental handicap and learning disability, to identify giftedness, to understand why a student is having learning problems, and to study the development of cognitive skills from 2-adult. There are 15 subtests, not dissimilar from those in the WISC-III, including Vocabulary, Quantitative, Memory for Sentences, Pattern Analysis, Copying, Verbal Relations, Memory for Objects, and others.

Strengths and Weaknesses:

There is surprisingly little research or review material on what has been a long established IQ test, perhaps because of the excellent reputation of its predecessors. The publishers claim to have responded to cultural-bias criticism directed at earlier versions. It is likely that time and experience will increase the use of this test as an alternative to the WISC-III.

Test of Reading Comprehension ("The TORC") (1978): Pro-Ed.

This is a standardized, norm-referenced test for individual or group, designed to give a normed measure of silent reading comprehension independent of specific curriculum, via eight sub-tests like Paragraph Reading, Synthetic Similarities, Social Studies Vocabulary, Reading the Directions of Schoolwork, etc. The age range is 6½-14½; it takes 1½-2 hours to administer and produces scaled (each sub-test) and standardized (total test) scores.

Strengths and Weaknesses:

Generally the test has come to be used at the upper age ranges because of the preclusive effect of very specific, subject-based vocabulary. Several of the sub-tests measure abilities not taught in classrooms and therefore the value of the results for school purposes may be questionable. Because the theoretical constructs underlying The TORC are new and complex, the worth of the scores, not to mention their interpretation, may well be suspect, especially in light of the intricate psycholinguistic base from which the tests are developed.

The Wechsler Intelligence Scale For Children - Third Edition ("The WISC-Three") (1991) The Psychological Corporation.

This is an individual, standardized, norm-referenced test designed to offer an ability score (IQ) and to offer information about a subject's skills in a variety of areas. Test results give three overall scores: *Verbal Scale, Performance Scale,* and *Full Scale.* The Verbal Scale is built on six subtests: (general) information, similarities, arithmetic, vocabulary, comprehension, and digit span. According to the publisher, these subtests evaluate such areas as attention span, analysis of relationships, social maturity, memory, and others. The Performance Scale has seven subtests: picture completion, picture arrangement, block design, object assembly, coding, symbol search, and mazes. Among the areas evaluated, according to the publisher, are attention to detail, visual sequencing, analysis of differences, etc. The Verbal Scale is much more closely correlated with classroom activities than the Performance Scale. *The Full Scale Score* is what is generally referred to as one's IQ.

It is usually irregular for classroom teachers to administer a WISC, but they may receive results. Ideally, teachers will be given the sub test results as well as the Full Scale, Verbal, and Performance Scores, for these may have diagnostic information on which a plan of remediation can be based.

Strengths and Weaknesses:

The WISC-III, like its predecessors, has wide acceptance in Ontario as a clinical and diagnostic tool, and both teachers and non-professionals are very familiar with it. Although the manual for the test states that the instrument is intended for use with people aged 6 years 0 months through 16 years 11 months, it is not uncommon for the test to be used with students who are older or younger. (Adult and older students should theoretically be tested on the WAIS, the Wechsler Adult Intelligence Scale, and younger children on the WPPSI, the Wechsler Pre-Primer Scale of Intelligence.)

Reliability and validity coefficients are high; it is particularly well standardized, and can produce some useful diagnostic information. Testing time is approximately 1½ hours.

Wide Range Achievement Test — Revised ("The WRAT-R") (1983): Jastak Associates.

This is an individual, norm-referenced, standardized test designed to assess skills in reading (actually, word recognition), written spelling, and arithmetic computation. The age range is 5 to adult; it takes 20-30 minutes to administer; and produces grade level, standard, percentile, and stanine scores.

Strengths and Weaknesses:

This test is very easy and very fast in administration and scoring, and can be a fairly efficient first step in an assessment. However it should never be used as the sole element in any evaluation, assessment or admission procedure (but often is!). The arithmetic computation sub-test does not test ability as much as it tests what the subject's curriculum offered. The spelling sub-test grants a grade level score of 1.3 for merely copying 18 marks and writing two letters from the subject's name. Finally, the reading sub-test asks the subject merely to read a list of single words. There is no measure of sentence or paragraph reading, or of comprehension. Reviewers also point out that overestimations of reading ability, at the primary level especially, are a weakness.

Woodcock-Johnson Psycho-Educational Battery ("The Woodcock") (1990): Teaching Resources Corporation.

This is an individual, standardized, norm-referenced test designed to measure cognitive ability, academic achievement and interests over a wide range. The age range is 3-adult; it takes 1½-2 hours to administer; and produces grade level, age level, percentile, and standard scores, along with scores the authors call 'functional level' and 'relative performance index'.

Strengths and Weaknesses:

This is a busy and involved instrument, with 27 sub-tests. Twelve are in "Cognitive Ability" (e.g., analysis-synthesis; quantitative concepts; memory for sentences, etc.) Ten are in "Tests of Achievement" (e.g., calculation, dictation, proofing, etc.). There are five in "Interest Level" (e.g., Reading Interest, Social Interest, etc.).

Clusters of sub-tests (e.g., reading) provide the primary analysis, with scores plotted on four profiles: the 'sub-test profile' for quick presentation of performance, the 'percentile rank profile' for comparison with age or grade; the 'instructional implications profile' for relating instructional range to current grade placement, and the 'achievement-aptitude' profile to compare actual and anticipated achievement. This is a comprehensive and interesting means of reporting which offers some interesting comparisons of cognitive ability with actual achievement.

To make this instrument work its best however, requires a major commitment from the examiner. It is difficult, complex and time-consuming. This fact, along with the concern over whether the scholastic aptitude clusters are reliable and valid measures of reading, math, written language, and knowledge, has restricted the popular use of the instrument. There is considerable research being conducted on it at present, and a major effort is being made by the publisher to add information for examiners, and to develop awareness among psychometrists.

Woodcock Reading Mastery Tests (1973): Guidance Service.

This is an individual, standardized, criterion and norm-referenced test designed to measure a wide range of reading skills. The grade range is K-12; it takes 30-45 minutes to administer; and it produces a wide set of scores including grade level, percentile, relative mastery, achievement index, and reading range.

Strengths and Weaknesses:

This test offers five sub-tests covering letters, words, and passages. The Word Comprehension sub-test uses analogy, and the Passage Comprehension makes use of the cloze procedures, both highly regarded techniques. A useful concept is the 'relative mastery' which provides a useful indication of what can be expected of a student. Another useful point is the concept of instructional range in which the test gives indication of where a student can be expected to perform. Reliability and validity data are very good.

As with all tests of reading skills however, the results must always be viewed with some circumspection simply because of the elusiveness of the task of measuring reading ability.

Some General Terms Used In Testing
(See Also Chapter 14)

Age Norm (Age Score) A score indicating average performance for students classified according to chronological age.

Correlation Coefficient (r) A statistical index that measures the degree of relationship between any two variables.

Mean (M) The sum of a set of scores divided by the number of scores.

Median (MD) The middle point in a set of ranked scores.

Mode (MO) The score that occurs most frequently in a distribution. In the distribution 18, 14, 12, 11, 10, 10, 7, the mode is 10. Its value is entirely independent of extreme scores.

Percentile Rank A type of converted score that expresses a student's score relative to his or her group in percentile points. Indicates the percentage of students tested who made scores equal to or lower than the specified score.

Projective Technique A test situation in which the student responds to ambiguous stimulus materials, such as pictures, inkblots, or incomplete sentences, thereby supposedly projecting personality characteristics.

Protocol The original record of the test results.

Raw Score The basic score initially obtained by scoring a test according to the directions in the manual.

Reliability The degree to which a student would obtain the same score if the test were re-administered (assuming no further learning, practice effects, or other change).

Scaled Score Usually this is a score which is used to measure students' growth from year to year. It is a useful comparison also with the norming sample.

Standard Deviation (SD) The most commonly used measure of variation. A statistic used to express the extent of the distribution's deviations from the mean.

Standardization In test construction, this refers to the process of trying the test out on a group of students to determine uniform or standard scoring procedures and methods of interpretation.

Standardized Test Contains empirically selected materials, with specific directions for administration, scoring, and interpretation. Provides data on validity and reliability, and has adequately derived norms.

Standard Score Derived score that transforms a raw score in such a manner that it has the same mean and the same standard deviation.

Stanine A weighted scale divided into nine equal units that represent nine levels of performance on any particular test. The stanine is a standard score.

Validity The extent to which a test measures what it is designated to measure. A test valid for one use may have negligible validity for another.

Definitions of Exceptionalities (Rev.1998)

The Ontario Ministry of Education presents five general groupings of exceptionalities with definitions and specifics within each grouping.

Behaviour

A learning disorder characterized by specific behaviour problems over such a period of time, and to such a marked degree, and of such a nature, as to adversely affect educational performance, and that may be accompanied by one or more of the following:

(a) an inability to build or maintain interpersonal relationships

(b) excessive fears or anxieties

(c) a tendency to compulsive reaction

(d) an inability to learn that cannot be traced to intellectual, sensory, or other health factors, or any combination thereof.

Communication

Autism

A severe learning disorder that is characterized by:

(a) disturbances in
* rate of educational development;
* ability to relate to the environment;
* motility;
* perception, speech, and language;

(b) lack of the representational-symbolic behaviour that precedes language.

Deaf and Hard-of-Hearing

An impairment characterized by deficits in language and speech development because of a diminished or non-existent auditory response to sound.

Language Impairment

A learning disorder characterized by an impairment in comprehension and/or use of verbal communication or the written or other symbol system of communication, which may be associated with neurological, pyschological, physical, or sensory factors, and which may:

(a) involve one or more of the form, content, and function of language in communication;

(b) include one or more of the following:
* language delay;
* dysfluency;
* voice and articulation development, which may or may not be organically or functionally based.

Speech Impairment

A disorder in language formulation that may be associated with neurological, psychological, physical, or sensory factors; that involves perceptual motor aspects of transmitting oral messages; and that may be characterized by impairment in articulation, rhythm, and stress.

Learning Disability

A learning disorder evident in both academic and social situations that involves one or more of the processes necessary for the proper use of spoken language or the symbols of communication, and that is characterized by a condition that:

(a) is not primarily the result of:
* impairment of vision;
* impairment of hearing;
* physical disability;
* developmental disability;
* primary emotional disturbance;
* cultural difference;

(b) results in a significant discrepancy between academic achievement and assessed intellectual ability, with deficits in one or more of the following:
* receptive language (listening, reading);
* language processing (thinking, conceptualizing, integrating);
* expressive language (talking, spelling, writing);
* mathematical computations;

(c) may be associated with one or more conditions diagnosed as:
* a perceptual handicap;
* a brain injury;
* minimal brain dysfunction;
* dyslexia;
* developmental aphasia.

Intellectual

Giftedness

An unusually advanced degree of general intellectual ability that requires differentiated learning experiences of a depth and breadth beyond those normally provided in the regular school program to satisfy the level of educational potential indicated.

Mild Intellectual Disability

A learning disorder characterized by:

(a) an ability to profit educationally within a regular class with the aid of considerable curriculum modification and supportive services;

(b) an ability to profit educationally within a regular class because of slow intellectual development;

(c) a potential for academic learning, independent social adjustment, and economic self-support.

Developmental Disability

A severe learning disorder characterized by:

(a) an inability to profit from a special education program for the mildly intellectually disabled because of slow intellectual development;

(b) an ability to profit from a special education program that is designed to accommodate slow intellectual development;

(c) a limited potential for academic learning, independent social adjustment, and economic self-support.

Physical

Physical Disability

A condition of such severe physical limitation or deficiency as to require special assistance in learning situations to provide the opportunity for educational achievement equivalent to that of pupils without exceptionalities who are of the same age or development level.

Blind and Low Vision

A condition of partial or total impairment of sight or vision that even with correction affects educational performance adversely.

Multiple

Multiple Exceptionalities

A combination of learning or other disorders, impairments, or physical disabilities, that is of such nature as to require, for educational achievement, the services of one or more teachers holding qualifications in special education and the provision of support services appropriate for such disorders, impairments, or handicaps.

Becoming a Special Education Teacher

For most qualified teachers in the province of Ontario, the path to becoming a Special Education Teacher is a very direct one. To be recommended to the Ontario College of Teachers, a candidate must complete Special Education Part 1. This course, offered at a variety of locations across the province, consists of two parts: core, and an elective (for example, learning disabilities or behaviour). Candidates wishing to complete a Specialist in Special Education are required to complete two more courses and two elective courses. Teachers moving here from out-of-province or out-of-country can apply to the Ontario College of Teachers for both basic teaching certification, and additional qualification course equivalency.

Supplementary Notes to the Fourth Edition: (1) The definitions of exceptionalities on pages 188-9 have been extant in Ontario since 1984 and have undergone only limited revision since then (as in 1998). In January 2000, the Ministry of Education announced its intention to develop province-wide standards for programs and services within each exceptionality. Among the proposed steps are revisions to the definitions.

(2) Also in January 2000, the Ministry issued a document describing new, province-wide standards that all school boards must meet henceforth in developing their Special Education 'Plans' (see page 12 for a brief description of 'Plans'). As of 2001, the Ministry will review plans to determine whether they comply with the standards.

Subject/Context Index

Author/Resource Index